The Nuclear Question
The United States and Nuclear Weapons, 1946–1976

To Samuel Weiss and in memory of Eva Weiss
and Samuel and Lena Mandelbaum – my grandparents

The Nuclear Question: The United States and Nuclear Weapons, 1946–1976

MICHAEL MANDELBAUM

Harvard University

CAMBRIDGE UNIVERSITY PRESS

CAMBRIDGE

LONDON NEW YORK MELBOURNE

Published by the Syndics of the Cambridge University Press
The Pitt Building, Trumpington Street, Cambridge CB2 1RP
Bentley House, 200 Euston Road, London NW1 2DB
32 East 57th Street, New York, NY 10022, USA
296 Beaconsfield Parade, Middle Park, Melbourne 3206, Australia

First published 1979

Printed in the United States of America

Library of Congress Cataloging in Publication Data
Mandelbaum, Michael.
The nuclear question.
1. United States — Military policy.
2. Atomic weapons. I. Title.
UA23.M277   358'.39   79-388
ISBN 0 521 22681 3 hard covers
ISBN 0 521 29614 5 paperback

Written under the auspices of the Center for International Affairs and
the Center for Science and International Affairs, Harvard University.

3/81

CONTENTS

v

Preface

This book is a history of American nuclear weapons policy. Little of what has been written about nuclear weapons is historical. Most of those who have concerned themselves with the problems that these armaments have raised since 1945 have, understandably, been more interested in the question "What is to be done?" than in asking what has happened, and why.

The Nuclear Question is intended to be more than merely a chronology. I offer several arguments about the development of American policy, drawn from the history of international politics and from what many still consider the greatest book on international conflict — Clausewitz's *On War*.

A secondary purpose of the book is to trace the similarities and differences between international politics before and after the coming of nuclear weapons, a task that I take up at greater length in a forthcoming volume.

I believe that technology and politics have combined to create what has been called a nuclear weapons "regime": "a system of international obligations (formal accords, tacit commitments, and informal understandings), and doctrines (when, where, why, how and which nuclear weapons ought to be used) that together govern the role of nuclear weapons in war, peace, and diplomacy,"[1] and that this regime constitutes the feasible obligations, force structures, and doctrines most likely to keep the nuclear peace. In this sense *The Nuclear Question* is the story of the evolution of the best of all possible nuclear worlds, although it is also the story of the failure to bring about the best of all *imaginable* nuclear worlds.

[1] David C. Gompert, "Approaching the Nuclear Future," in Gompert et al., *Nuclear Weapons and World Politics* (New York: McGraw-Hill, 1977), p.6.

I hope that this book will be of interest to those who do not take part in debates about nuclear policy, and who do not feel at home in discussions of throw-weights, cruise missiles, and MIRVs. A kind of allergy to anything connected with nuclear weapons is not uncommon, even among people who follow politics and international affairs attentively. Such an allergy may be founded on the conviction that the doctrines and concepts of nuclear strategy and arms control lie beyond the power of ordinary people to comprehend. This is not so. By describing the origins and development of these concepts and doctrines, I hope to contribute to reducing this allergy.

The book is also written for the specialists who follow the technical developments and the political responses to them that make up the politics of nuclear weapons. I have drawn upon the declassified archival material and the Oral History collection of the John F. Kennedy Library. But most of what is significant for my purposes appears in the public record. By no means all the information on American nuclear weapons policy is yet available. I am confident, however, that when it is, the general picture that I have drawn will not have to be altered significantly.

A word is in order about the book's historical span. Why end in 1976? From a practical viewpoint, a thirty-year span carries the account through the life of the most recent Republican presidency, and the presidential term is a useful way to divide the history of postwar American foreign policy. But the date 1976 is in some respects arbitrary. The SALT II negotiations began before 1976 and continued afterward. Bringing the account to a close in 1976, however, is in keeping with the book's argument that the main lines of nuclear weapons policy were laid down between 1961 and 1963. The following 13 years, as I argue in Chapter VIII, confirmed what the Kennedy administration had established, both deliberately and inadvertently. This remains true in the most recent years as well.

Initially President Carter tried to chart a new course for nuclear weapons policy. He proclaimed the goal of ridding the world entirely of nuclear weapons, and in April 1977 submitted a SALT proposal to the Soviet Union that differed markedly from those previously considered. He was soon forced back to the patterns his predecessors had followed, however, by the Soviet refusal to accept his new proposals.

Like everyone who writes on these matters, I do so in part because I do not want the bombs to go off. Like everybody else, I do not know whether, or when, or between which countries the next nuclear war will be fought. The task of keeping the nuclear peace is, alas, neither simple, nor easy, nor the province of a single nation. I have written The Nuclear Question, however, on the presumption that this task is one to which an account of three decades of American nuclear weapons policy can contribute.

It is a pleasure to acknowledge the debts that I have incurred in writing this book.

I have received help of various kinds from Edward K. Hamilton, Robert Jervis, William W. Kaufmann. Carl Kaysen, Anne Hebald Mandelbaum, David G. Mandelbaum, Gary R. Orren, David Riesman, Michael Schaffer, Edward Skloot, John Steinbruner, Strobe Talbott, Daniel Yergin, and especially from Stanley Hoffmann.

Three research centers generously provided office space, useful libraries, and congenial environments in which to think and write. I am grateful to the Center for International Affairs of Harvard University, and its Director, Raymond Vernon; to the Center for Science and International Affairs at Harvard, and its Director, Paul Doty; and to the Research Institute on International Change at Columbia University, and its Director, Zbigniew Brzezinski, and Acting Director, Seweryn Bialer. I spent part of a year on a Rockefeller Foundation Fellowship in the Humanities largely devoted to other matters working on the book.

The staff of the John F. Kennedy Library, and especially Sylvie Turner, Ann Travis, and Susan Landy, were exceedingly diligent in locating materials there for me.

Barbara Brennecke, Pamela Squires, Barbara Falgoust Williams, Martha Ockenfels, Kenji Gleason, and Eva Morvay typed the manuscript, in its various incarnations, with skill and dispatch.

When I first began to read books like this, I noticed that the author frequently included a special, fulsome tribute to his wife, and wondered why. Now I know.

MICHAEL MANDELBAUM

The Nuclear Question

We find ourselves with an explosive that is far from completely perfected. Yet the future possibilities of such explosives are appalling, and their effects on future wars and international affairs are one of fundamental importance. Here is a new tool for mankind, a tool of unimaginable destructive power. Its development raises many questions that must be answered in the near future.... These questions are not technical questions; they are political and social questions, and the answers given to them may affect all mankind for generations.

Henry De Wolf Smyth, *Atomic Energy for Military Purposes: The Official Report on the Development of the Atomic Bomb Under the Auspices of the United States Government, 1940–1945*[1]

The bomb and the international system

The history of the nuclear age is usually written with a tragic theme at its center. It begins with the discovery by scientists of the technique of liberating the stupendous energy stored in the very heart—the nucleus—of matter. The technique is then used to make explosives more powerful than any ever before known, and two of them are used against Japanese cities in the fateful year 1945. But national leaders, who control the fruits of scientific discovery, miss the chance to trammel this new power, to ban explosives based on it, and thereby to keep mankind safe from the perils of the atom. With this chance tragically missed the threat of annihilation is loosed upon the world.[2]

It is hardly surprising that the history of the nuclear age has been interpreted in this way. An unprecedented threat of annihilation has become a part of modern life. Nuclear weapons have the power to destroy more lives and property more quickly than any of the wars, natural disasters, or plagues of

1

recorded history. They are the most powerful explosives that have ever been devised; indeed, unless the present understanding of the physical world turns out to be radically incomplete, they are the most powerful explosives that can be made by man.

The power of nuclear weapons can be expressed by numbers. One of the commonest kinds of nonnuclear explosives is TNT. The first two bombs, which struck Hiroshima and Nagasaki, were equal in force to about 20,000 tons of TNT. The TNT equivalences of the nuclear weapons that became standard fifteen years later are rendered in the millions of tons. So one such explosive – and the United States and Soviet Union both have thousands – exceeds in power all the bombs that all the allied powers dropped on all of Germany during World War II.[3]

Numbers are abstractions. The power of nuclear weapons can be described more graphically. Exploding shells are a particularly lethal feature of twentieth century warfare. They produced novel, startling, and grisly effects in World War I when they were widely used for the first time. A British soldier recorded a grotesque battlefield scene: "A signaller had just stepped out when a shell burst on him, leaving not a vestige that could be seen anywhere near."[4] A human being simply disappeared. Thirty years later a participant in another war witnessed a similar disappearance. But there was one important difference in 1945: What disintegrated was not a single combatant but an entire city. "The visual results of Hiroshima as seen from the ground were awe-inspiring and tremendous. A city of approximately 300,000 was essentially destroyed."[5]

The devastation of Hiroshima could, in theory, have been accomplished without the atomic bomb. As Thomas Schelling has noted, "Japan was defenseless by August 1945. With a combination of bombing and blockade, eventually invasion, and if necessary the deliberate spread of disease, the United States could probably have exterminated the population of the Japanese islands without nuclear weapons . . . . Against defenseless people there is not much that nuclear weapons can do that cannot be done with an ice pick."[6]

But there is a difference between the kind of bomb used against Hiroshima and Nagasaki and all other instruments of destruction. "Nuclear weapons can do it quickly."[7] The history of warfare is a bloody and terrible history, but it is the history of conflicts that took their tolls in lives and treasure over days, months, and years. The annihilation of Hiroshima took place almost literally in an instant. The bomb exploded at 8:15 a.m. on August 6, 1945; the blast and resulting shock waves lasted only a few minutes, yet both they and the fires that raged in the hours afterward accounted for the "desert of clear-swept, charred remains," the "vast expanse of desolation" that the city became.[8]

So numerous and so powerful are the nuclear weapons of the United States and the Soviet Union today that either could perpetrate several thousand Hiroshimas in a single afternoon. And this, as Schelling went on to point out, makes "the bomb" an entirely different military proposition from all other weapons.

To compress a catastrophic war within the span of time that a man can stay awake drastically changes the politics of war, the process of decision, the possibility of central control and restraint, the motivations of the people in charge, and the capacity to think and reflect while war is in progress. It is imaginable that we might destroy 200,000,000 Russians in a war of the present, though not 80,000,000 Japanese in a war of the past. It is not only imaginable, it is imagined. It is imaginable because it could be done in a moment, in the twinkling of an eye, at the last trumpet.[9]

Indeed, so drastic are these changes that they call into question the very purpose for which all weapons have been used in the past — the conduct of war. According to its foremost student, the nineteenth century Prussian soldier Carl von Clausewitz, war is always and everywhere "an act of force to compel the enemy to do our will."[10] In theory the violence builds to a terrible climax — a blind, furious explosion. In theory, war ends only when one party to it (or both) is crushed. The logic of war, as Clausewitz defined it, is Hiroshima, for nothing in its definition restrains war's essential violence from attaining this extreme, which Clausewitz called "absolute war."

But real wars do not become absolute. There are natural

barriers that limit war's violence.[11] And there is a man-made barrier as well; the political control of force. This is expressed by the best-known phrase in Clausewitz's On War: "War is nothing but the continuation of policy with other means."[12] The phrase is both a statement of fact and an exhortation. Responsible leaders do keep control of their troops during battle. They try to tailor the force they expend to the goals they seek, rather than dispensing violence indiscriminately. To do otherwise would render warfare an absurdity rather than an extension of policy.[13]

The power of nuclear weapons is such as to challenge both the statement and exhortation in Clausewitz's dictum. It jeopardizes both the natural limits on violence, and the prospects for imposing further, political controls, that Clausewitz believed kept all actual wars from mounting to horrible, senseless, "absolute" extremes.

Such is the destructive force of nuclear weapons; awesome, revolutionary, frightening. It is a destructive force that existed before 1945 only in mythology, or in the contemporary equivalent, science fiction. It is a force so great that it is a kind of curse on its possessor. It is only natural to wish, as do historians of the nuclear age, that the world had been spared such force. It would be surprising to discover any other immediate reaction to the invention of these armaments.

But the wish begs a question: What would have been required to spare the world from having to live with the possibility of a nuclear holocaust? The nuclear curse might in theory have been lifted by turning back the advance of science that imposed it. But this was scarcely possible in 1945 or afterward. The modern world could not, and cannot, simply choose to forget the laws of nature whose discovery made possible the manufacture of nuclear explosives, as medieval Europe lost, although not by choice, much of the learning of antiquity.

Alternatively, again in theory, governments could have chosen not to use these discoveries to make weapons. But this self-restraint would have required nothing less than a revolution in international politics, a revolution that has often been

hoped for and occasionally predicted, but that has never occurred. An unbreakable logical chain connects the structure of
international politics with nuclear weapons. The individual
nation — states of the world form a system. Their fates are
joined together. With few exceptions they cannot carry on
their affairs in isolation from their neighbors, or in ignorance
of what other states do. But as well as being interdependent,
they are independent. No central authority exists to guide and
regulate their relations, to set rules for their interactions. The
international system is "anarchic," where anarchy means not
chaos or disorder but the absence of formal organs of government to enforce order, as the instruments of the state do for
domestic society.

The anarchic structure of the international system has a
momentous consequence for its members. It means that with
membership comes insecurity. The inherent insecurity of international life does not arise simply from the logic of their
common predicament. Without an overarching authority,
none can feel wholly protected from the threat of war. Because
this is so, states feel obliged to prepare for war. They arm
themselves, with the best weapons they can get. Since 1945
the most formidable weapons have been nuclear. States may
worry about the devastation sophisticated armaments can
cause. But they will also worry about what their neighbors
will do if they themselves do not have these weapons. The
United States and Great Britain experimented feverishly to
produce atomic bombs during World War II because they
feared that Germany was acquiring them. (Indeed, the Germans did start a nuclear weapons program.) After the war the
mutual fear that the other would draw decisive political advantage from its arsenal spurred competition in nuclear
weaponry between the United States and the Soviet Union.

A world in which no nation would take up arms, including
nuclear arms, would have to be a world without insecurity.
And a world without insecurity would have to be a world
without anarchy. No state would finally renounce armaments
without being certain that all other states would make the
same renunciation. And no state *could* be certain of all the

others as long as the others retained their sovereign independence. For nuclear weapons to be abolished, sovereignty would have to be abolished.[14]

This connection was recognized by one of the important figures of the nuclear age, the Danish theoretical physicist Niels Bohr. Bohr's scientific work helped to harness atomic power. The perils presented by atomic energy deeply troubled him. He carried on a personal campaign during the war to alert the leaders of the United States and Great Britain to these perils, and to persuade them to put the new force under international supervision. He wanted to remove atomic energy from the control of individual nation–states. He understood this would be a revolutionary development. He believed the revolutionary advance of man's mastery of nature represented by the bomb made not only necessary but feasible a comparable revolution in the world's political arrangements.

Bohr had a brief audience with Churchill in May 1944 to present his views. The meeting had no impact on the course of history. But it has a symbolic importance. It was the earliest moment when the most basic issue of the nuclear age was joined. The two men came from different worlds. Bohr was a man of science. His hope for putting atomic energy under an international authority bespoke his roots in the community of scientists, a community that operated according to principles quite dissimilar to the ones that governed the community of nations. No national barriers separated Bohr from his colleagues. Ideas flowed freely among them. Every new discovery became public property, to be shared by all. The community of scientists was a fellowship of openness and cooperation dedicated to a common enterprise – the pursuit of truth. Bohr believed the invention of the bomb offered the occasion for making over the international system in the image of this community.

Churchill did not share this belief. The British Prime Minister was in the midst of a brutal war, and had already spent a long lifetime in the treacherous pathways of international politics, whose code of conduct was altogether harsher than the one to which Bohr was accustomed. Theirs was a dialogue of the deaf. In fact, Bohr scarcely got the chance to open his mouth. There is no record that Churchill took what he had to say very seriously. As the physicist ruefully noted afterward, the two of them did not speak the same language.[15]

The meeting with Churchill was the first, not the last, hearing that Bohr's ideas received. After the war they attracted support that reached into the highest councils of the American government. They were incorporated into public proposals that the United States made to the international community. But the meeting was a portent of things to come.[16] The international system did not change. Nothing remained as sovereign, the system of states as anarchic after World War II and after the dawn of the nuclear age as before. Why was this so?

The shortsightedness of American leaders is sometimes cited as the stumbling block to international reform.[17] They had the bomb, and therefore they had both the opportunity and the responsibility for finding a way to control or abolish it. The Soviet Union has also come in for a share of the blame.[18] The suspicious, narrow-minded Soviet leaders — or, perhaps more properly, the supreme Soviet leader, Joseph Stalin — rejected the proposals for international control that the United States did put forward without trying seriously to find common ground with the Americans. Both these changes carry some weight. But the difficulty of altering the very structure of international politics goes beyond the obstinacy of one or another set of political leaders. The resilience of the sovereign state has a primordial quality. The tendency of people to sort themselves into national groups and to claim wide authority for the governments of these groups has been a force of almost Newtonian power and regularity, as Hobbes and Rousseau, among others, have noted.[19]

Albert Einstein is supposed to have been asked once why man had had the wit to make bombs of unimagined power but could not order his political affairs in such a way that such weapons could never be used. The answer is simple, the great scientist is said to have replied: Politics is more difficult than physics.[20] Why this is so, why the natural world yielded to scientists while the political world resisted the efforts of political leaders, is a question that has no simple answer. That it is so is incontestable. It proved possible to release the energy stored in the nucleus of matter, impossible to reorganize the world so that the energy could never be put to warlike use. The nuclear age is the child of both politics and physics. It is, therefore, the product of the two most powerful forces of the modern age – science and nationalism. And since this is so, its history is not most appropriately understood as a lost opportunity for the transformation of international politics.

As J. Robert Oppenheimer, the scientific head of the wartime Manhattan Project, which produced the first bomb, watched the first atomic explosion in the New Mexico desert, a line from the Hindu epic, the *Bhagavad Ghita*, passed through his mind: "I have become Death, Destroyer of worlds."[21] But the atomic bomb, fearsome and terrible though it was, did not destroy the world of sovereign states. Nuclear weapons became part of an international system whose members had the power to use them. And because the anarchic world of independent nations was preserved, the most pressing of the "many questions" to which what became known as the "Smythe Report" alluded, the question around which the history of the nuclear age has revolved, became not how to *abolish* nuclear weapons but how to *live with* them.

How was the world to live with nuclear weapons? They were unprecedentedly powerful. And yet the direction in which the question led was not entirely unfamiliar. The threat of force and the possibility of war were, after all, as old as the system of independent but interrelated political communities that made such a threat ever-present. And over time, sovereign political communities had developed two instruments of statecraft for managing this threat. One was the art of using force – strategy. The other was the technique of resolving disputes, of transacting the business of the international system without resorting to force – diplomacy. Strategy has to do with wielding military force, diplomacy with talking. But there has always been more to each of them than just that.

The three questions of strategy

In making a strategy, a state must settle upon answers to three questions. What are the political purposes to which its military force will be put? How is that force to be deployed to serve those purposes? And how will the force be used once hostilities have begun?[22]

The political purposes chosen by states have varied widely. Every state seeks security. But security is a highly variable concept. What it takes to make a state feel secure depends upon size, geographical location, domestic structure, and the character of the international milieu. And security is difficult to separate from the panoply of other political ambitions that a state can have, which includes conquest, domination, economic sway, religious and political evangelism, and the reform of the international system itself.

The answers to the second question of strategy, how to deploy force, follow from the answers to the first. These answers, too, have varied widely, especially according to geography and to the state of the military art. How a state has deployed its military might has depended on what political goals it has sought, where it has been located, and what forces have been available for deployment.

There is no pattern or formula that tells how states choose their political purposes, and none for the way they deploy their armed might, either. But the answers to the third question of strategy involve some general considerations. Like the definition of war, these come from Clausewitz. He acknowledged the impossibility of constructing a scientific theory of the political purposes of military force, or of its deployment. There were no hard and fast rules for actually fighting wars, either. But he did provide a set of categories for analyzing and comparing wars, categories that encompass the search for an answer to the question of how to use nuclear force.[23]

Every war, according to Clausewitz, is not only a struggle between two political communities, or groups of communities. It is also, for each party, a contest between the violence that it can master and the natural limits to man-made violence that always keep real wars from reaching "absolute" extremes. The violence of war has three ingredients. The first is physical force. In Clausewitz's day, before the industrial revolution made technology the crucial component, physical force was tied to manpower. A state's military might depended upon how large an army it could put in the field. The second ingredient is morale. The more strongly motivated an army, the better it would fight. Clausewitz gave greater emphasis to the role of morale in war than did other commentators on military affairs of the time. The third ingredient of military violence is what Clausewitz called the commander's "genius for war." By this he meant skill at choosing the proper moment to fight and at inspiring and maneuvering troops.[24]

The natural barriers that have historically modified the violence of war are also three in number. The first of them is the fragmented character of real wars. War never consists of a single blow. A commander cannot concentrate all his forces in a single spot, and pulverize the enemy with one mighty salvo.[25] The second is the natural superiority of the defense over the offense. "It is easier to hold ground than take it,"[26] and this diminishes the power that the attacker can bring to bear. The third barrier to absolute war is what Clausewitz termed "friction" — which is composed of the innumerable unforeseen and unpredictable difficulties that crop up during battle and that prevent plans from being fully translated into action.[27]

Since every nation lives with the threat of war, each must respond, somehow, to the three problems of strategy. Like Molière's bourgeois gentleman, who discovered that he had been speaking prose all his life, every nation has found answers to the three. Every nation has had a strategy, which historians can reconstruct.[28] But not every nation has worked out its strategic policies coherently, self-consciously, or publicly. The political purposes to which most states have put force have usually remained more or less fixed, changing only very slowly, if at all. The deployment of force has often been a matter of custom and tacit assumption rather than explicit doctrine, and it, too, has changed only gradually at most times and in most places. The accepted methods of fighting wars have also frequently been matters of custom, at which nations arrived through trial and error.

The power of nuclear weapons was so vast that their appearance forced an urgent rethinking of all three questions. Even this rethinking was not entirely without precedent. Military innovation was hardly unknown before 1945. New military inventions had prompted strategic revision throughout history. Perhaps the closest parallel to the coming of nuclear weapons was the switch from sail to steam propulsion of naval vessels in the nineteenth century. This shift helped to alter the foreign policies of the European powers by making trade both accessible and profitable with parts of the globe previously guarded by difficult ocean currents and uncertain wind patterns. The age of steam helped to touch off the surge of European imperial expansion in the latter part of the century. The deployment of navies changed as well. Naval squadrons were based on colonial ports that could reliably supply them with fuel in wartime, whereas sailing war ships had not required such an extensive system of bases. The location of its coaling stations determined a fleet's range. And battle tactics had to be completely revamped. Previously everything had depended upon the direction and strength of the wind. With steamships this was no longer so, and a whole new set of rules had to be worked out.[29]

But the shift from sail to steam took place over a century. The nuclear revolution came much more swiftly, and the increment of destructive power that nuclear armaments placed in the hands of political leaders was far greater. The invention of nuclear weapons was part of an ongoing trend, that of using the discoveries of science to make ever more powerful armaments. But the power of these weapons, the power to destroy entire cities "in the twinkling of an eye," made them a sharp departure from the pattern of the past. Strategy could not be adapted to nuclear weapons leisurely, or through trial and error.

The drama of the nuclear age is the account of how a new strategy was devised to accommodate this revolutionary force to the uncertainties and the dangers of politics in the anarchic system of nation — states. But that is only half of the story. The other half of the history is the adaptation to changes in international politics brought about by the new weapon of the other traditional instrument of statecraft – diplomacy.

The two schools of diplomacy

War has not, ordinarily, been the favored means of resolving disputes between nations. Diplomacy, the management of international relations by negotiations, has usually, although not always, been preferred. Churchill put it succinctly: "Better jaw jaw than war war." The two are not wholly separate. The possibility of war bends diplomats to their task. Negotiations are often carried out with the threat of violence lurking in the background. And, as Clausewitz noted, diplomatic contact continues even while battles are taking place. Diplomacy has the same root as strategy; the "anarchic" international system that gives all its members a measure of independence and confers upon each a corresponding measure of insecurity.

Like strategy, diplomacy has three parts. There are three requirements for the successful resolution of disputes between nations through negotiation. The first is a common frame of reference. The parties must agree on what is negotiable, and on how to proceed. The second requirement is that the terms of a diplomatic settlement must apportion benefits and sacrifices more or less evenly to the nations receiving them and making them. History is, of course, filled with negotiated settlements with manifestly unequal effects on the parties concerned. But these settlements involved nations quite unequal in power: Either one country had defeated the other in war or could easily have done so. These unequal accords are the result of dictation – not diplomacy, which must take place between equals. Of course no two states or groups of states are ever precisely equal in strength. But diplomatic partners, like the United States and the Soviet Union after 1945, are equal enough – that is, each is strong enough – not to be brow-beaten by the other. Each can credibly threaten to go to war rather than submit to dictation. Neither can enforce its will upon the other without paying an appreciable price. The third requirement for successful diplomacy is the political will to agree.

Even with a common frame of reference and terms that affect all parties equally, agreements do not come automatically. The diplomatic process is in this respect like a piece of machinery; no matter how good the working order of its parts, it requires a source of energy to run. Political will is the gasoline, or the electricity, of diplomacy.

As with the first and second questions of strategy, no formula or general pattern encompasses the many ways in which the second or third requirements for successful diplomacy have been met in the history of relations among sovereign states. But in modern times two variants of the first requirement have appeared; there have been two different frames of reference for diplomacy.

The origins of the first, "traditional" style of diplomacy lie in north and central Italy in the fifteenth and sixteenth centuries. There separate city–states emerged and were thrust up against one another; together they constituted a distinct system, just as the nation–states of today do. They had governments capable of raising and sustaining armies, which, partly to consolidate power, partly because of the exuberant, aggressive character of the era, were constantly fighting with each other. And with the demise of medieval Christendom there was no overarching authority with the power to restrain them.

These city–states began stationing ambassadors at each other's courts. At first the ambassadors served to gather public information, otherwise unavailable to their distant countrymen, and to subvert the political plans of their hosts. Occasionally they helped to forge alliances – *combinazioni* – but these seldom lasted for long. In general, Renaissance diplomacy was a continuation of the conflict between states by other, less violent, but no less ruthless, means.[30] But gradually the possibility of using diplomacy to moderate, as well as to prosecute conflicts between states, became apparent and attractive. The Peace of Lodi, signed in 1441, recognized the mutual interest of the signatories in restraining themselves and preserving the status quo. And although they did not always observe that interest, the second half of the fifteenth century was a more tranquil period than the decades that preceded the agreement.[31]

The assumptions implicit in the Peace of Lodi spread beyond the borders of Italy and came to dominate the relations between the principal nations of Europe during the seventeenth, eighteenth, and nineteenth centuries. The era of traditional diplomacy spanned the decades between the Peace of Westphalia, in 1648, and the outbreak of the First World War, in 1914. The several treaties signed at Westphalia enshrined the single most important principle on which traditional diplomacy was based – the immutable sovereignty of the nation–state.[32] Traditional diplomacy came to full flower after the Congress of Vienna, in 1815, when the principal members of the international system made the adjustment of differences without general war and the maintenance of an international equilibrium the chief goals of their foreign policies.

The establishment of the agent of diplomacy, the ambassador, as a permanent official signaled the common presumption that the anarchy of the international system was a permanent condition, and that the adjustment of discord would be perpetually necessary. The decline of the Renaissance practice of expecting the envoy to stir mischief in the capital where he was posted testified to the respect each member of the international system was increasingly prepared to pay to the sovereignty of the other. And when the Treaty of Utrecht gave international recognition to England's revolution of 1688, a nation's sovereignty was effectively severed, in the eyes of the international community, from the person of any particular ruler.[33] The supremacy of the nation–state was complete.

An intricate cocoon of etiquette came to surround the conduct of traditional diplomacy. Partly this was because diplomacy became the preserve of the aristocracy, a class given to ritual both to emphasize its own distinctive importance and to use and display its wealth in the era before economic growth offered more productive uses for affluence. But the formal aspects of the diplomatic method also served to emphasize, in the absence of an authority to enforce them, the obligations that international agreements entailed. Diplomatic ritual, especially in the nineteenth century, particularly stressed the hierarchy of nation–states. Great powers had larger prerogatives and responsibilities than lesser ones. The strong paid greater heed to each other, and assumed the common right to intervene in the affairs of the weak.

Traditional diplomacy did not abolish political conflict, or even war. It was not intended to do so. It was intended to keep war from becoming eternal, and from consuming all of Europe's energies. But it did not prevent this from happening in the first years of the nineteenth century, when Napoleon's conquests and the resistance that they aroused plunged the continent into the largest conflict it had ever seen. Still, the aftermath of the Napoleonic wars saw the reaffirmation of general faith in the tenets and procedures of classical diplomacy. It seemed the best solution available to the perennial problem of security that the anarchic character of the international system bequeathed to the nation–states that comprised it.

But as traditional diplomacy came to govern the relations between the principal countries of Europe, a current of opposition to it developed that took issue with the fundamental traditional assumption, the primacy of the nation–state. This dissenting view sought to do away with national sovereignty, the feature of international politics that permitted wars to break out from time to time despite the best efforts of professional diplomats at prevention. The proponents of this view wanted to replace the bewigged, perfumed gentlemen and the selfish governments they represented with a more reliable mechanism for averting international conflict. The opposition to national sovereignty and the advocacy of some alternative to the international anarchy existed for most of the heyday of traditional diplomacy in the writings of a few critics and visionaries, who attracted relatively little interest and few followers.

This opposition had three main variants. In the seventeenth and eighteenth centuries, when the memory of a unified community of Christian nations still persisted, some vision-

aries called for the establishment of a world state, or at least a
state encompassing all the major European powers. There
were proposals to pool all separate sovereignties in one towering international Leviathan.[34] In the early nineteenth century,
with the rise of the philosophy of laissez-faire liberalism and
its hostility to government of any sort, the hopes of many who
wished to do away with national sovereignties turned to the
expectation that individual governments, which were artificial in the first place, would disappear, leaving the naturally
harmonious impulses of the world's societies free to usher in
perpetual peace.[35]

In the latter half of that century, however, as the resilience of
the nation–state and the strength of nationalist feelings made
themselves felt, both positions lost their force. The champions
of a world state had to concede that individual nations placed
a high value on their separate identities. And those who
awaited the withering away of the various states of the international system had to confront the fact that national governments were, contrary to their hopes and expectations, mul-
tiplying and prospering. Thus an approach midway between
the two became popular: a confederation of states to which its
members would surrender at least some of their authority. The
dissenters from the founding assumption of classical diplomacy gave up the idea of submerging or abolishing national
sovereignty completely and concentrated instead on trying to
moderate it.[36]

A confederacy, an international organization that would
keep peace by regulating relations between states, became by
the end of the nineteenth century the principal goal of the
proposed alternative to the traditional method of international
negotiation, an alternative that may be called "liberal diplomacy." It deserves the title "liberal" because it was born of the
optimistic belief in human progress that is characteristic of
liberal thought and the equally characteristic faith that great
problems could be solved by political reform. It was liberal,
too, in foreseeing a world government drawn along the lines of
the political institutions of the liberal state, foremost among
which was the representative assembly, or parliament. The

member states, it was assumed, would have liberal constitutions. And the alternative approach to diplomacy was characteristically liberal because it was most popular in the liberal nations of Western Europe and North America. By the end of the nineteenth century, several of these countries had incorporated the tenets of liberal diplomacy into their national policies. The goal of replacing the international anarchy with some sort of international organization ceased to be the reverie of a few eccentrics.

The goal of reducing and even abolishing national armaments was an expression of the liberal approach to diplomacy. The influence of this approach showed most clearly in the meetings, held with increasing frequency as the nineteenth century gave way to the twentieth, to abolish, reduce, and control such armaments.[37] It reflected the supposition, akin to the liberal faith in progress, that armaments caused war, and that abolishing them was the way to bring peace. Armaments were the essence of national sovereignty because they were its ultimate guarantors, so restricting weapons seemed a logical way to moderate sovereignty. And schemes to reduce armaments invariably raised the need for some sort of international mechanism of enforcement. Finally, efforts to put limits on military might evoked the greatest enthusiasm from the liberal states of the international system, especially the United States of America.

Traditional diplomacy presumed that the nations of the international system would remain independent, free of the overarching authority that the state imposes in domestic politics, and that disputes among them would have to be resolved within the framework of the "international anarchy." Liberal diplomacy proceeded from the opposite premise. It took as its principal task the eradication of national sovereignty, so that the sovereign prerogative to go to war, and thus war itself, would no longer exist. This premise became increasingly attractive as wars became ever more destructive. Both diplomatic methods were alive in historical memory at the dawn of the nuclear age. And just as the advent of atomic weapons made it necessary to recast the principles of national strategy, so it prompted the urgent reconsideration of diplomacy. Conflict between nations had become extraordinarily dangerous because war had become, potentially, so destructive.

Two prophets

The task of finding a strategy and a diplomacy appropriate to the age of nuclear weapons fell to the United States. America was the first nuclear power. And it remained the leading nuclear nation even when others acquired atomic weapons. Because the new instruments of destruction came first into American hands, the United States was the leader in working out strategic principles that incorporated them. And because, among other reasons, the horrors of nuclear war were vivid to Americans, especially those who had had a hand in making the first bomb, the United States pressed ahead with the search for a diplomacy that could make certain that another nuclear assault would never occur. The United States has shared the summit of nuclear strength with the Soviet Union for most of the nuclear age. It is arguable that the Soviet Union has largely followed the American lead in coming to grips with the problem of nuclear weapons.[38] It is certain that the Americans fashioned a nuclear strategy and a nuclear diplomacy more openly, and more self-consciously, than did the Soviets. The story of how the United States adapted the venerable instruments of statecraft, strategy and diplomacy, to the fearsome armaments that science created in the second half of the twentieth century is not the full story of the nuclear age. But it is a good part of that story, and the part that can most readily be told.

The American reaction to the news of Hiroshima and Nagasaki was swift and sharp. The feeling spread quickly that international politics had changed dramatically, that a new age was at hand, and that entirely new measures were required for nations to survive and prosper. But there were different notions of what these new measures should be. In the national discussion about the proper policies for the atomic age that took place immediately after the bombs were dropped two voices proved to be prophetic. Two men foresaw the lines of strategy and diplomacy that would enable the world to live with nuclear weapons.

The strategic seer was Bernard Brodie, who had written before the war on the impact of the industrial revolution upon seapower,[39] and who edited a book published in 1946 entitled *The Absolute Weapon: Atomic Power and World Order*,[40] to which he contributed two prescient essays. Brodie foresaw the principal features of the nuclear age before they had come fully into being. "Everything about the bomb," he wrote, "is overshadowed by the twin facts that it exists and that its destructive power is fantastically great."[41] He correctly assumed that the new bombs would become available in relative abundance.[42] And he foresaw two other important developments: "No adequate defense against the bomb exists," he asserted, "and the possibilities of its existence in the future are exceedingly remote."[43] Neither sophisticated antiaircraft batteries nor the superiority of one air force over another could prevent grievous damage to both sides in a war between nuclear-equipped states.

The defenselessness of all states against nuclear assault was the first development. The second was the likelihood of what came subsequently to be known as "nuclear proliferation." Whatever the wishes of the United States, Brodie predicted, "other powers besides Britain and Canada will possess the ability to produce the bombs in quantity within a period of five to ten years hence."[44]

Niels Bohr's colleagues, the atomic scientists, also foresaw these developments. J. Robert Oppenheimer concluded that the bomb would prove to be a weapon for aggressors. Brodie disagreed. Oppenheimer's gloomy judgement that the bomb introduced a profoundly dangerous and unstable element into world politics depended, Brodie pointed out, on "one vital but unexpressed assumption; that the nation which proposes to launch the attack will not need to fear retaliation. If it must fear retaliation," he reasoned, "the fact that it destroys its opponent's cities some hours or even days before its own are destroyed may avail it little."[45] A state could guard itself against nuclear attack if it had the ability to retaliate in kind. This was the central insight of Brodie's essays. It has some claim to being the foremost strategic proposition of the nuclear age.

The rest of the strategic wisdom that Brodie offered was summed up in a single sentence: "Thus far the chief purpose of our military establishment has been to win wars. From now on its chief purpose must be to avert them. It can have almost no other useful purpose."[46] Together with his emphasis on the ability to retaliate, that sentence foreshadowed a particular nuclear strategy. The purpose of nuclear force would be to prevent wars. A state could prevent them by deploying its forces so as to be able to respond to a nuclear attack with a nuclear salvo of its own. And as for using nuclear armaments (although not necessarily other weapons) in battle, there would be no fruitful or sensible way to do so.

These are the answers to the three strategic questions upon which the American government eventually decided. But the decisions were not taken in 1945. This was partly because the conditions Brodie foresaw had not yet come fully into existence. There was only one nuclear state. And the United States owned, at most, a few relatively primitive atomic bombs. Scientists and social scientists could discern the nuclear future. But generals and political leaders could not act on it until it had arrived. Ten years were required for the features of the nuclear age that Brodie had predicted to be wholly realized, and ten more for the strategic principles that his early analysis had suggested to be widely accepted.

And the eventual answers to the three strategic questions did not become official policy immediately after the end of the war because American hopes for easing the danger that nuclear weapons presented rested, at first, on diplomacy. The style of diplomacy upon which the United States ultimately came to rely also had its prophet. He was the American Secretary of War, Henry Stimson. He knew of the Manhattan Project and realized even before Hiroshima how deeply the bomb would influence the future of international politics. A month after the war had ended he put his thoughts about what to do with the new explosive in a memorandum to President Truman. Much depended, he noted, on how the bomb affected relations with the Soviet Union. "My idea of an approach to the Soviets," he wrote, "would be a direct proposal after discussion with the British that we would be prepared to enter into an arrangement with the Russians, the general purpose of which would be to control and limit the use of the atomic bomb as an instrument of war and so far as possible to direct and encourage the development of atomic power for peaceful and humanitarian purposes."[47]

Stimson's recommendation was notable for what it did not include. It did not envision abolishing the new weapon altogether. There was no suggestion that an attempt be made to keep the rudiments of nuclear technology secret. Nor did Stimson think it wise to try to use the bomb to compel the Soviets to conduct their affairs in a way more in keeping with American preferences. After the Potsdam Conference with the Soviets and the British in 1945, he wrote, he had briefly entertained the thought of employing "the atomic 'secret'. . . to win concessions from the Russian leaders as to their cherished, if frightful, police state."[48] But he had rejected this idea. And he warned against one of the hallmarks of liberal diplomacy, the placing of nuclear questions in the hands of an international organization. "Action of any international group of nations," he said, "including many small nations, who have not yet demonstrated their potential power or responsibility in this war would not, in my opinion, be taken seriously by the Soviets.[49]

Stimson did not have a formula for answering the nuclear question. He offered, rather, an approach to finding one. What he suggested amounted to an extension of the diplomacy of World War II, when the leaders of the United States and the Soviet Union, along with Great Britain, were forced together in common cause by a dangerous enemy. He hoped that the fearful potency of the new weapon would clear away some common ground, and make for a modicum of mutual trust between them, just as Fascism had. And his recommendations followed the lines of traditional diplomacy: the recognition of hierarchy in the international system, with some of its members carrying greater weight than others; the practice of transacting business among nations directly and in private rather than in public international forums; and the understanding that states would not interfere in each other's internal affairs – that they would respect each other's sovereignty.

Stimson retired from active government service soon after submitting his memorandum to the President. His colleagues and successors honored his career, but ignored his advice. Hiroshima and Nagasaki had dramatized, far more emphatically than any memorandum could, the need to find some way to control the military use of atomic energy. But to try to control it the American government drew first upon a different approach to international negotiation. The initial American nuclear policy was squarely in the tradition of liberal diplomacy. It proceeded from the fundamental liberal premise; it took as the central task of American diplomacy the transformation of international politics in such a way that nuclear weapons would disappear.

The Failure
of Liberal Diplomacy

You come up to face these terrible issues and you know that what is in almost everybody's heart is a wish for peace, and you want to do *something*. . . .
Dwight D. Eisenhower[1]

The Baruch Plan

The first official American approach to the problems that nuclear weapons posed was presented to the newly formed United Nations organization in 1946. The allied powers had laid the groundwork for the UN while the Second World War was still in progress. It was the international organization in which American hopes for a peaceful and orderly postwar world rested. The scheme was called the Baruch Plan, after the man President Truman chose to present it, Bernard Baruch — financier, philanthropist, and purveyor of advice to several chief executives. The Baruch Plan called for the creation of an "International Atomic Development Authority" that would take control of "all phases of the development and use of atomic energy," from the mining of the necessary raw materials to the operation of reactors to the conduct of nuclear research and development.[2] The Baruch Plan proposed to keep atomic bombs out of the hands of sovereign states by placing the means to make them under the supervision of a

supranational body. That body would have the power, as
Baruch envisioned it, to mete out "immediate, swift and sure
punishment" to any nation that attempted to acquire them.
The UN had been created as a two-tiered body. In the General
Assembly every state had a single vote, and a majority was
sufficient to pass any measure. But above the General Assembly stood the Security Council, made up of the most powerful
states in the international system, including the United States
and the Soviet Union. And any permanent member of the Security Council could defeat a proposal with a negative vote.
Baruch stipulated that the new Atomic Development Authority would not report to the Security Council, thereby making
its dictates immune to the veto of one of the Council's permanent members.[3]

The Baruch Plan bore the stamp of Niels Bohr's ideas. He
was its spiritual father, and his scientific colleagues played
important roles in its creation. The substance of the Plan
emerged from a series of memoranda, declarations, and reports that scientists helped to shape. It was they who pressed
upon government officials the idea of international control,
which the Plan incorporated. Indeed, after the war they
formed an organization to lobby for this idea.[4]

The scientists had a hand in fashioning important markers
on the trail that led from Bohr's vision to the Baruch Plan. At
the end of September 1944, Vannevar Bush, chairman of the
Manhattan Project's Military Committee, and James Conant,
his deputy, both prominent scientists, sent a memorandum to
Secretary of War Stimson suggesting that atomic weapons be
turned over to some sort of international agency after the war's
end.[5] By November of 1945 the war was over, the feasibility
and the power of the atomic bomb had been conclusively
demonstrated at Hiroshima and Nagasaki, and President Truman was meeting with the Prime Ministers of Great Britain
and Canada to consider, among other things, the future of
atomic energy. Bush was instrumental in preparing a statement issued in the names of all three leaders declaring their
readiness to take steps to put this new force under international control, and calling for the establishment of a UN com-

mittee to work out specific steps in this direction. To prepare
an American position for this UN inquiry, President Truman
appointed a committee headed by Under Secretary of State
Dean Acheson and the Chairman of the Tennessee Valley Authority David Lilienthal. Both Bush and Conant sat on the
Acheson–Lilienthal panel. The report that the panel produced had a central theme – the international control of
atomic energy – and it became, with a few modifications, the
basis for the Baruch Plan.

The Baruch Plan made a generally favorable impression on
the members of the United Nations. There was, however, a
notable exception: It did not favorably impress the Soviet
Union. Five days after Baruch offered his formula the Soviet
delegate, Andrei Gromyko, tabled a counterproposal. It called,
initially, for an international convention "prohibiting the
production and employment of weapons based on the use of
atomic energy."[6] Parties to the convention would promise not
to use, produce, or store atomic weapons in the future and to
destroy all present stocks within three months from the day
the convention entered into force. Gromyko also proposed the
creation of two committees under UN auspices; one to work
out channels for circulating scientific information, the other to
devise a system of safeguards against violating the initial convention. But the safeguards would come only *after* the
weapons, which the United States alone then possessed, had
been destroyed. And Gromyko made it clear that whatever
organization came into being to monitor atomic energy had to
include a provision for a veto.[7]

Months of discussion and negotiation followed. But no
common ground could be found. Neither side would move far
enough from its initial position to accommodate the other. A
technical committee was set up, and it issued several reports.
The Security Council considered the matter. The General Assembly encouraged the talks to go on. But the deadlock remained unbroken. Finally, in November 1949, more than three
years after they had begun, the deliberations of the United
States Atomic Energy Committee were discontinued. Their
failure had been sealed the month before, on September 23,

when the Soviet Union had set off, for the first time, a nuclear explosion of its own.

Even if the Soviets had found the Baruch Plan more attractive than they did, it is not at all clear, in retrospect, that the American government would have been willing to carry out its provisions. The Americans were cautious about revealing the "secrets" of atomic energy and there was a reluctance, strongly felt by members of the Acheson–Lilienthal group and reflected in the rejection of the Soviet counterproposal to the Plan, to divulge useful atomic information before a workable system of international control was in place.[8] Moreover, any agreement on international control would have come under close congressional scrutiny, and the Congress was not happy about the dissemination of the discoveries made by American scientists and their foreign colleagues working under American auspices. The May–Johnson bill for the control of atomic energy, which left open the possibility of military supervision, which made no provision for sharing with other nations what American scientists had learned, and which included criminal penalties for the disclosure of classified information, had been defeated – but only after a spirited political battle.[9] And the McMahon Act, which the Congress had passed in its stead, did not mandate an entirely open-handed approach to nuclear matters. Truman had appointed Baruch as his special representative to the UN meetings in the hope that the financier's stature in the country and in the Congress would help to blunt suspicions of any plan for international control. Public opinion on the subject of atomic energy, although diffuse, uncertain, and susceptible to the influence of political leaders, especially the President, seemed to favor keeping atomic information secret.[10] And the American armed services, which took almost no part in preparing the Baruch Plan, had deep reservations about relinquishing control of a potentially decisive weapon.[11]

The Baruch Plan is important not as an end but as a beginning. It was not the last chance to put the new fearsome power of the atom under international supervision – although it represents the apogee of hope for international control – but the first of many failed attempts to do so. The Baruch Plan, and the Soviet response to it, served as models for the nuclear diplomacy of the next fifteen years. In that period the two sides tabled dozens of schemes and spent hundreds of hours discussing them. Almost all resembled, in crucial respects, the original positions. And this resemblance doomed them. None led to an agreement. Throughout the 1950s nuclear negotiation was a soufflé that never rose, because the United States and the Soviet Union followed the recipe, with the same principal ingredients, that had failed in 1946.

The nuclear diplomacy of the 1950s

The Baruch Plan was a liberal proposal. It bore three distinct liberal trademarks that characterized its successors as well. It was, first of all, sweeping in scope, in contrast to the traditional practice of concentrating on a few concrete issues. It was intended to bring all facets of nuclear energy everywhere under international control. Baruch strongly implied that his scheme was to be understood as the first step toward the abolition of *all* weapons.[12] Successor plans had similarly broad goals. Even after both the United States and the Soviet Union had accumulated sizable stockpiles of nuclear weapons, at least rhetorical homage continued to be paid to the goal of "general and complete disarmament." The British and French floated a proposal to that end in 1954 and 1955. In 1959 Soviet Prime Minister Khrushchev called for the abolition of all weapons of war over a period of four years in a speech to the United Nations. And two years later, from the same rostrum, President Kennedy announced a plan for full-scale disarmament.

The Baruch Plan was liberal, as well, in its manner of presentation — before the United Nations. Despite Stimson's warning, the task of controlling nuclear energy was entrusted to the international organization that the victors had created at the end of World War II. And even after the glow that surrounded its birth had faded and bright hopes for its success had been tempered by the harsh realities of postwar interna-

tional politics, the UN remained the principal forum for nuclear diplomacy. Every nation, large or small, thereby received
the opportunity to air its views on nuclear weapons.

And the Baruch Plan was most characteristically liberal –
and this was the most telling point for the future of nuclear
diplomacy – in its provision for the dilution of national sovereignty. It required every state to surrender the prerogative of
acquiring the most powerful of all weapons, and to submit to
the authority, in nuclear matters, of a supranational body. It
therefore envisioned a partial transformation of international
politics, of the kind that Bohr and his scientific colleagues had
anticipated. The transformation was not complete. While an
international authority governed all nuclear matters, the rest
of the world's business would presumably continue to be
transacted by sovereign, independent states. But coexistence
between those two ways of doing business might not be easy.
Walter Lippmann wrote: "... There cannot be a system of world
law that is unique for atomic energy and a different and conflicting system for the maintenance of peace."[13]

Dean Acheson believed that when the two systems con-
flicted, sovereignty would win out. Indeed, he believed that
no international body would be able to restrain a great power
bent on acquiring nuclear weapons. He, and others, saw the
international authority as a kind of warning system to alert the
world when a state was launching a nuclear weapons program, not as the foundation of world government.[14] But
Baruch regarded the Plan as a means of implementing the
scientist's vision. He made no bones about this. He asserted
that it was time for Americans "to start freeing ourselves from
the fetish of national sovereignty."[15]

The Soviets understood what the Baruch Plan required them
to give up. Gromyko denounced the American proposal on the
grounds that it would "lead to interference by the (proposed)
control organ in the internal affairs of States and eventually
would lead to arbitrary action by the control organ in the solution of such problems as fall completely within the domestic
jurisdiction of a state."[16] The United States favored the restriction of national sovereignty. The Soviet Union opposed it.
This impasse persisted through the 1950s.

The Americans insisted that any disarmament plan had to have some enforcement mechanism. There had, in the American view, to be safeguards of some sort to prevent violations of the terms of any nuclear treaty, or at the very least to detect violations. And these safeguards always involved some intrusion upon sovereignty. The Soviets refused to accept any such intrusion. This difference was an obstacle to agreement that no nuclear negotiation ever managed to overcome.

Liberal diplomacy held out the same appeal at the beginning of the nuclear age as before. It seemed to offer a way to put an end to war once and for all. The invention of nuclear weapons seemed to have made the survival of civilization itself contingent on doing so. Before 1945 the "anarchic" structure of international relations had endured, despite the obvious connection between the absence of world government and the persistence of war. But the blast of the first nuclear weapons was powerful enough to knock down the walls of national sovereignty. Or so it seemed in the United States.

The logic of liberal diplomacy was particularly compelling to Americans. For the child of Europe had embraced with enthusiasm the dissenting strain in European diplomacy. Their country's history predisposed Americans to the attitude toward war and peace that the liberal approach implied. For the first century and a quarter of its life the United States had gone about its business in relative isolation from the main currents of international affairs, towering over its immediate neighbors, with whom it had no need to hammer out terms of coexistence, and sheltered from the maelstrom of European politics by the Atlantic Ocean and the British Navy that patrolled it. Americans had slight acquaintance with the stubborn persistence of conflicting interests among different nation – states. American history, unlike the history of Europe, did not testify to the durability of the international anarchy and its consequences.

And if the traditional principle that force was an inevitable part of international politics rang false to Americans, the liberal belief in the pooling of separate sovereignties struck a responsive chord. For the United States, after all, had had its origins in a confederation of previously autonomous units.

The founding of their republic offered to Americans the same hopeful precedent for a world without artificial barriers and the conflict they bred that the international scientific community offered to Bohr and his associates. The United States itself was, in the words of an American treatise on international affairs written at the beginning of the twentieth century, "an exemplification of international organization."[17]

When the United States broke out of its isolation and entered into the thick of world politics, traditional diplomacy had fallen into disrepute, absorbing much of the blame for the catastrophic bloodletting of the First World War,[18] a war that America had entered late enough to avoid most of the carnage but early enough to claim a voice in the peace settlement. The American President, Woodrow Wilson, made his presence felt in the meetings that followed the end of hostilities. And he made his characteristically American ideas heard. He became the zealous champion of liberal diplomacy, bent on replacing the international anarchy with a compact that would bind all the states of the world together. Wilson proposed the establishment of a League of Nations to resolve international disagreements and punish blatant transgressors, thereby rescuing the world from the perpetual insecurity and the periodic wars that the international system permitted. He expected that member states would adopt liberal domestic procedures and that the international organization would operate according to similarly liberal rules.[19]

The League of Nations embodied the principles of liberal diplomacy. It was the first real trial they received. And it failed. The United States, despite Wilson's efforts, did not join. The organization's meager powers could not sustain its vast ambitions and the forces that culminated in the second great war of the century tore the League apart. When World War II ended the United States was again deeply involved in European politics. This time there would be no retreat into isolation. And 1945, even more than 1918, seemed an auspicious moment for a fresh vision of international affairs. For the second World War had finished what the first had begun — a sweeping change in the distribution of power in the international system. The two wars had enfeebled some previously mighty members of that system and swept others away altogether. What had happened since 1918 had reinforced American faith in liberal diplomacy. World War II proved not that the liberal approach would not work, but that it was needed all the more urgently. And the atomic bomb underscored that urgency.

No other nation embraced the tenets of liberal diplomacy with the enthusiasm of the United States, for no other national history seemed to bear them out so emphatically. But it is doubtful that any member of the international community regarded them with quite the same measure of distaste as the Soviet Union. Liberal diplomacy ran counter to the deepest convictions of the Soviet leaders. Openness was one of its hallmarks. Americans associated secrecy with skulduggery at home and war abroad. The Soviet state, on the other hand, had been founded on secrecy. A conspiratorial party had seized power in 1917 and had never abandoned its habits of wariness. The power of the Communist party rested, in its own view,[20] on sealing off its borders from foreign influences and keeping the government's transactions concealed from public view. Bloody internal purges, two invasions within 25 years, and an ideology that posited a death struggle with the capitalist nations of the world, all fed Soviet distrust for the liberal precepts in which the Baruch Plan was grounded. The Soviet government did not wish to relinquish its sovereign powers. Its chief postwar aim was to reinforce them. It was intent, in 1946 and afterward, upon closing its country off from the rest of the world, not opening it up. The American commitment to liberal diplomacy, rooted in American history and strengthened by the horror of nuclear weapons, and the Soviet distaste for the liberal approach, equally firmly grounded in Russian history and comparably strengthened by Soviet fears, meant that the Baruch Plan did not meet the first requirement of successful diplomacy — a common frame of reference. Like Bohr and Churchill, the United States and the Soviet Union, where nuclear matters were concerned, did not speak the same language.

The Baruch Plan did not meet the second requirement –
equal terms – either. It affected the two principal nations quite
differently. The difference was partly that one of them accepted the liberal vision of world order while the other rejected it. But there was another asymmetry in the two positions. In June 1946, the United States had already built and
tested an atomic bomb. The Soviet Union had not. The Soviets
would not commit themselves to a plan that would have left
the United States with an understanding of how to make a
bomb, even if not with its fruits, while preventing any other
country from acquiring either.[21] And the Americans did not
propose to give up their weapons until all parts of the international nuclear authority were in place and running smoothly.
"We should not throw away our gun," Truman wrote to
Baruch, "until we are sure that the rest of the world can't arm
against us."[22] First came the international organization, in the
American scheme of things, and then the surrender of existing
weaponry. The Soviet plan reversed the order: first it proposed
to eliminate the bombs, and then the world could devise a
system for keeping others from being manufactured.

The pattern persisted. The United States continued to insist
that ground rules for prohibiting atomic weapons be established before existing arsenals were abolished. The Soviets
stuck to the reverse preference. And each put forward other
proposals that would have worked to its own advantage. The
American "Open Skies" plan of 1957 called for each side to
permit unimpeded aerial surveillance of its territory. But since
much more was known about American than about Soviet
military power this would have amounted to a concession by
the Soviets, who would have been disadvantaged further because the extent of American nuclear superiority would have
become known. The Soviets, for their part, several times
suggested the removal of atomic armaments from Germany
and the drawing down of conventional forces in Europe. Both
of these measures would have had a greater effect on the
United States and its allies than upon the Soviet bloc, for the
Western powers had assigned a greater role in their defense
plans to nuclear weapons, and could mobilize nonnuclear
forces less rapidly than the Soviet Union and its allies.

It was difficult, during the decade and a half after the Baruch Plan made its debut, to find potential nuclear agreements that conspicuously favored neither side. And after a time both great powers ceased to search for compromises as energetically as they might have. The third requirement for successful diplomacy, the political will to agree, was also missing after 1946. Nuclear negotiations were overtaken by the increasingly bitter rivalry between the United States and the Soviet Union. This was the final fatal flaw in the Baruch Plan: It was bound up with the Cold War.

The Cold War and the nuclear age were in fact born twins. And they influenced each other. The Baruch Plan helped to start the Cold War, for it collapsed at an important moment in the sequence of events that led from joined hands to drawn swords. It came at a time, just after the initial American chagrin over the forcible installation of Soviet dominated governments in Eastern Europe, and before the ringing declaration of the Truman doctrine that the United States would resist the spread of Communism everywhere, when the American attitude toward the Soviet Union was hardening and those responsible for American foreign policy were deciding to "get tough" with the Russians.[23] The brusque Soviet rejection of Baruch's proposal was taken as one among a growing number of signs that the Russians did not intend to cooperate with the Western democracies. And the Cold War, in turn, dimmed the prospects for adoption of the nuclear proposals that followed the Baruch Plan. It prevented the development of the good will that is the precondition for any diplomatic agreement between equals. Every plan and proposal that passed between the two great powers became tainted by their mutual suspicions. Even a purposely friendly gesture could be interpreted as a tactical maneuver in the ongoing struggle between the Soviet Union and the United States.

The search for a "first step"

The fifteen years following the introduction of the Baruch Plan were filled with proposals for controlling nuclear weapons, and with international meetings to discuss them.

None was enacted. But plans continued to be drafted even when they had no chance of adoption; and conferences continued to meet even when the participants had no hope of producing an agreement. Nuclear diplomacy went forward in the 1950s partly because neither the United States nor the Soviet Union wished to seem less devoted than the other to the cause of peace. The leaders of each country strove to impress their own people, and the leaders and citizens of third countries, with their sensitivity to the perils of the nuclear age and their ardent desire to find a way to avoid them. Each, in fact, wanted to put the other in a bad light, and so each put forward proposals that it felt confident the other would reject. Nuclear diplomacy turned into a battleground of the Cold War, and offering proposals and counterproposals became a form of political warfare.

But the persistence at nuclear negotiations in the Eisenhower years, at least on the American side, was inspired by more than the hope of seizing an advantage in the conflict between East and West. It grew as well out of the same horror at the destructive power of nuclear weapons, and consequent hope of finding some way to bottle up that power, that had given rise to the Baruch Plan.

"We are here to make a choice between the quick and the dead," Baruch had told the United Nations Atomic Energy Commission in presenting the plan to which he had lent his name.[24] Five, ten, and fifteen years later Armageddon had not arrived. But the choice that Baruch had held out continued to loom as the choice that the world faced. In 1959 Eisenhower told a group of science advisors that he always came back to "the basic truth": The United States had to find ways of cooperating with other countries, "or else."[25]

Out of Eisenhower's passionate desire to find some way to ease the burden of nuclear danger that the two great powers bore came several personal initiatives to the Soviet Union, which he put forward outside the formal framework of nuclear diplomacy. Upon the death of Stalin he issued a public call for Soviet–American cooperation in a well-received address that came to be called the "Chance for Peace" speech. Shortly afterward he laid before the United Nations a plan for sharing with all nations the industrial and commercial benefits of atomic energy—the "Atoms for Peace" proposal—that he hoped would divert the world from the competition in nuclear armaments that had already gathered considerable momentum.

In 1957 came the "Open Skies" proposal, which was designed to give each side confidence that the other was not planning to launch a surprise attack. And as President, Eisenhower twice met personally with the highest leadership of the Soviet Union. Each of these initiatives seemed, for a time, an oasis in the barren landscape of the Cold War. But each proved to be a mirage.

The Atoms for Peace Plan showed the intensity of Eisenhower's wish to find common ground of some kind with the Soviet Union. For its terms had nothing directly to do with disarmament, or war, or even with nuclear weapons. Its rationale was that an agreement on something — on anything — would begin to break down the barrier of mistrust that separated the two principal nuclear powers, and would thereby lead on to other agreements.[26]

This rationale appealed, as well, to the scientists whose hopes for international control of atomic energy had crucially influenced the Baruch Plan. It became, for them, the "first step" approach to nuclear diplomacy. The first step approach was based on the realization that wholesale nuclear disarmament would not come all at once, but only by stages that, in turn, would only be possible with improving political relations between the United States and the Soviet Union. And it was based, as well, on the feeling that a breach in the wall of suspicion between the two could gradually be widened. It was well, therefore, to concentrate, according to this approach to nuclear diplomacy, on initial steps that would push them toward disarmament while building the mutual confidence that would encourage them to continue the journey.

The measure upon which efforts to take a first step came to focus was the prohibition of atomic tests. Hiroshima and Nagasaki had proven to be the first of a series of nuclear explo-

sions that were touched off by the United States and then by
the Soviet Union. Only the first two were military operations.
The rest were conducted for experimental purposes, to perfect
the weapons that the two powers were accumulating. Even
though they took place far from populated areas, these nuclear
tests had lethal side-effects. The radioactive debris that they
spewed into the air was highly toxic. Its poisonous properties
became dramatically apparent from the unforeseen consequences of the detonation of the first fission—fusion bomb, by
the United States, on a small island in the Pacific Ocean in
1954. A group of Japanese tuna fishermen aboard the trawler
"Lucky Dragon" was dusted with the fallout from the explosion and became horribly ill, with one of them finally dying.

Scientists subsequently discovered that the radioactive material could cause genetic damage even to people far away
from the site of the blast itself. One radioactive isotope, strontium 90, had a long half-life and properties similar to cal-
cium so that it passed through plants and the cows that ate
them into the milk that children all over the world drank.
Once within the human system strontium 90, it was feared,
could produce leukemia.[27]

Nuclear testing symbolized the horrors of the nuclear age. It
concerned others besides the two great powers, because
everybody everywhere was, potentially, prey to the poisons
that testing produced. And the first public suggestion for an
end to all tests came not from the United States or the Soviet
Union, but from Prime Minister Jawaharlal Nehru of India, in
1954. The Democratic candidate for President in 1956, Adlai
Stevenson, proposed that the United States unilaterally halt
tests as an inducement to the Soviet Union to renounce them
also. But Eisenhower dismissed the suggestion on the grounds
that a test ban could only come about as part of a comprehensive disarmament agreement. On April 30 of the following
year, however, the Soviet Union proposed that the question of
nuclear testing be considered separately from other disarmament matters,[28] and the next month the Soviet government
declared itself willing to agree to a mutual suspension of tests
for two or three years. The American government then joined
in negotiations on a treaty to make the suspension permanent.

The most prominently stated reason for seeking to suspend nuclear testing was properly liberal; it was to be the first step on the path to nuclear disarmament. But the proposed step itself was closer in form and substance to traditional than to liberal diplomacy. It took place mainly in direct and largely private exchanges between the United States and the Soviet Union. A test ban was a relatively modest measure. It did not promise a revolution in world affairs. It did not aim at doing away with all nuclear weapons, or infringing directly upon the right of states to have them. And in 1959 the United States formally withdrew its insistence that progress on other disarmament measures accompany the cessation of weapons tests.[29] But the test ban bogged down just as efforts to conclude more grandiose disarmament schemes had stalled.

In fact, although the rhetorical commitment to abolish all nuclear weapons remained, with the efforts to secure a test ban the thrust of nuclear diplomacy shifted from the search for total disarmament to attempts to agree on measures to restrict the arsenals of the United States and the Soviet Union,[30] measures that came to be grouped together under the rubric "arms control." The first had necessitated the submergence of individual national sovereignties and the rise of a powerful international authority. The second was far less ambitious. Arms control measures required no supranational body to enforce their terms. Enforcement was no longer in question. If others violated its terms, the recourse available to a party to an arms control agreement was simply to withdraw.

But this did not set aside the issue of sovereignty in nuclear diplomacy. For a signatory to an arms control accord had to be able to know when a violation had taken place. This had not been difficult in the past. Monitoring the handiwork of traditional diplomacy had been a straightforward task. A treaty characteristically assigned a patch of territory to a country, which then occupied it. Arms control affected the disposition of weaponry within a nation's borders, and so checking on compliance meant breaching those borders. But in the case of the test ban, when the state in question was the Soviet Union, the issue of "inspection" proved to be a sticking point.

Inspection had been part of the Baruch Plan, which had

envisioned that while "dangerous" nuclear activities—making bombs—would fall wholly under the control of the international authority, "safe" nuclear pursuits, like the generation of electrical power, would be carried on by individual nations. To make certain that none of the facilities for these "peaceful" undertakings was being secretly used for warlike purposes, one of the reports of the United Nations Atomic Energy Committee in 1946 had recommended that the international authority have unfettered access to them.

Inspection of this kind constituted, of course, an infringement on national sovereignty. It attracted little attention in 1946, since a powerful supranational body that meant an even more dramatic eclipse of the traditional practices of sovereignty was being contemplated. But when the idea for such a body was abandoned, inspection took on added importance. It became the only means of monitoring a nuclear accord. The United States insisted on it. The Americans were unwilling to take Soviet compliance with a test ban on faith. They wanted the right to see for themselves that the Soviets were not conducting secret atomic tests, especially underground. But the Soviet government refused to commit itself to allowing foreigners to enter their country and poke around as they pleased.

How could the American demand for effective monitoring and the Soviet insistence on absolute territorial integrity be reconciled? The two sides spent long hours wrestling with the problem.

At Eisenhower's behest, a conference of Soviet and American scientists with expertise in nuclear explosions and the detection of earthshocks convened at Geneva in 1958. By bringing them together he hoped to remove some of the political contentiousness from the search for a system of inspection. The conference recommended a series of "control posts," equipped with instruments to monitor tremors and to distinguish tests from earthquakes, as the safeguards for a treaty prohibiting nuclear testing.

But the scientists' recommendations did not break the deadlock as Eisenhower had hoped. Technical disputes arose. Subsequent American research suggested that the task of distinguishing between natural and man-made earth tremors was more difficult than had been believed, and that more control posts than the Americans had originally proposed would be necessary. There was another difficulty. The details of the monitoring scheme provoked controversies that were unhappily familiar. The Soviets insisted upon the power of veto over the activities of the commission that would staff the control posts. They wanted the right to deny access to Soviet citizens. They wanted, in sum, a system of inspection that left undisturbed the sovereignty of the Soviet Union. To the United States this amounted to no inspection at all.

The test ban negotiations seemed more promising than any other nuclear discussions during the 1950s. They proceeded in a spirit of purposefulness and relatively good faith. They met the second requirement of successful diplomacy; a test ban would have had a roughly equal effect on the two great powers. But the negotiations failed the first test of nuclear diplomacy, a common frame of reference; a vestige of liberal diplomacy, the insistence upon inspection, remained. And this failure was closely related to the absence of the third requirement — political will.

For the spirit that surrounded the test ban negotiations was the exception, not the rule, in the decade and a half following the introduction of the Baruch Plan. The climate of the Cold War was frigid. The Korean conflict and the suppression of the Hungarian uprising, rather than the personal encounters between Eisenhower and Khrushchev, set the tone for relations between the United States and the Soviet Union. And distrust of the Soviets was crucial in blocking American agreement to a test ban. The number of control posts and annual inspections that the United States deemed essential rose after the "Conference of Experts" when calculations showed that if a nuclear explosion were set off in an underground cavern hollowed out of resistant material, the shock would be muffled and therefore difficult to detect. This process of "decoupling" was expensive and elaborate. The Soviets could not hope to glean much information from such a disguised test. At least one American

scientist was embarrassed to raise the matter with his Soviet
counterparts, since it implied that the Soviets would go to
fantastic lengths to evade the letter of a test ban.[31] But suspicion of the Soviets was such that only an absolutely foolproof
accord, under the terms of which no nuclear explosion could
even theoretically go undetected, had a hope of winning political approval in the United States.

Nuclear negotiations in the 1950s resembled wartime diplomacy. But this was not the wartime diplomacy that Henry
Stimson had hoped could be recreated in the nuclear era. It
was not the grudging but necessary partnership between allies
fighting a common foe. It was, rather, the communication that
takes place between enemies even as they fight.

Governments at war keep in touch with each other, as
Clausewitz noted, in the hope, however faint, that their differences can be resolved without further bloodshed, and sometimes to reassure their citizens that the responsibility for the
conflict lies elsewhere. But as the fighting proceeds, settling
matters becomes increasingly difficult. And in war it is fighting, not talking, that is central. The United States and the
Soviet Union did not do battle directly with one another in the
Cold War; they did not fire their nuclear weapons. But they
invested heavily in building them. And they thought long and
hard about how to deploy and use them. In the 1950s diplomacy was secondary in the nuclear policies of the United
States – as well as the Soviet Union. The American government devoted more to the task of working out a nuclear
strategy.

The Origins of Strategy

The history of invention shows that at the time of a particular discovery the
social effects to come from that invention can only be judged as the size of an
iceberg is judged with seven-eighths of its whole below the surface of visibility.
Comment in a Symposium on the "Social Adjustment to Atomic Energy,
November 16, 1945[1]

From Hiroshima to the nuclear age

Scientists were discussing the need for nuclear diplomacy and
the virtures of a liberal approach to it even before the first
nuclear explosion took place; before, indeed, it was certain
that there could be such a thing as a man-made nuclear explosion. Nuclear strategy developed differently. The first fully
worked out American plan for the military uses of nuclear
energy did not take shape until eight years after the end of the
first nuclear war. That war ended on August 9, 1945, when
Japan accepted the terms of surrender offered by the United
States. The two atomic bombs that had been dropped on
Hiroshima and Nagasaki had achieved their common purpose.
They had brought World War II to a conclusion.

Although Japan had lost all hope of winning the war that
had begun at Pearl Harbor, American leaders feared that an
invasion that might well meet stiff, even fanatical resistance,
and cost thousands of American lives. The bomb appeared a
substitute for that grim project. Accordingly, the Americans

41

decided to use it against two cities with substantial industrial and military activity, and with some political importance. On August 6 an atomic bomb struck Hiroshima. Three days later another hit Nagasaki.

The same day, the Japanese Emperor, in an unprecedented radio broadcast, informed his people that his government was giving up. He told them that "the enemy has begun to employ a new and most cruel bomb, the power of which to do damage is indeed incalculable, taking the toll of many innocent lives. Should we continue to fight, it would not only result in an ultimate collapse and obliteration of the Japanese nation, but also it would lead to the total extinction of human civilization."[2] His words helped to persuade the American leaders that their decision to drop the bomb had been wise. Two years afterward Henry Stimson said that "all the evidence I have seen indicates that the controlling factor in the final Japanese decision to accept our terms of surrender was the atomic bomb. . . . The bomb thus served exactly the purpose we intended."[3]

The first, and so far the only, time that the atomic bomb was used in combat turned out to be the last time its use as an instrument of policy was clear and straightforward. In 1945 it was simply the most powerful explosive yet developed. And it was used for precisely the same purposes as its less powerful predecessors; to force the Japanese to accept defeat by destroying both their capacity and their will to continue fighting.[4] The bomb's success made further investigation of nuclear strategy unnecessary, or so it seemed in 1945. The Axis powers had been conquered. The victorious allies had no challengers anywhere; and the allies, including the Soviet Union, were committed to peace. The United Nations organization that was being formed under their sponsorship would carry out that commitment – or so at least the Americans believed. The Baruch Plan, which would be administered under UN auspices, would cope with the special danger of nuclear energy.

The balmy political climate of the summer of 1945 did not endure. But it did not change suddenly. The Cold War set in by stages, like the changing of the seasons. The realization that war had not been abolished forever, that the use of force between nations would continue, that one of the requirements for effective membership in the international community would be military might, and that an armed collision with the Soviet Union was distinctly possible, all came upon the American public and the American government gradually, not at once.

Their disenchantment with the Soviet Union was touched off by the forcible incorporation of the nations of Eastern Europe into a Soviet sphere of control beginning in 1945, and was codified by the Truman Doctrine in 1947, which proclaimed American willingness to assist free peoples to resist the encroachment of communism. And disenchantment was brought to the brink of battle in 1948 over the question of the future of Germany. The Potsdam Conference in 1945 had established separate zones of occupation for each of the four major victorious allies. Disputatious wrangling about what to do next followed for more than two years, with neither side having a clear idea about what kind of postwar Germany it wanted to create.[5] At the end of 1947 the United States, Britain, and France began to consolidate their zones, and to press for the creation of a West German state.

These measures alarmed the Russian authorities, who claimed that they violated wartime agreements and threatened the security of the Soviet Union. Tension centered on the city of Berlin, the former capital of the Reich, where the Western nations had entry rights, although the city lay one hundred ten miles inside the Soviet zone. Harassment of traffic into Berlin turned into a full-scale blockade on June 24, 1948. The United States decided to maintain a Western presence in Berlin by supplying the city by airlift, and did so for eleven months, until the road was finally opened again. In the early days of the blockade, especially, fears of the outbreak of war ran high.[6] And even as it ended, the United States, Canada, and most of the nations of Western Europe formed the North Atlantic Treaty Organization, a military alliance aimed against the Soviet Union — the first military alliance the United

States had ever joined in peacetime. The ticklish, vexing relationship with the Soviet Union had become a military problem.

In 1950 confrontation with the Soviet Union received an
official imprimatur within the American government. In
January of that year President Truman ordered a sweeping
reappraisal of American foreign policy. Officials in the State
Department and the Department of Defense worked on a paper
to which Truman gave his approval in April, 1950. It was
known as "NSC-68". It noted the aims of the Soviet Union,
and found that "The United States, as the principal center of
power in the non-Soviet world and the bulwark of opposition to Soviet expansion, is the principal enemy whose integrity and vitality must be subverted or destroyed by one means
or other if the Kremlin is to achieve its fundamental design."[7]
It urged that American and Western European military
strength be built up.[8] And it concluded with a call for "a
presentation to the public of a full explanation of the facts and
implications of the present international situation."[9] Administration officials proceeded to make that presentation throughout the country. They hammered home the message that the
Soviet Union posed a grave threat to the United States, which
demanded an immediate and forthright response. Events reinforced the message. By the end of 1950 the United States was
at war with North Korea and the People's Republic of China —
two Asian states governed by Communist parties and allied
with and encouraged and supplied by the Soviet Union.

So American leaders had to come to terms with a postwar
world that was not a world without war. But their military
preparations did not at first include a special role for nuclear
weapons. Between 1945 and 1950 American war plans, such
as they were, resembled the aerial campaigns of World War II.
They called for the Air Force to try to destroy Russian industry
and military support facilities, in much the same way that
military authorities believed the German war machine had
been slowly but steadily crippled between 1942 and 1945.[10]
There was some recognition that the next war would not be an
exact replica of the last. The "Finletter Report" of 1948 em-

phasized the increased importance of air power and it called for a dramatic expansion of Western air forces. But it set forth no coherent strategic program, nor did it come to grips with the special features of nuclear weapons.[11]

The military hesitated to rely on nuclear weapons for the defense of the United States and her allies partly out of professional conservatism. Military men prefer to fight with weapons that they know, and that have served them well in the past. The American armed forces in the first years of the nuclear age were dominated by men who had won World War II, and that experience weighed heavily upon them.[12] Retrospective surveys made after 1945 downgraded the contribution of strategic bombing to the defeat of Germany and Japan. And it was possible that advances in the art of air defence would keep pace with the growing sophistication and power of air forces in the postwar world.[13]

But the most important reason why the United States did not develop a full-fledged nuclear strategy immediately after 1945 was that the nuclear age had not fully arrived. The American stockpile of atomic bombs was small.[14] The transformation in international politics that the power to destroy two hundred million Russians "in the twinkling of an eye" would bring had not occurred because, in the early postwar years, the American atomic arsenal was not large enough to wreak that much destruction.

The development of the American nuclear arsenal parallels the development of other industrial inventions, like the airplane and the automobile. The first bomb marked the beginning of nuclear development: Hiroshima showed that a nuclear explosion was possible, just as the Wright brothers proved that man-made machines could fly. Then came improvements of two sorts. First, more efficient models came into production. Second, the successors to the first two bombs were more powerful and compact, so easier to transport. And they became available in greater numbers and at lower cost. There is a lag between invention and mass production; between a new device as a curiosity and as an integral part of everyday life. Carl Benz made the first modern automobile. But it remained for

Henry Ford to make the automobile age, forty years later. It was not the Manhattan Project, but research and development of atomic weaponry after the end of World War II, that truly made the nuclear age.

After 1950 the iceberg rose increasingly into view. The scientists and engineers turned out ever more – and ever more efficient – nuclear weapons. The "progress" that they made was to continue throughout the first three decades of the nuclear age. And that progress gave rise to the principles of nuclear strategy. Strategy followed technology. But this was not an automatic process. Strategy depended upon technology, but was not altogether determined by it. Politics shaped the American response to the three strategic problems as well. And since the political process in the United States is public, and subject to controversy, so was the forging of American nuclear strategy. The problem of war in the nuclear age might or might not have been too important to be left to the generals. In the American political system it was impossible to leave it only to them.

The "New Look" of 1953

The first detailed American nuclear strategy did not, however, come from the generals. It came from the politicians. And political as well as technical considerations shaped it. The newly installed Eisenhower administration produced the first nuclear strategy in 1953, in a series of public pronouncements, internal memoranda, and budget decisions that came to be known, collectively, as the "New Look." Like everything else under the sun the New Look was not entirely new. The strategic ideas it incorporated had been aired previously. The weapons upon which it depended had been designed and in some cases manufactured before 1953. But the New Look drew doctrine and hardware together, and gave them an official stamp, for the first time. And it marked, as well, a shift in emphasis in American defense policy, toward atomic weapons. For the first time the American government gave a formal answer to the first two questions that the atomic age had pressed upon it: What political purposes would atomic weapons serve? And how should they be deployed to serve these purposes?

The answer to the first question turned out to be deterrence. The concept of deterrence is simple: prevention by threat. One side advertises the damaging consequences of an act, to prevent an adversary from acting. Deterrence is not peculiar to politics among nations. It is, for example, one of the rationales for punishing criminals. One burglar sent to prison is supposed to serve as a cautionary lesson to other would-be thieves. Nor is deterrence in international politics a special feature of the nuclear age. States have often fortified themselves to discourage their neighbors from attacking. *Si vis pacem bellum para* – if you want peace, prepare for war – was an ancient Roman maxim. Deterrence is the strategy of the hedgehog, who bares his bristles to keep other animals away. The sharper the bristles are, the greater the caution that they presumably induce.[15]

If not unique to it, however, deterrence was particularly well suited to the foreign policy of the United States in the postwar period. It fit the principal American international goal. This was the "containment" of the Soviet Union – an idea first given prominence by a foreign service officer named George Kennan in an influential magazine article in 1947,[16] ratified as government policy by NSC-68, and reaffirmed by the Eisenhower administration in 1953.[17] The policy of containment sprang from the conviction that the internal dynamics of the Soviet form of government led to a pushful foreign policy. The Soviet Union could be counted upon to press outward, to try to expand its sphere of dominion. The United States would have to serve as a bulwark of resistance against this, to "contain" the Russians.

The policy of deterrence – prevention by threat – fit the technical features of nuclear weapons as well as the main goal of American foreign policy. For if the political task of the United States was one of prevention – of Soviet expansion – the bomb constituted a mighty threat. The prospect of an atomic attack was bound to encourage any nation to be cautious. The strategy of nuclear deterrence that the Eisenhower administration adopted as part of the New Look was designed to promote caution in Soviet foreign policy, to restrain what the Americans regarded as the Soviets' natural aggressive impulses.

The American nuclear arsenal, according to their strategy of deterrence, was to serve as a kind of giant club. It was to be wielded menacingly, with the threat of smashing it down upon an adversary in reprisal for a misdeed. And by threatening to swing the club the United States was counting on not having to do so. The power of even the first crude atomic bombs was apparent from the moment that one of them devastated Hiroshima. Atomic deterrence may have begun to operate the moment that news of the destruction of Hiroshima reached the Soviet Union.[18] The bomb certainly impressed the Soviet leaders, and probably entered into their foreign policy calculations, although how it did so, and whether the exclusive American atomic franchise in the early years of the nuclear age prevented the Soviets from doing anything they would otherwise have done, are questions that cannot be answered with the information now available.[19]

The accumulation of a modest store of Hiroshima-type bombs made it feasible to rely on nuclear weapons in the conduct of American foreign policy. And a technical breakthrough in weapon design made a strategy of deterrence virtually inevitable. This was the perfection of the first fusion or hydrogen bomb, which drew its power not from splitting apart the material in the nucleus of matter, but from fusing them together. Scientists could generate up to 1000 times more energy from fusion than from the fission process upon which the Hiroshima and Nagasaki bombs had been based. And so the hydrogen bomb was far more powerful than the first atomic weapons had been. Its explosive power was measured by millions rather than thousands of tons of TNT, by "megatons" rather than "kilotons." The first fission bombs had devastated two medium-sized cities. Their successors could reduce large metropolises like Tokyo, or Moscow, or New York, to rubble and ashes.

The first atomic bombs could be regarded as simply the latest, most powerful explosives in a chain that stretched back at least seven centuries to the first Chinese experiments with gunpowder; their appearance could be seen as a refinement, but not a decisive change, in the art of warfare. It was not possible to place hydrogen weapons in this evolutionary context. The atomic bomb was built to be used. The decision to proceed with the hydrogen bomb provoked controversy because there was no apparent point to using it. Its champions did not dispute this, but argued that its power made it a threat so formidable that it would not have to be used.[20] The fusion bomb was supremely, and perhaps exclusively, a weapon of deterrence.

The deterrent value of nuclear weapons came from the two characteristics that Brodie had pinpointed in 1946: "Everything about the bomb is overshadowed by the twin facts that it exists and that its destructive power is fantastically great."[21] By 1953 these were indisputably facts, not predictions. The American arsenal had grown beyond the few bombs that had been available immediately after the war. And the fusion explosive had confirmed beyond doubt what the first fission models had portended — the extraordinary, unprecedented, revolutionary power of nuclear weapons. Churchill put the proposition in dramatic fashion: "There is an immense gulf between the atomic and the hydrogen bomb. The atomic bomb, with all its terror, did not carry us outside the scope of human control or manageable events in thought or action, in peace or war. But... (with) the hydrogen bomb, the entire foundation of human affairs was revolutionized."[22]

Deterrence was formally proclaimed the first principle of American nuclear strategy in 1953, and so it has remained ever since. Through technical progress, doctrinal disputes, thaws and freezes in the Cold War, and changes of administration, the United States has kept to a policy of deterrence. Containment of the Soviet Union has continued to be one of the animating purposes of American participation in international affairs. Occasionally there have been demands for a more "positive" policy, like the "rollback" of Soviet power from

Eastern Europe.[23] But these have gone unheeded at the upper reaches of the government. And whatever the vicissitudes of political opinion in the United States, the sheer physical power of nuclear weapons gave these armaments a deterrent force. As the American stockpile grew, the possible penalty for war with the United States became more and more severe. A nuclear arsenal was bound to have a deterrent effect whatever the avowed intentions of its owner. A club so large was bound to appear menacing.

Brodie had also written in 1946: "Thus far the chief purpose of our military establishment has been to win wars. From now on its chief purpose must be to avert them. It can have almost no other useful purpose."[24] This prophecy for nuclear weapons was not as rapidly borne out. In 1953, whether the prevention of war was the only useful purpose of nuclear weapons remained to be seen. But the New Look established the *chief* purpose of the growing American nuclear arsenal as the deterrence – the prevention – of war.

The New Look supplied an answer to the second strategic question; how to deploy nuclear weapons to achieve the designated political ends. Deployment had two parts. The first was the array of weapons tnemselves. The Eisenhower administration made plain its intention to place primary emphasis on nuclear, rather than on nonnuclear or "conventional" weapons to thwart the Soviets. The second part was the doctrine that specified when and how those weapons would be used. The American nuclear deterrent was not a brick wall, a Maginot Line obviously solid enough to check any assault and thus sufficient to discourage one. It was a club, whose deterrent power lay in the threat of reprisal, of punishment. To make deterrence effective, the American government had to set out the conditions that would bring the club into action, and to say how and where the blow would fall. It had, in sum, to say with some precision just what it was threatening to do to the Soviet Union, and when.

The doctrinal part of the New Look had its most authoritative presentation in a speech on January 12, 1954, by Secretary of State John Foster Dulles. He announced that local defenses against communism the world over would be reinforced by "the further deterrent of massive retaliatory power." Thereafter, he said, the United States would seek to deter the Soviets by having "a great capacity to retaliate, instantly, by means and at places of our own choosing."[25] Dulles did not give details, but he seemed to imply that the class of acts that could bring the American nuclear club into play was a broad one. In response to Soviet misconduct falling into this broad category, the United States was, it seemed, prepared to respond with the full force of its nuclear arsenal. The threat upon which the American government was relying to keep the Soviet Union in check was the threat of "massive retaliation."

The speech met a stormy reception and Dulles subsequently hedged and qualified what he had said. But the impression remained that the administration reserved the right to bring its nuclear club down with a terrible thump as punishment for a wide variety of Communist acts of aggression.[26] And other Eisenhower policies gave credence to that impression. The budget of the Air Force, which had charge of most of the American nuclear arsenal, was pushed upward in the first years of the Eisenhower administration, while the other armed services found their appropriations reduced.[27] Newly designed "miniaturized" atomic warheads, known as "tactical" nuclear weapons, were transported to Western Europe and stationed there. These packed a smaller punch than the stupendous hydrogen explosives that were also being made, but represented a quantum step beyond nonnuclear armaments in destructive power. And the President issued a directive to the Joint Chiefs of Staff, entitled "NSC-162/2," informing them that they could plan to use nuclear armaments of all shapes and sizes in the future whenever this would work to the advantage of the United States.[28]

Deterrence, the response to the first strategic question that the New Look embodied, sprang from a mixture of political goals and technical imperatives. The threat of massive retaliation, the answer to the second question, had its roots in the political theories and historical interpretations of its authors. It jibed with Dulles's belief that the great conflicts of history had arisen from the aggressor's miscalculation of the opposition he would meet.[29] "If we had had the capacity to retaliate instantly," he told a news conference in March 1954 in answer to a question about his landmark January speech, "in my opinion there would have been no Pearl Harbor."[30]

Massive retaliation had another kind of appeal for the Republican administration. It offered a way of saving money. This was popular politically. The desire for economy in government, particularly in defense spending, ran deep in American public opinion, and the Truman administration had felt it acutely through demands for rapid demobilization immediately after World War II. But fiscal frugality was also a matter of firm conviction for the conservative businessmen who dominated the higher councils of the Eisenhower administration. They devoutly believed that government profligacy would wreck the nation's economy. And that, they thought, would endanger the republic. Eisenhower himself spoke of the need to maintain the "great equation" between military requirements and economic soundness. In his "massive retaliation" speech Dulles warned against "military expenditures so vast that they lead to 'practical bankruptcy.'" It was cheaper to build a few hundred bombs to deter an attack on Europe than to pay hundreds of thousands of soldiers to stand guard there. And by keeping those bombs continuously ready for delivery the United States could deter the Soviet Union over "the long haul," rather than periodically having to launch feverish military build-ups in anticipation of a crucial moment when the chances for war were high, as the Truman administration had done.

The New Look closely resembled the defense policy that Britain had adopted three years before, and for similar reasons. Faced with a budget squeeze upon his return to power, Churchill told his Chiefs of Staff to find ways to cut costs. They suggested that NATO adopt a policy of deterrence resting principally on American and British nuclear firepower.[31] The Chief of Staff of the British Air Force, Sir John Slessor, failed to sell the new concept to his American counterparts during the last years of the Truman administration. But it proved attractive to the Republicans.

American military policy between 1945 and 1953 had amounted to an extension of the practices of World War II. The New Look drew upon the Korean War, reflecting what the Eisenhower adminstration took to be the lessons of that conflict. Its outbreak seemed to bear out Dulles's ideas about the beginnings of major wars. Shortly before the North Korean armies marched south, the then-Secretary of State Dean Acheson had given a speech in which he had drawn the American defense perimeter and conspicuously left South Korea outside it. This omission was widely believed to have confirmed the North Koreans in their aggressive plans.[32] The Korean War was fought without nuclear weapons, and it dragged on inconclusively. As the fighting continued and American casualties mounted, the American public grew restless, and impatient in particular with the men responsible for conducting the war. Harry Truman's popularity plunged. Mindful of his fate, the Eisenhower administration was leery of getting bogged down again. On the other hand, when, upon inheriting the war, Eisenhower hinted that he might employ nuclear weapons, a settlement followed.[33] The settling of the Korean War provided another piece of evidence in support of the effectiveness of a threat of "massive retaliation."

The New Look, and the strategy of deterrence through the threat of massive retaliation that it set forth, constituted the analogue for nuclear strategy to the Baruch Plan and nuclear diplomacy. Both were first efforts. Each was fertilized by both technology and politics; in the case of diplomacy, the infant state of the art of nuclear weaponry and the American monopoly of it made international control seem feasible, and the liberal tinge to the American outlook on world politics made it seem wholly desirable; for strategy the overwhelming power of the hydrogen bomb made a policy of deterrence almost inevitable, and the Eisenhower administration's beliefs about the beginnings of past wars and the conditions for fiscal soundness in the United States led to deterrence through the threat of massive nuclear retaliation.

Both came under challenge. But the two challenges differed. The Baruch Plan had a real trial, and it failed. This was not true of the New Look. No war broke out during the Eisenhower

years. No nuclear weapon was ever used. But the logic of the
New Look was cast into doubt all the same. The most important criticism came from within the United States, rather
than, as had happened with the Baruch Plan, from the Russians. And whereas the American approach to the problem of
nuclear diplomacy changed gradually and rather quietly,
strategic issues were the subject of a full-scale political debate during Dwight Eisenhower's two presidential terms.
Questions of nuclear diplomacy hovered, for the most part, on
the fringes of American political discourse during the 1950s.
Strategic issues found their way to the center. The problem of
how to deploy the American nuclear arsenal in order to deter
the Soviet Union grew in importance during that decade, and
by its end had become one of the most important issues in
American politics.

Strategic revisionism

Criticism of the New Look came first from a small group of
men who took a professional interest in the study of strategy,
especially strategy in the nuclear age. These "nuclear
strategists" played a role for nuclear strategy similar to one the
atomic scientists took in the development of nuclear diplomacy. Like the scientists, they inhabited universities and independent research institutions, such as the RAND Corporation, which was founded after the war with the encouragement of the Air Force. Like the scientists, they established
both formal and informal networks of communication. Like
the scientists, they stood halfway between public and private
life. They had access to, and, as the decade wore on, some
influence on the nation's defense programs; but they were not
bound by official routine. They addressed themselves to questions that the government wanted to answer; but they had the
freedom to look beyond those immediate concerns, and to dis-
sent from government policy.

The emergence of the cadre of nuclear strategists, like the
movement of scientists from their laboratories into the political arena, was an event without precedent in American poli-

tics, and one that underscored the singularity of the nuclear age. For most of the recorded history of warfare, strategic thought had been an intellectual backwater, the province of a few, often rather eccentric, military officers. Nuclear weapons changed this. Working out their implications became a far more formidable intellectual task than deciding how to assault fixed emplacements of machine guns, or to deploy a group of tanks. Just as nuclear diplomacy was too important, in the eyes of the atomic scientists, to be left to the diplomats, so nuclear strategy, on the evidence of the work of the strategists, had become too significant — and too complicated — to remain the preserve of the professional military. Like the scientists, the ideas of the strategists became the foundations of official policy, when passed through the wringer of politics.

The strategists concurred with the Eisenhower administration that the principal purpose of nuclear weapons was the prevention of war. They accepted deterrence as the response to the first question of strategy. But they found fault with the Eisenhower administration's response to the second strategic question — how to deploy them. Their objections had a single source. The principles of the New Look, in the opinion of the strategists, failed to take sufficient account of the growth of the Soviet nuclear arsenal. In the early years of the nuclear age the Russians did better in equipping themselves with nuclear weapons than most American officials thought they would. The first Soviet atomic explosion came in 1949. By 1953, a fusion device had been detonated. And the Soviets were able to produce increasingly sophisticated means of delivering their bombs sooner than the Americans had thought possible. The New Look, the strategists believed, was suitable only so long as the United States enjoyed a monopoly of nuclear hardware. Once the monopoly was broken, they charged, the Eisenhower administration's response to the second strategic problem became dangerously outmoded.

The strategists took issue with massive retaliation on two counts. Their initial criticism was an elaboration of Brodie's 1946 rule that a nuclear nation's first duty in facing another similarly equipped was to safeguard its retaliatory force. With the growth of Soviet nuclear might, the resilience of the American nuclear arsenal – its capacity to weather a Soviet assault with enough firepower intact to deliver a devastating blow in return, thereby discouraging such an assault – became a matter of immediate concern. The strategists wanted to have the "survivability" of the retaliatory force accepted as the cardinal principle upon which the design and deployment of the American nuclear forces were based. And throughout the 1950s they monitored the two arsenals to make certain that the American one could indeed survive a Soviet attack. Since the adversary had fashioned its own nuclear "club," it was imperative to see that the American club could not be smashed to splinters with a surprise blow.

A 1951 report by the RAND Corporation to the Air Force made this point. The report was prompted by a request that RAND study the most effective ways to build and use air bases in foreign countries. A philosopher and economist turned strategist named Albert Wohlstetter took charge of the project. Wohlstetter recast the question in broader terms. The important problem seemed not how to build air bases in foreign countries, but "where and how to base the strategic Air Force and how to operate this force in conjunction with the base system chosen."[34] He and his associates made calculations based on what appeared to be the most important factors: the costs of installing bases at varying distances from the United States; the range of American aircraft; and Soviet military capabilities.

The group came to the preliminary conclusion that a system of overseas air bases, ringing the Soviet Union, would maximize American strategic power. They then added another element to their calculations: the vulnerability of bases to enemy attack. This changed their findings. For the closer a base lay to the Soviet Union, the more susceptible to Soviet attack it turned out to be. Whatever savings the Air Force might make by positioning its aircraft close to the borders of the Soviet Union would be more then cancelled out by the costs of protecting overseas bases against a Soviet strike. The group finally recommended that the Air Force base all its planes in the continental United States, and use overseas facilities only for refuelling them.

The Wohlstetter report was one of those documents, like the Kennan "Mr. X" article, NSC-68, and the Dulles "massive retaliation" speech, that pulled together into coherent and accessible form ideas that had been circulating within the government. It was distributed and discussed in the higher echelons of the Defense Department.[35] The Air Force adopted its main point – the importance of allowing for the enemy's striking power in deploying strategic forces – and revised its program for constructing strategic bases in accordance with the suggestions that it made.[36]

The first critique of the strategists, then, was that the New Look did not give enough emphasis to the need to protect the American nuclear club against a shattering blow from its Soviet counterpart. The second critique was that the club was too unwieldy to carry out the range of chores that the New Look had assigned to it. The American nuclear arsenal, asserted this argument, could not reasonably be expected to deter every challenge that the Communists could mount. The case was put cogently by an alumnus of RAND named William Kaufmann, in an essay in a 1956 volume called *Military Policy and National Security*. The New Look, he noted, was intended to put the Communist nations, and above all the Soviet Union, on notice that any hostile act would call forth a nuclear volley from the United States. But they had strong reason to expect that only the most extraordinary acts would in fact touch one off. "An examination of our recent diplomatic record, and indeed of the course of American foreign policy during the past fifteen or twenty years," Kaufmann wrote, "suggests that it is quite out of character for us to retaliate massively against anyone except in the face of provocations as extreme as Pearl Harbor."[37]

In the days of the American nuclear monopoly, an American pledge to hurl its nuclear thunderbolts in punishment for an international misdemeanor might have been credible enough to keep Communist designs in check. But by 1956 those days were forever gone. An American government would hence-

forth have to turn its nuclear force loose with the knowledge
that its adversaries could retaliate. This put the United States,
in the face of provocation, in an uncomfortable position: "If
the Communists should challenge our sincerity, and they
would have good reasons for daring to do so, we would either
have to put up or shut up. If we put up, we would plunge into
all the immeasurable horrors of an atomic war. If we shut up,
we would suffer a serious loss of prestige and damage our
capacity to establish deterrents against further Communist expansion."[38]

Kaufmann conceded that the threat of massive retaliation
probably did deter a direct attack against the territory of the
United States, or against "areas that have come to be regarded
as of vital interest to us."[39] But he foresaw other contingencies
that the "Great Deterrent" would not cover. He predicted that
the Soviet Union and the People's Republic of China would
push into "peripheral areas not only for gain but for the purpose of discovering what constitutes the limits of our toler-
ance."[40] In fact, two Communist probes into the "peripheral
areas" on the fringes of the two great blocs in the international
system had, in the estimation of Kaufmann and the other
critics of the Eisenhower defense policy, already taken place
since 1945 – in Korea and in Indochina.[41] In both places the
United States had intervened – and rightly, in their view. In
neither case had the government brought nuclear weapons
into use. This, too, had been sensible: "Korea was a tragic and
painful experience; with its 137,000 casualties, it scattered
suffering throughout the country. But even so, a hundred
Koreas would still be cheaper than an American – Soviet exchange of atomic and hydrogen blows."[42]

The Republican Administration and the strategists drew
quite different lessons from Korea. For Eisenhower and Dulles
the war had been a political, military, and economic disaster.
The United States, in their judgement, could not afford to fight
another such war. By assembling a nuclear striking force of
extraordinary power and threatening to use it to punish a wide
range of misdeeds, the Administration believed that it could
avoid more Koreas. The nuclear strategists, by contrast, believed that the United States could not afford not to be able to

wage more wars like the one in Korea. For more were surely on
the way. The Communist nations were disposed by political
temperament to fight them. Communist doctrine, with its
broad definition of conflict and its emphasis on flexible tactics, was well suited to launching many different kinds of
challenges. The United States, the strategists maintained,
needed to prepare for many types of nonnuclear or "limited"
war. This involved outfitting the American land, sea, and air
forces with "conventional" armaments to supplement the nuclear weapons that the New Look prescribed, no matter what
the cost. And it meant, as well, preparing the American people
for the frustrations of protracted nonnuclear conflict.

Being able to fight limited wars could have, according to the
strategists, two salutary consequences. First, the United States
might not have to fight such wars. Once the Communists saw
that they could not stir up rebellions in Asia or seize a slice of
Western Europe with impunity, they might not attempt to do
so. But if the lesser threats to American interests did develop,
these could be met without facing the dreadful choice between
"humiliation" – giving in to them – or "holocaust" – starting a
nuclear war.[43]

The nuclear strategists and the Eisenhower administration
differed over the requirements of deterrence in the nuclear
age. The government placed its faith in the accumulation of an
ever-growing stockpile of atomic weapons, and the threat to
unleash these weapons at the time and place of its choosing to
keep the Russians at bay. The strategists believed that the requirements of deterrence were more complicated. A formidable nuclear striking force was needed to ward off an all-out
Soviet attack. But this had to be constructed with an eye not
simply to size but to the ability to survive an attack. And a
serviceable deterrent force needed to have a large nonnuclear
component as well, to discourage continually and perhaps
even to meet occasionally less apocalyptic challenges than
nuclear attack. The United States needed more than a huge
club; it needed clubs of various sizes.

The prescriptions for the requirements of deterrence differed because the concept of deterrence differed. For the
strategists it was "proportional" or "graduated" in character;

different varieties of aggression were possible, and so a corre-
spondingly diverse array of responses was necessary to deter
them. Eisenhower conceived deterrence in much more "absolute" terms; a large threat, he thought, would prevent even
small acts of mischief.

The strategic debate

By themselves the strategists could not have aroused much
public reaction to their ideas. Their audience was not large.
But part of that audience was influential in its own right. Both
of the strategists' criticisms got a sympathetic hearing from the
armed services. The Army found the case for preparing for
limited war particularly persuasive. For the Army, like the
other services (and in the solipsistic fashion of many large
organizations), tended to see the national interest and the nation's security wrapped up in the military mission that it was
uniquely qualified to perform. "Limited war" stressed the
Army's role. Ironically, the defense doctrine of its former
highest-ranking officer, Dwight Eisenhower, gave the Army
a much smaller part in the nation's defense than the one that it
had played in World War II and in Korea. Its leaders came
naturally to the view that strategic nuclear forces, which happened to come chiefly under control of the Air Force, could
not by themselves adequately protect the interests of the
United States.

The Army Chief of Staff when the Eisenhower administration came into power was Matthew Ridgeway. He was plainly
unhappy with the share of the budget his service was allotted.[44] Ridgeway's successor, Maxwell Taylor, also ques-
tioned the soundness of massive retaliation, and tried to persuade his civilian superiors to spend more money on nonnuclear forces. Having lost the argument within the government
he put his case to a wider audience when he left his post, in a
1959 book he called The Uncertain Trumpet. The book re-
stated the case for preparing for limited war, proposing a
"Strategy of Flexible Response" to provide "a capability to
react across the entire spectrum of possible challenge, for cop-

ing with anything from general atomic war to infiltrations and aggressions such as threaten Laos and Berlin in 1959."[45]

The Air Force, on the other hand, was particularly interested in the first of the strategists' criticisms, since it centered on air power. In the mid-1950s the Air Force aired publicly its fears that the Soviets would so far outstrip the United States in the production of long-range bomber aircraft that the American retaliatory force would become prey to a disarming blow. This danger called for more American aircraft, and thus a larger budget for the Air Force. And a larger Air Force budget followed, as well, from the contention that in order to deter the more ruthless and aggressive Soviets, the United States needed to have strategic superiority — the capacity to inflict far more damage on the Soviet Union than the Soviets could hope to visit on the United States.[46] Some Air Force officers plumped for superiority.

Even fortified by the discontent of the military, however, the strategists' criticisms, although more widely distributed, did not reach the front pages of the nations' newspapers until 1957. In that year they were catapulted to the center of American politics by the Soviet Union's launching of the first earth-orbiting satellite. Sputnik jolted the collective American psyche. The reaction had something in common with the financial "panics" of the nineteenth century, when the worth of stocks and the solvency of banks were suddenly called into question, and thousands of people rushed to cash in their certificates or withdraw their deposits. It resembled even more closely the moment in the nineteenth century when the fear suddenly spread in Britain that the French had built a fleet that could defeat the Royal Navy, form a "steam bridge" across the channel, and spearhead an invasion of the British Isles.[47]

Sputnik was proclaimed "another Pearl Harbor."[48] It did not begin a war. But it was like Pearl Harbor in that the world suddenly looked quite different to Americans than it had before. They had presumed that their scientific and technical capabilities far exceeded those of the Soviet Union, and that that superiority offered a margin of safety in the nuclear age. Sputnik shattered that complacent presumption. The Soviets stepped into outer space before the Americans. That step seemed to portend other, unknown advances that might put the security of the United States at risk. If the Russians could use space as a launching area, they might be able to annihilate the United States without warning.

Generals, scientists, educators, political and community leaders propounded their views on the challenge that Sputnik posed to America. Magazine and newspaper editorials and the reports of specially assembled civic commissions echoed them. The Democrats moved to take advantage of the outcry. Many of them had had reservations about the New Look. Now they saw the chance to lay in some political capital by proclaiming their doubts. The Democratic Party controlled the Congress, and Democrats used Congressional forums to investigate the state of American "preparedness." Several prominent Senators launched inquiries.[49]

The second precept of the strategists, the need for nonnuclear forces to deter, and to fight if necessary, a broad assortment of "limited" wars, was consistently rejected by the Eisenhower administration. And just as consistently the administration resisted attempts by Congress to appropriate funds to assemble such forces.[50] As the Soviet nuclear stockpile grew in the 1950s a nuclear war seemed increasingly likely to annihilate both the United States and the Soviet Union. But Eisenhower stuck to his "absolute" concept of deterrence. He continued to believe that the threat of annihilation, even though both sides would be annihilated if the threat were carried out, would restrain the Soviets. He and his associates affirmed that any wars the United States fought would be nuclear wars.[51] He issued several more or less explicit nuclear warnings: when the People's Republic of China shelled the islands of Quemoy and Matsu that were held by the government of Taiwan; and again when the Soviets put pressure on Berlin in 1959.[52] In fact, in neither case was the United States forced to carry out its warning, although whether this was because the Chinese and the Russians recoiled at the prospect of a nuclear engagement — whether, that is, the threat of massive retaliation succeeded in deterring them — can be neither proven nor disproven.

To the strategists' first precept – the need to protect the nuclear arsenal against a disarming blow – the Republican government was more accommodating. In fact, the administration publicly embraced the principle of the "survivability" of the retaliatory force that Brodie had first set forth, albeit in a rather backhanded way and for mixed reasons. In 1956 the Secretary of the Air Force, Donald Quarles, made a speech in which he defined the standard that the American nuclear arsenal had to meet. It did not necessarily have to be larger than its Soviet counterpart: "Neither side can hope by a mere margin of superiority in airplanes or other means of delivery of atomic weapons to escape the catastrophe of such a war. Beyond a certain point, this prospect is not the result of *relative* strength of the two opposed forces. It is the *absolute* power in the hands of each, and...the substantial invulnerability of this power to interdiction."[53] "Invulnerability to interdiction" was precisely Brodie's "security of the retaliatory force."

But Eisenhower did not choose to bolster with his personal support what came to be known as the doctrine of "sufficiency" that Quarles had laid down, although other high officials did return to it.[54] And the Quarles speech was designed as a political rejoinder to an Air Force request for enough strategic hardware to keep the United States unmistakably superior to the Soviet Union in nuclear weaponry. It was intended not so much to enshrine the principle of an invulnerable retaliatory force as the first requirement of deterrence as it was to serve the goal that Eisenhower and his associates valued most highly – restraining government expenditures.

Still, the administration was sensitive to the assertion that the requirements for deterrence – the measure of invulnerability – were not fixed, but varied according to the size of the attack the enemy could mount. And Eisenhower in fact presided over both a steady expansion of the American nuclear arsenal and a rapid and pronounced change in its composition, especially between 1957 and 1960. The driving force behind both was not the sting of the strategists' criticisms but the rapid advance in the technology of nuclear weapons. Not one but two dramatic changes in the design of nuclear armaments took place in the 1950s. The fabrication and successful test of a fusion bomb was the first; the second was the advent of the ballistic missile.

The fusion bomb confirmed the enormous expansion in human destructive power that the first fission explosives had portended. The missile stood in the same relationship to the airplane. It promised to be a far more efficient vehicle for delivering bombs. Unlike an airplane, a missile needed no pilot on board to guide it. Unlike an airplane, a missile could make most of the journey from take-off to target in outer space. So a missile could have a longer range than an airplane, it could arrive on target far more swiftly and hence with much less warning, and could be manufactured more cheaply. And since missiles could strike so suddenly, and because a state could equip itself with a large missile fleet and augment these with decoys difficult to distinguish from the real vehicles, missiles were even more difficult to repel than jet airplanes. The power of atomic explosives tilted the balance in air warfare between offense and defense sharply in favor of the offense, since only a few atomic bombs would have to evade antiaircraft batteries to cause vast damage. The appearance of the missile decisively confirmed the tilt, further increased the explosive power the attacker could deliver, and complicated the task of resisting the attack.

With the ballistic missile, as with the fusion bomb, technology influenced strategy. The hydrogen weapon was so powerful as to be readily usable for nothing except making threats, and so it pushed the United States toward deterrence. Similarly, the design of the ballistic missiles that came into production in the second half of the 1950s bore upon the requirements for deterrence.[55] The earlier, "intermediate" range models had to be stationed in Europe to be able to reach the Soviet Union. These first missiles were powered by liquid fuel. They were cumbersome, they could not be launched quickly, and they were vulnerable to sabotage, to malfunctioning, and to preemptive attack. In many ways they were less efficient instruments of deterrence than the long-range bombers upon which the United States had relied for the first decade of the nuclear age, and continued to rely well into the second, and the third as well.

But the second generation of missiles bolstered rather than undercut deterrence, for they incorporated special features that appreciably reduced their vulnerability to attack. The most important of the second generation of missiles was the Minuteman, which drew its power from solid fuel, and so was less susceptible to accidents and attacks than its liquid-powered predecessors. Minuteman's range was such that it could be deployed in the United States, where it could be better protected against both accidents and attacks. It was less vulnerable than previous missiles because a special guidance system permitted it to be launched while housed underground in a solid concrete bunker. And shortly after the advent of the Minuteman came the weapon – or more properly, weapon *system*, a term that came into common use in recognition of the extraordinary complexity of nuclear weaponry – that seemed to qualify as the foolproof deterrent – the Polaris submarine. The submarine included missile firing tubes and could launch the missiles from under water. The Polaris could prowl the ocean floor with its retaliatory arsenal at the ready. And the enemy could not hope to cripple it – or at least not the entire Polaris fleet – with a surprise attack. The mobility of the Polaris and the vast caverns of water in which it could move about made it virtually immune to attack. The nuclear-equipped submarine was the perfect technical fulfillment of Brodie's injunction and the strategists' first principle; it was as close to an absolutely invulnerable retaliatory force as could be imagined.

Dwight Eisenhower presided over momentous changes in the composition of the American strategic arsenal. The first liquid-fueled intermediate range missiles were deployed during his term of office. And as it drew to a close, the investment in research and development of Minuteman and Polaris was on the point of bearing fruit. As these changes were in motion, he steadfastly insisted that the fleet of bombers, upon which the United States would have to depend for deterrence until its missiles were fully operational, was adequate to deter the Soviet Union from any adventure inimical to American interests. But events, notably Sputnik, conspired to make difficult the task of persuading the American people that this was so.

Shortly before Sputnik, Eisenhower commissioned a panel of prominent private citizens to study the nation's defenses and report their findings to him. He hoped that the report would reinforce his own conviction that the country was more than adequately protected. But the Gaither committee, as it was called after its chairman, a California lawyer named H. Rowan Gaither, sounded a note of alarm rather than reassurance. It strongly recommended a series of measures "to secure and augment our deterrent power."[56] Although the report was officially classified as secret, its major conclusions found their way into public print, and heightened rather than calmed the anxieties that Sputnik had stirred up. These anxieties crystallized around the fear that a "missile gap" was opening between the United States and the Soviet Union.

At the root of this fear was the strategists' first principle of deterrence – the need for a survivable retaliatory force. Sputnik seemed to show that the Soviets were far ahead of the Americans in developing nuclear-carrying rockets, and there was no way of being certain how many missiles Soviet factories were producing. A pessimistic appraisal of both trends could, and did, lead to the conclusion that the American fleet of bombers and missiles was, or would be during the late 1950s and early 1960s, perilously susceptible to a sweeping, crippling Soviet strike.

A RAND study in 1955, a successor to the 1951 Air Bases report supervised by Albert Wohlstetter, had warned that the addition of missiles to the Soviet arsenal would complicate the problem of guarding the American nuclear striking force. In 1958, with the shock of Sputnik still palpable in the United States, with the dimensions of the Soviet fleet unknown, and with the sturdier second generation of American missilery not yet in place, Wohlstetter published an article about the requirements of deterrence in the missile age. It was entitled "The Delicate Balance of Terror," and it appeared in the January issue of the widely read quarterly journal *Foreign Affairs*. Wohlstetter reiterated the central importance of a "protected retaliatory capacity."[57] And he offered several suggestions for safeguarding the American force, which he believed (and as the title of the piece implied) was in danger of becoming vulnerable to Soviet assault. The article reached a wide audience, and further aggravated the doubts about the adequacy of the American nuclear force that Sputnik had kindled.

In the presidential election year of 1960, the Democrats seized upon the missile gap as a major theme in their campaign to turn the Republicans out of the White House. Their candidate, Senator John F. Kennedy of Massachusetts, told audiences across the nation that the incumbents had given the nation a "cheap, second-best defense."[58] He referred to the "missile lag," in which the United States trailed behind the USSR. And he echoed the other of the strategists' criticisms – the inability to fight "limited" wars.[59] Presidential campaigns are curious, hybrid creatures, part gladiatorial engagement, part beauty contest, part great debate. They test public sentiment on the pressing political issues of the day only imperfectly. But insofar as any presidential contest can focus squarely upon a question of the moment, the 1960 election was a referendum on military policy in the nuclear age. When a Gallup Poll asked the question, "What do you think is the *most* important problem facing the country today?" over two-thirds of the respondents listed matters having to do with foreign policy and defense.[60] Within a decade the problem of the requirements of deterrence had moved from the speculations of a narrow group of specialists to the center of attention in the world's mightiest political community.

But by the time it arrived there the debate had become one-sided. Not only Kennedy, but his Republican opponent embraced the strategists' views. As Eisenhower's Vice-President, Richard Nixon was awkwardly placed to join the chorus of criticism of the New Look. But he was induced to do so by his chief rival for the Republican nomination, Governor Nelson Rockefeller of New York. Rockefeller had become an enthusiastic champion of the strategists' (and the Democrats') criticism. After Sputnik he had assembled a group of prominent citizens, under the auspices of the Rockefeller Brothers Fund, to ponder "the problems and opportunities confronting American democracy." One panel had investigated "Interna-

tional Security: The Military Aspect," and had made the familiar recommendations for beefing up the nation's nuclear striking force and girding for nonnuclear conflicts as well. In July
of 1960, just before the Republicans were to convene, Rockefeller lured Nixon to his Manhattan apartment with the implied threat of an active candidacy or a floor fight at the convention. The two issued a joint communiqué that said that
"new efforts" were needed in the field of defense, and that the
"two imperatives of national security in the 1960s" were "a
nuclear retaliatory power capable of surviving surprise attack
to inflict devastating punishment on any aggressor, and a
modern flexible and balanced military establishment with
forces capable of deterring or meeting any local aggression."
And they called for new and larger programs to fulfill those
imperatives.[61] The strategists' critique could hardly have been
more succinctly put.

Kennedy won the election. As he prepared to take office, he
faced a set of circumstances similar to those that his two predecessors had confronted eight and sixteen years before. Each
had had to cope with a new section of the rising "iceberg" of
nuclear destructiveness: Each had come into office with a new
weapon in his possession and with the task of accommodating
American policy to its technical characteristics. Harry Truman
had inherited the atomic bomb, and he had set the nation on a
course of liberal diplomacy with the aim of eliminating
the weapon entirely from international politics. Dwight
Eisenhower was presented with the hydrogen bomb, and he
made it the centerpiece of a strategy of deterrence through the
threat of massive retaliation. John Kennedy assumed power at
the beginning of the missile age. And he entered the White
House with a mandate to refashion the nation's defenses, and
thus to rethink the answers to the three strategic questions that
the invention of nuclear weapons had thrust upon the United
States.

The Foundations of Stable Deterrence

Only when our arms are certain beyond doubt can we be certain beyond doubt that they will never be used.   John F. Kennedy, *Inaugural Address, 1961*[1]

The Kennedy administration

Tracing continuity and change from one historical period to another is a favorite game of the historian. Usually both are present. This is true of the strategic policies of the administrations of Dwight D. Eisenhower and John F. Kennedy. At first glance the differences between them stand out. Kennedy emphasized these differences. He presented his government as a sharp break with the past all across the spectrum of national policy. He summoned his countrymen to a "New Frontier," to new national challenges for which novel political departures were necessary. And new men were needed too. The Kennedy administration supplied them. "The torch has been passed," the President proclaimed in his inaugural address, "to a new generation of Americans." The men who filled the ranks of his government were younger than their predecessors. They had formed the junior officer corps during the Second World War. While Eisenhower was supreme commander of all the allied forces in Europe, Kennedy was commanding a PT boat in the

Pacific. And they had more enthusiasm, vision, and—to use the favored word of the time—vigor, than the Republicans, whom they pictured as tired, complacent, and dim. Kennedy and his men formed an administration of football players— touch football, to be sure, not the grinding violent combat of the college and professional athletes, but football all the same—in energetic contrast with the stolid golfer (who, unlike Kennedy, had been a college football player of note, but in the distant past) who sat in the White House for most of the 1950s.

The contrast between Eisenhower and Kennedy seems especially vivid—again at first glance—in the area of military policy. The heart of the Democratic case against the Republicans was the charge of inadequate attention to the nation's defenses, a charge that underpinned the general themes of youth against age and energy versus torpor. Kennedy was borne into office on the wave of national concern about Sputnik, and the fear of a missile gap. He presumed that he had a mandate for changing the design of America's defenses. And he took immediate steps to make changes. He delivered three major addresses on defense and security in his first four months in office. Each sounded a note of alarm. The net result was a sharp increase in federal expenditures for defense.

He broke with precedent by giving a State of the Union Message just ten days after his inauguration. "I must inform the Congress," he said, "that our analyses over the last ten days make it clear that—in each of the principal areas of crisis—the tide of events has been running out and time has not been our friend." "The news will be worse before it is better," he warned later in the speech, "and while hoping and working for the best, we should prepare ourselves now for the worst."[2] As part of that preparation he ordered a sweeping reappraisal of the nation's defenses. With the preliminary results of the review in hand[3] he sent a Special Message on the Defense Budget to Congress on March 28, which requested increases in military appropriations. And he followed that with a "Special Message on Urgent National Needs" on May 25, his second assessment of the "State of the Union,"[4] which he made in a further break with precedent, because the tradition of a single annual message "has been broken in extraordinary times [and] these are extraordinary times." Again he requested further outlays for military purposes. All in all Kennedy increased the Eisenhower defense budget for fiscal year 1962 from $49 to $51 billion.

With their reappraisal of the nation's defenses in the beginning of 1961, Kennedy and his men had, in their view, "compressed fifteen years of postwar history into four weeks."[5] Their purpose had been to reexamine and rethink the central problems that nuclear weapons had raised. But the conclusions that emerged were not altogether different from the ones at which the previous guardians of the nation's security had arrived. There was as much continuity as change in the transition from Eisenhower to Kennedy.

This was so in part because the broad political commitments of the United States did not change in 1961. Neither Eisenhower nor Kennedy was sympathetic to the aims, as they understood them, of Soviet foreign policy. Neither wanted the United States to retreat into isolation. Neither favored dismantling the American armed forces. Foreign policy debates between Republicans and Democrats since 1945 had not been about what the nation's role in the world should be but about how to carry out the agreed-on role; not, that is, on what to do but on how best to do it.[6]

The continuity from one administration to the other was also due to the continuity of the weapons that served as the basis for strategy. The American nuclear stockpile did not disappear when Kennedy took office. He had the same material with which to work as his predecessor. And in the nuclear age weapons had come to circumscribe strategy; the technology at hand shaped the political choices of what to do with it. This reversed the usual pattern. In the past, the more troops and arms a nation had the more strategic options it could pursue. But the more nuclear weapons a state had, and, crucially, the more weapons its chief adversary owned, the narrower its range of strategic maneuver became. The growth of the American nuclear arsenal was like the building of a house; the higher the structure rose, the less variation became possible in the overall design.

But if Kennedy embraced some of the same strategic principles as the Eisenhower administration, he implemented them differently. The Democrats found some of the same answers to the strategic questions that nuclear weapons posed, but they gave those answers more formally and emphatically than had the Republicans. Strategic principles achieved an official status in the 1960s that they did not have in the preceding decade.[7]

The Eisenhower response to the questions of strategy in the nuclear age was like the British constitution; it was a matter of custom as much as principle, and it had to be deduced from the day-to-day policies of the government. The Kennedy responses to these same strategic questions were closer, by contrast, to the American constitution — systematic, explicit, and clear. Kennedy declared in his Special Message on Defense Policy his intention to set out "basic policies or principles" to "constitute the essential guidelines and standards to be followed by all civilian and military personnel who work on behalf of our Nation's security,"[8] and he and his chief lieutenants proceeded to do so.

This difference in emphasis and in manner of presentation had its roots in the differences in style between the two administrations. Kennedy and his associates had a taste for constitution-making. They eagerly turned their attention to the exploration of all the ramifications of nuclear weapons, and to the search for as clear and precise rules for making, deploying, and using them as it was possible to find. The symbol of this predilection and the agent for carrying it out was the man Kennedy appointed to be Secretary of Defense, Robert McNamara.

McNamara became the dominant member of the cabinet, and the second most powerful man in the federal government.[9] He possessed a generous share of the fresh reservoir of energy that the Kennedy men brought to Washington. He became famous for it, for his impressive memory, his Herculean appetite for work, his quick mastery of the details of defense issues, and above all his fondness for — indeed his insistence upon — precision in dealing with those issues. A tribute to his qualities of mind and character was his reputation as a "human Univac," a man who could retain and use information with the facility of a computer. Under Eisenhower strategy tended to be a series of presumptions, which were neither exactly stated nor rigorously tested. McNamara ushered in strategy by calculation. Kennedy relied heavily upon him, and he became the most authoritative spokesman on nuclear weapons matters in American history — authoritative both in the sense of understanding the pertinent issues and in having the power to speak for the government.

In his second year at the Pentagon, McNamara began the practice of preparing a summary and an explanation of the Defense Department's plans for the upcoming fiscal year. The summary, which appeared annually, became known as the "Posture Statement," and it provided a detailed public record of American military policy. In addition McNamara spent hours testifying, again in detail, before congressional committees. (It was estimated that he spent the equivalent of over three months of every work year either testifying or preparing to do so.)[10] Out of what he as well as the President said emerged a clearer picture than had ever before been available of the American responses to the three questions of strategy in the nuclear age.

There was another reason why Kennedy's answers to those questions were more precise and emphatic than those of the Eisenhower administration. The Democrats did not have to cope with quite the same uncertainties that the dizzying pace of technical improvement in armaments had produced during the 1950s. When they assumed office the art of nuclear weaponry had undergone three revolutionary changes in little more than a decade. The first was the fabrication of the initial bomb, which showed that explosives drawing their power from the nucleus of matter could in fact be made. The second was the hydrogen bomb, which ratified the promise of extraordinary destructive power that the first fission devices held out. And the third was the ballistic missile, which made it possible for nuclear explosives to be delivered with unprecedented swiftness, and in great numbers. Each of these leaps in technical sophistication reinforced the truth and magnified the importance of Brodie's observation of 1946: "Everything about the new weapon is overshadowed by the twin facts that it exists and its destructive power is fantastically great." Each affected the American response to the questions of strategy that the nuclear age raised. But the three innovations had a progressively diminishing effect on the possibilities of warfare, and thus on American defense policy. If the first atomic bomb was an earthquake in international politics, the hydrogen explosive and the ballistic missile were its after-shocks. Each tremor was less disturbing than its predecessor; with each development, that is, the necessary adjustment was smaller. Kennedy took office after the third major leap – the coming of the missile age – was well under way. He and his associates came to believe no further leaps were imminent.

They came to see themselves as resting on a plateau of technical refinement, or, if not a plateau, at least a point from which further progress would be gradual and predictable. "The prospect that remarkable new weapons can provide a sudden change in the margin of superiority," McNamara told a congressional committee in early 1963, "is not, in my judgment, likely."[11] Because he could see the future more clearly than had been possible previously, and could tell that it looked very much like the present, he could set down principles that could endure.

And that is what happened. The life of the Kennedy administration was short; it lasted barely a thousand days, only a little more than a third the length of Eisenhower's stay in the White House. But it was a momentous period for American nuclear strategy. Because of its approach to the formation of defense policy, and because it held power when the curve of innovation in nuclear weaponry was flattening out after more than a decade of precipitous upward climb, the Kennedy administration laid down principles of nuclear strategy that endured well beyond 1963. By circumstance and by temperament it fell to this administration to make the definitive American response to the problem of nuclear weapons.

A "survivable" striking force

Kennedy embraced the Eisenhower response to the first question of nuclear strategy. He reaffirmed the political purpose of the nuclear arsenal that he inherited. That purpose was deterrence, the prevention of war by the threat to punish Soviet aggression, and the new President emphasized the defensive intent of the United States. "The United States will not strike first," he told a news conference in early February, and he repeated the pledge in his Special Defense Message at the end of March: "Our arms will never be used to strike the first blow in any attack."[12] This promise touched off a minor uproar in the capitals of Western Europe, since it seemed to remove the threat of an American nuclear salvo against a Soviet conventional assault, a threat on which the Europeans counted to keep the Soviet ground forces at bay. The mighty Red Army, they feared, would roll over its puny Western counterpart without having to fire a single nuclear shot unless the Soviets believed that moving their tanks westward would provoke a nuclear attack in return.

Kennedy clarified his intentions and soothed the Europeans by drawing a distinction between a first strike – attacking the Soviet Union by any means – and the first use of nuclear weapons. The United States would foreswear the former, but not the latter. The American Commander-in-Chief would not start a war with the Soviet Union – the overriding political purpose of the American arsenal remained deterrence – but if the Soviets themselves attacked, he would reserve the right to bring that arsenal into play if the Western forces were being defeated.[13]

President Kennedy's wishes on the deployment of nuclear weapons were faithful to the first strategic criticism of the Eisenhower administration, which he had made an important part of his campaign platform. He wanted a secure retaliatory force. He and McNamara both stressed this. "If we are to keep the peace," he said in his January 30 State of the Union address, "we need an invulnerable missile force powerful enough to deter any aggressor from even threatening an attack that he would know could not destroy enough of our force to prevent his own destruction."[14] "What we have and must continue to have," he reiterated in the Special Message on the Defense Budget eight weeks later, "is the ability to survive a first blow and respond with devastating power."[15] McNamara hammered home the point in congressional testimony. In one of his earliest appearances he said, "In this age of nuclear-armed intercontinental ballistic missiles, the ability to deter rests heavily on the existence of a force which can weather or survive a massive nuclear attack, even with little or no warning, in sufficient strength to strike a decisive counter-blow."[16] "We are emphasizing survivability," he said a few weeks later in explaining the supplements to the Eisenhower defense budget that he was recommending.[17]

"Survivability" was not altogether an alien concept to American strategic policy. It was at least a first cousin to the notion of "adequacy" that Secretary of the Air Force Quarles had announced as the heart of the nation's policy in 1956. And as recently as the year before Eisenhower's last Secretary of Defense, Thomas Gates, had cited the need for "an assured retaliatory capability."[18] But where the Eisenhower administration had, in effect, suggested "survivability" as the goal toward which the deployment of nuclear weapons should aim, Kennedy and McNamara loudly proclaimed it. They engraved it in stone and set it up in public view. Brodie's insight of 1946, Wohlstetter and his associates' criterion for locating air bases of 1951, and the ever-louder criticism of American defense policy in the latter half of the 1950s became, in 1961, a fundamental principle of American nuclear strategy, as important as the concept of deterrence itself.

And Kennedy and McNamara moved quickly to bring the American arsenal into conformity with the principle of "survivability." Kennedy had said in his campaign that this was an urgent matter. And McNamara stressed, as had Wohlstetter and other critics of Eisenhower's strategic policies, that the missile age made the task of deterring an all-out attack "vastly more complicated."[19] Much of the flurry of defense activity in the first months of 1961 was directed toward ensuring that the American nuclear force would weather a Soviet assault in sufficient strength to launch a devastating counterattack on the Soviet Union. The administration took steps to see that the retaliatory arsenal that already existed would survive a preemptive strike. Most of the American hydrogen bombs

were still carried in the bays of long-range bomber aircraft,
which were managed by the Strategic Air Command. In the
first weeks of 1961 Kennedy ordered that half of these aircraft
be put on permanent "alert status," so that they could take
off upon warning of enemy attack and escape being struck
and destroyed on the ground should the warning prove
accurate.

At the same time, Kennedy and McNamara decided to emphasize, in the procurement of further nuclear hardware, the
most "survivable" kinds of weapons – those that "could ride
out a massive nuclear attack."[20] This meant investing heavily
in the Polaris and Minuteman systems that had come into
production at the end of the Eisenhower period. The schedule
on which the Polaris was being produced was speeded up, and
the number ultimately to be deployed was increased.[21] Two
years later the Polaris seemed to McNamara to have been an
exceedingly wise investment. The submarines, he told the Senate Armed Services Committee, could "be stationed in a wide
area of the ocean, so wide that we see no possibility that they
can be detected under today's conditions."[22] If they could not
be detected they could not be destroyed, and would always be
ready to fire their missiles in response to a Soviet attack on the
United States.

McNamara and Kennedy did not want to place all of the
American deterrent force on submarines and airplanes. The
United States, they believed, needed a fleet of land-based intercontinental missiles as well. The Minuteman appeared
more "survivable" than the other available models. The President ordered the opening of a second production line for the
Minuteman, so that more of them could be available sooner
than the Eisenhower administration had planned. And the
missiles themselves were deployed in a "hardened" fashion.
They were stored underground in concrete shelters, as further
insurance against being destroyed by a surprise attack.
McNamara's plans for an increase in the number of bombers
on alert status, for "hardened" Minuteman missiles, and for
more Polarises than the Eisenhower administration had envisioned, added up, he estimated for a House subcommittee in

April 1961, to a 50 percent increase in American destructive
capability in the "critical period of 1961 through 1963," the
period when, some feared, the nation's retaliatory force would
be vulnerable to enemy assault.[23]

The adoption of "survivability" as the essence of deterrence
and hence as the guiding principle of the American nuclear
arsenal had an important consequence: It reinforced the Kennedy administration's penchant for declaring its strategic
policies openly and in detail. Publicity fitted the logic of deterrence. "We should acquaint the Soviets with our strengths
so that they cannot misjudge our strengths," McNamara said
in 1963. "It is for this reason, for example, that we have given
as much information as we have to the press on our future
missile procurement and Polaris system procurement programs. . . [which] serves as a foundation for our statement,
repeatedly made in public, that we have enough strategic nuclear power to absorb fully a Soviet strike and survive with
sufficient power to destroy utterly the Soviet Union. We have
made that statement. We wish them to believe it. They should
believe it. It is true. And we have documented it by release of
information that really could be considered highly classified,
but we think it is in our national interest to release that kind of
information."[24] Deterrence required not only a huge nuclear
club that was shatter-proof, but one that was well known to be
shatter-proof.

Weapons procurement and bureaucratic "friction"

The first stage of strategic policy – deciding upon the specifi-
cations for a "survivable" nuclear arsenal – was a straightforward enough undertaking for Kennedy and McNamara. The
second – carrying it out – proved more difficult. As warfare
came to depend more upon machines and less upon men, the
art of deployment came to involve producing war machines of
the best possible design. The adept commander was no longer
the one who moved his troops into the most favorable positions, but rather the one who had had the wit to order the
proper weapons in the first place.

This presented a problem for Kennedy and McNamara. They had several kinds of weapons from which to choose. The combination of American ingenuity in the research and design of nuclear hardware and the energy of the nation's defense industries produced a cornucopia of nuclear weapons, of different shapes and sizes, beginning in the latter half of the 1950s, The task of the President and the Secretary of Defense was like that of the man shopping for a new car who faces an array of different models, with different features and different prices but with the same basic purpose, who cannot afford them all, and who therefore needs some means of selection.

The Eisenhower administration had had to make such choices also. But it had made them on fiscal rather than on strategic grounds. The President and his chief adviser had set the general limits for military expenditure and then given the armed services a relatively free hand in deciding how and where to spend the funds available within the designated limits.[25] Their procedure reflected the belief that fiscal prudence was of supreme importance: How much the government spent mattered at least as much as what it bought. The principle of deterrence through the threat of massive retaliation had, after all, been adopted because it could be sustained at a price the Republicans were prepared to pay. Kennedy and McNamara put things the other way around: Strategic principle was to govern expenditure. They were not prepared to tolerate fiscal profligacy, and as time went on McNamara worried more and more about the size of the defense budget. But the question of what the United States bought for defense would precede the question of how much weapons would cost. This approach to buying weapons was summed up in Kennedy's charge to McNamara to "develop the force structure necessary to our military requirements without regard to arbitrary or predetermined budget ceilings. And secondly, having determined that force structure. . . procure it at the lower possible cost."[26]

McNamara did not propose to permit the services to choose whatever armaments struck their fancy. That violated his understanding of his proper role. The manager in any enterprise, public or private, he told an interviewer, "has the option of following one of two major alternative courses of action. He can either act as a judge or a leader. . . In the one case, it is a passive role; in the other it is an active role. . . . I've always believed and endeavored to follow [sic] the active leadership role as opposed to the passive judicial role."[27] McNamara believed in subordinating important tasks, like the procurement of weapons systems, to a common standard, rather than letting each administrative unit select its own guidelines and act accordingly, with the manager interfering only to resolve intractable disputes. The common standard he chose for long-range nuclear weapons was "survivability." He took as his responsibility the supervision of the process of acquiring armaments in order to see that the United States was getting the most survivable nuclear force possible per dollar of federal expenditure.

McNamara brought several managerial techniques to the Defense Department to carry out his philosophy of management. One was "systems analysis," a way of measuring different weapon systems against the nation's broad strategic requirements. Another was "program budgeting," which carried the same purpose into the preparation of the department's annual budget requests. Each was a way of joining strategic precept to fiscal policy, which the Eisenhower administration, in the view of its successors, had allowed to become separated. Each was a way of ensuring that the weapons that the government acquired conformed to an overall design. The design for long-range nuclear weapons was based on the principle of survivability, which was thus transformed from the answer to the question of how to prevent war to a managerial axiom for one of the largest enterprises in the world.

But the principle was not always and everywhere applied. In assembling the American nuclear arsenal there was a gap between theory and practice, a gap that recalls a problem of the battlefield commander that Clausewitz identified. Before the nuclear age, a nation's safety rested ultimately on the skillful use of its weapons in battle. But in combat it was never possible to carry out battle plans precisely to the letter. Clausewitz termed "friction" the thousand hindrances to the smooth execution of previously laid plans that crop up in the heat of battle. For nuclear weapons, security came to depend less on the use of force than on the threat to use it. Deployment — the design of a nuclear arsenal by scientists, engineers, and professional strategists — took the place of the tactical virtuosity of generals at the heart of military policy. And in the nuclear age, the American government encountered considerable interference in the application of strategic principles to its arsenal — interference analogous to the "friction" of the battlefield described by Clausewitz.

Resistance to the straightforward application of principle in acquiring nuclear weapons came not from numerous, random, and unpredictable sources, like battlefield "friction." It was put up rather by parts of the federal government itself, especially the armed forces, which had their own views on how the United States ought to arm itself. The armed services are often bent upon increasing the resources at their command and expanding their roles in the nation's affairs, however that sorts with the wishes of the President, despite the fact that he is their Commander-in-Chief. For example, in the 1950s the Army had been distressed at the New Look because the Eisenhower administration's strategy downgraded the foot soldier, and promised less money and institutional prestige for the service of which he was the heart.

The armed services not only have their own independent interests; they also have the means to pursue them, even when this brings them into conflict with the President and his cabinet. There are logistical obstacles to controlling defense policy. The Pentagon is so vast and its business so complicated that no Secretary of Defense can keep fully abreast of all that happens there. And there are political difficulties as well. The armed services often have influential friends elsewhere in the political system. They have been able to count on a friendly hearing from certain Congressmen on pet projects about which the President and the Secretary of Defense were not enthusiastic. And by testifying before congressional committees, dissenting officers have been able to put their cases directly to the public. The armed services have established sufficient independence to be described as "quasi-sovereignties."[28]

The emergence of "quasi-sovereignties" is due to the confluence, after 1945, of several features of political life that, separately, predate the nuclear age. One is politics within government, which is as old as government itself. Courtiers schemed for the king's favor, or the favor of king's favorite, long before the rise of the modern state. Today nations are governed not by courts but by large, complicated organizations, within and between which jockeying for position, bargaining and trading – the stuff of politics – goes on. The phrase "bureaucratic politics" has been coined to refer to these activities. It seems at first glance a contradiction in terms. The commanding principle of bureaucracy, in Max Weber's classical description, is hierarchy, which is antithetical to the conflict that is the essence of politics. Bureaucracies, and their constituent parts, are supposed to be subordinate to higher authority, not sovereign in their own right. "Bureaucratic politics" attests to the fact that the constituent parts of the American Federal Government have strayed from the Weberian norm by developing independent political purposes.

Similarly, the appetite of the armed forces for men, material, and the resources to procure them did not appear suddenly after 1945. It was George Bernard Shaw in "Man and Superman," not a latter-day critic of the American "military-industrial complex," who said "when the military man approaches, the world locks up its spoons." But in the United States in the nuclear age, the size and political prestige of the armed services grew dramatically, and vast sums became available for the purchase of the expensive, frightening weapons of contemporary warfare. The United States Congress has traditionally engaged in the process of bargaining, trading favors, and dividing up federal largesse among different regions and interest groups, the process that has come to be known as "pork-barrelling" and "log-rolling." In the nuclear age, the determination of the defense budget joined the authorization of highways, dams, and other public works projects as part of that process.

So the American nuclear arsenal was not cut precisely to the pattern that Kennedy and McNamara designed. The history of weapons procurement is not identical to the history of the evolution of strategic principles.[29] While the second has been geared to calculations of the political aims and military capacities of the Soviet Union, the first has been deeply influenced by the parochial interests of constituent parts of the federal government, in particular the armed forces. The degree of congruence between the two has depended on the determination of the Secretary of Defense to have his way, his political acumen, and the authority the President has been willing to grant him.

McNamara had, especially during John Kennedy's term of office, a generous share of all three. And despite the "friction" of parochial interests interfering with his labors, he did manage to impose a measure of doctrinal coherence on the American nuclear arsenal. The initial decision to stress the Polaris and Minuteman programs meant that the United States arsenal would have weapons that could ride out a Soviet assault, however fierce it was. But the Secretary of Defense wanted to go further. He wanted to prune away armaments that could not be expected to survive. He had some success. He cancelled two planned squadrons of Titan missiles, which were both more expensive and more liable to preemptive destruction than the Minuteman.[30] He also attempted, and finally succeeded after two years, in having the liquid-fueled Jupiter intermediate-range missiles removed from their stations in European bases close to the Soviet Union. As well as being exposed to Soviet attack, the Jupiters were vulnerable to sabotage.[31] McNamara even prevented the placement of Minuteman missiles on moving railroad cars. The "rail–mobile" Minuteman would have been even surer of weathering an assault than the stationary variety. But McNamara and his staff calculated that the gain in survivability would not have been worth the extra cost in development, operation, and protection that the mobile version would have required, and so they decided against it.

Because the Minuteman succeeded the Titan, and additions to the Polaris fleet took the place of the recalled Jupiters, these

measures to eliminate redundant nuclear hardware did not
arouse significant opposition from the other constituencies of
American strategic policy. But elsewhere McNamara did run
into a curtain of political friction in trying to cut the American
nuclear arsenal to fit, but not to exceed, the requirements of
survivability. He refused, for example, to authorize the production of a new long-range manned bomber, originally called
the B-70, to replace the B-52 models that had been built in
the 1950s. The airplane was a far less suitable "launching
platform" for nuclear warheads aimed at the Soviet Union
than was the ballistic missile, he believed, and the nation
should invest its resources accordingly. But the manned aircraft was the very soul of the Air Force, the appliance that had
called it into being and that justified its continued existence.
The service and its congressional friends fought hard to get a
new, up-to-date version.[32]

McNamara had his way in the B-70 controversy, however,
and he succeeded in cancelling another expensive strategic
weapon that did not meet the administration's standard of
strategic worth, this time over the objections of the British
government. This was the Skybolt air-to-ground missile, on
which Britain had been counting to maintain its status as a
full-fledged member of the "club" of nuclear weapon states,
and which would have helped prolong the strategic life of
American manned bombers as well. Since it took off from a
platform moving hundreds of miles per hour, Skybolt was less
reliable and accurate than Minuteman, or even Polaris, and
hence less desirable. The price of strategic purity here was,
potentially, a rent in the fabric of the Atlantic alliance, but the
Secretary of Defense was willing to pay it.[33]

McNamara was not always able to override the wishes of the
other constituencies of American nuclear strategy. The American military forces in the 1960s were shaped by the parochial
preferences of the armed forces, the Congress, and the nation's
allies, as well as by the principles of strategy that the Kennedy
administration officially adopted.[34] But McNamara did make
the American nuclear arsenal the realization, albeit an imperfect one, of the principle of the capacity to retaliate in kind

after an enemy attack that Brodie had stipulated as the key to survival in a world of more than one nuclear nation. The Kennedy administration embraced that principle and fixed it in concrete; literally — in the concrete siloes that encased the Minuteman fleet and guaranteed that it could ride out a Soviet attack and pulverize the Soviet Union in reply.

The principle of survivability lent itself not only to the choice of which of several similar weapon systems to acquire, but to the decision of how many of them to deploy. At the very beginning of the Kennedy administration McNamara ordered the development of quantitative requirements for strategic weapons.[35] "In contrast to most other military requirements," he told the Congress, "these lend themselves rather well to reasonably precise calculation."[36] As he explained it, this involved determining the targets in the Soviet Union and elsewhere to be hit, the forces best suited to hit them, and the fraction of the striking force that would exist after an enemy first strike. Each of these could be assigned a numerical value. Each in fact received several values, which included both optimistic and pessimistic estimates of the performances of the weapons on both sides. McNamara and his associates then calculated the results of nuclear exchanges between the United States and the Soviet Union under a wide variety of conditions.

"Out of these 20 or 30 primary factors, each with a set of 6 to 10 different alternative assumptions, we carried on a series of analyses to try to determine whether our forces were adequate to accomplish our objectives under all reasonable situations that we might face."[37] The objectives they set for the retaliatory force were the destruction of 50 percent of the Soviet Union's industrial capacity and 25 percent of its population.[38] This far surpassed the damage to any of the belligerents in the Second World War. The certainty of suffering it, they decided, would deter the Soviet Union from attacking the United States.

The calculations were not entirely free from all uncertainties. The assumptions on which they were based were only assumptions — they could not be tested. Neither side could predict with absolute precision how well its own weapons or the weapons of the enemy would work in the hour of truth. But the calculations were not mere guesses either. McNamara and Kennedy could, and did, have some confidence in them.[39]

McNamara came to have enough confidence in the calculations to believe that he and his colleagues had provided the nation with more nuclear firepower than was needed. Since the United States was pledged not to strike first, and needed a nuclear arsenal only to survive a first strike and retaliate, the proper size of the American force depended upon the kind of attack the Soviets could mount. And that, of course, depended upon the size of the Soviet nuclear stockpile. When Kennedy took office, only fragmentary evidence about its size was available, and estimates varied widely. The highest estimates formed the basis for the fears of a missile gap that were prominent in the last years of the Eisenhower presidency. But in the first months of 1961 the picture of Russian nuclear strength became much clearer. Photographs from newly launched reconnaissance satellites provided better evidence than American authorities had ever had before. And these revealed that the lowest estimates were the correct ones. There was no missiles gap.[40]

But when Kennedy and his chief advisors met in October 1961 to fix the total number of missiles the United States would eventually deploy, they settled on a number greater than what would have been appropriate, given the size of the existing Soviet striking force. The reason, once again, was the "friction" that surrounded the weapons procurement process. Political pressure pushed the American nuclear stockpile higher than strategic principle prescribed. Kennedy would have courted political embarrassment if, after having hammered away at the shortcomings of the nation's nuclear forces during his campaign, he admitted upon taking office that his charges had been unfounded. And he had to take into account the view of the armed services, especially the Air Force, which had a proprietary interest in the missile program. A lower figure than the 1000 that Kennedy selected for Minuteman deployment might have sent the Joint Chiefs scurrying to their congressional allies, and stirred up trouble for the administration there.[41]

Whether or not the United States had more than enough deterrent power as a result of Kennedy and McNamara's efforts, it certainly had enough. "There is no question," McNamara said at the beginning of 1962, "that, today, our Strategic Retaliatory Forces are fully capable of destroying the Soviet target system, even after absorbing an initial nuclear surprise attack,"[42] He repeated the statement the following year.[43] Indeed, with the defense budget he presented in 1963, he said, "we begin to encounter the law of diminishing returns, where each additional increment of resources applied produces a smaller increment of overall defense capability."[44] This marked a milestone of sorts in military history. Nations had assembled mighty armies to discourage their neighbors from mischief in the past, but never had the means to inflict retaliatory punishment been so firmly assured.

In his inaugural address Kennedy had said that "only when our arms are certain beyond doubt can we be certain beyond doubt that they will never be used." McNamara's nuclear policies had fulfilled Kennedy's condition. Eisenhower had been confident of the deterrent effect of the American nuclear arsenal. Because of the additions to that arsenal and the elaborate calculations of its destructive potential that McNamara and his associates had made, Kennedy felt certain of it, a certainty rooted in the extraordinary, unprecedented power of nuclear armaments.

"We do not have complete knowledge under all circumstances of the survivability of our hardened sites," McNamara said in early 1963, "but when one is facing a Soviet force of the size that we are proposing, such gaps as exist in our knowledge, and they are not very great, in my opinion, offer no risk to our security."[45] The mechanical and human errors that had plagued battlefield commanders in the past might occur during a nuclear exchange. The Soviets might knock out part of the American striking force on the ground. Missiles could misfire, or explode in the air, or miss their targets. None of this would matter. The United States could still inflict more dam-

age on the Soviet Union more quickly than any nation had
ever suffered before. The Soviet leaders had to operate on the
assumption that the worst imaginable performance of the
American retaliatory force after the mightiest attack on the
United States that they could mount would still annihilate
their country.

This achievement had a momentous implication, which was
not lost on McNamara. If the United States could build a nuclear retaliatory force that could be certain of devastating the
Soviet Union after any conceivable assault, the Soviets could
do the same. The techniques for rendering long range
weaponry "invulnerable" were available to them as well. And
a prudent defense planner would have to assume that if his
opponent could protect his retaliatory force he would do so.
This assumption came to the surface in McNamara's 1963
congressional testimony. Asked whether the Soviets could follow the American pattern of nuclear weapons deployment, he
affirmed that they could.[46] "I believe that they are moving
toward more invulnerable missile systems," he said a short
time later. "I think there is ample evidence that they are moving to sub-launched missiles. I think they are probably direct-
ing a movement toward hardened missile sites."[47]

This, he added, was not necessarily a bad thing. "As a nation we should not assume that our position is worsening as
they do that. As a matter of fact, it will put less pressure on
them to carry out a preemptive strike in a time of crisis and
this is to our advantage."[48] With secure retaliatory forces on
both sides neither would need to fear a disarming blow from
the other, and this could help to smooth relations between
them. "When both sides have a sure second-strike capability,"
he had said in an interview in late 1962, "then you might have
a more stable balance of terror."[49] McNamara shied away from
stating bluntly and unequivocally that a nuclear stalemate was
in prospect. He was sensitive to the political risks of acknowledging that the Soviet Union was, for all practical purposes,
the nuclear equal of the United States.[50] But if he was hesitant
to admit it publicly, there can be little doubt that he understood privately that the Soviets could assemble a nuclear striking force as "survivable" as its American counterpart.

Ironically, the moment when McNamara accepted the inevitability of a nuclear standoff was the point in the nuclear age when the balance between the two giants was most lopsided. The increase in American striking power that Kennedy had ordered had the effect not of closing the missile gap, which did not exist, but of opening one up, to the disadvantage of the Soviet Union. The Soviet arsenal was not absolutely certain to weather an American surprise attack. At the end of 1963 the Soviets had fewer than 100 operational intercontinental ballistic missiles; the United States had over 550.[51] But in 1963, knowing that the United States would not launch such an attack, and obliged to plan for a period of five years into the future, McNamara presumed – correctly – that the Russians would take steps to protect their retaliatory force and close the gap. When they did, part of the nuclear problem – the problem of how to live in a world with both nuclear weapons and independent nation–states – was solved, with a standoff between the United States and the Soviet Union. The two nuclear giants stood facing each other, their huge clubs poised, each prevented from smashing the other by the certainty of being smashed in return.

This was not entirely unforeseen. In 1955 Winston Churchill had noted the "process of sublime irony" – the march of technological advance in the design of weapons systems – that was ushering in an age "where safety will be the sturdy child of terror, and survival the twin brother of annihilation."[52] That same year the atomic physicist Leo Szilard had foreseen an "atomic stalemate," where neither the United States nor the Soviet Union "could knock out, by a surprise attack, the capacity of the other to retaliate." "And with no reason left to fear an attack," he predicted, "the Atomic Stalemate may acquire a certain degree of stability."[53] Eisenhower's defense policies at times had implied the acceptance of a nuclear stalemate with the Soviets. The Kennedy administration made the stalemate explicit. But the nuclear standoff that McNamara recognized in 1963 carried with it an important question: How far did it extend? Each side was or would soon become equipped to deter a large, direct surprise attack. Neither would be able to launch a "nuclear Pearl Har-

bor" without suffering terrible retribution. But the critics of
the Eisenhower defense policies had held that the achievement of this invulnerability by the protection of the retaliatory
force was only half the task. Kennedy and McNamara subscribed to the strategists' graduated conception of deterrence
and took seriously the responsibility for carrying out the other
half – the resistance to "limited" challenges – as well.

"Flexible response" and beyond

Being prepared to fight nonnuclear wars – giving the United
States the capacity for "flexible response," as Kennedy and
McNamara called it – was the twin of protecting the nuclear
retaliatory force. The two had similar histories, starting as
criticisms of the defense policies of the Eisenhower administration and ending as principles around which the Kennedy
defense budgets were organized. Flexible response was the
second tenet of the strategic critique of the Eisenhower administration, of which the need for a survivable retaliatory force
was the first. Without a versatile, flexible military force,
McNamara said, adopting the logic of graduated deterrence as
the strategists had propounded it in the 1950s, "the Soviets
may well conclude that they can use lesser forms of military
and political aggression without the danger of an all-out nuclear response." If on the other hand the NATO nations had
prepared themselves in advance to fight nonnuclear conflicts,
the level of violence might be kept within bounds even after
war had broken out. "Escalation to a higher level of war,"
McNamara said, "is probably more likely to occur if we go into
these limited actions 'ill equipped and ill prepared' to support the political positions and political objectives that have
been previously established."[54]

Eisenhower had skimped on forces for limited war because
of his fixation with fiscal restraint, in the view of the Kennedy
administration. In his campaign, as well as pledging to reinforce the nation's nuclear stockpile to guard against a missile
gap, Kennedy promised to bolster the nation's nonnuclear
arms. Upon taking office he and McNamara stressed the importance of these "conventional" forces, and took steps to up-

grade them. In the early statements in which the new President addressed himself to defense matters — the State of the Union and Special Defense Messages and the message on "Urgent National Needs" — he moved to make the United States better able to fight in limited wars. He requested an increase in airlift capacity, additional funds for meeting threats posed by guerilla forces, the expansion of research on nonnuclear weaponry, the reorganization and reequipment of the Army, and the recruitment of more men for both the Army and the Marine Corps.[55]

The parallel between the capacity to fight a nonnuclear war and the "survivability" of the nuclear forces goes further. As with the Soviet missile fleet, improved means of gathering and evaluating intelligence yielded an estimate of Soviet nonnuclear strength early in the life of the Kennedy administration that was considerably below most of the guesses that had been current until then. This meant that NATO could match Soviet conventional might more easily than had been commonly presumed.[56] And there is a final correspondence between the fates of the two principal criticisms of the Eisenhower defense policies: "friction" in the form of political pressure hindered the translation of each from principle to policy. But the friction that inhibited the implementation of the policy of flexible response was different from the friction that affected the acquisition of a survivable retaliatory force. Whereas the Kennedy administration found itself compelled to produce too many missiles, it was able to field too few foot soldiers for its purposes. The allied governments of Western Europe balked at raising their contributions to Western defenses, as indeed they had since the North Atlantic Treaty Organization had been formed.[57] They were not anxious to conscript any more sons of the voters who had put them in office than were already serving in their armed forces. And there was another reason for their reluctance: They did not entirely share the Kennedy view of nuclear strategy. The Americans believed in being prepared to fight subnuclear wars all around the world, including in Europe. The Europeans did not want to fight any sort of war on their soil. They were convinced that, whatever the weapons used, a third major war in the twentieth century was bound to leave their homelands devastated. They wished to avoid such a war at all costs, and therefore wanted to devote all their energies to deterrence. And they were more attracted to the absolute than to the graduated concept of deterrence. They regarded the threat to use nuclear weapons as the heart of credible deterrence, and they did not want to risk vitiating that threat by being visibly ready to resist the Soviets by non-nuclear means. So the Europeans did not rally to Kennedy and McNamara's call for bolstering NATO's nonnuclear defenses.

That call became fainter as time went on. American enthusiasm for the policy of flexible response – or rather for the measures that the policy required – began to wane. Americans were not much more anxious to be drafted into the army than were Europeans. And the administration began to worry about the burden that the maintenance of a large European garrison placed on the American balance of payments. Finally, in the middle of the 1960s, the American drive for more conventional strength the world over was completely overtaken by the soaring quantities of men and material that the war in Indochina consumed.

What would happen if war broke out, in Europe or elsewhere, and both the United States and the Soviet Union became involved? Would nuclear weapons come into play? The thrust of the Kennedy – McNamara defense policies was to prevent both from happening: They were aimed at discouraging war by assembling a credible deterrent force, and at erecting a wall between conventional and nuclear conflict by building a serviceable nonnuclear arsenal. But neither effort was guaranteed to succeed. And if both failed, how was nuclear war to be fought? This was the third strategic question that the creation of nuclear weapons forced the United States (as well as the Soviet Union) to consider. The Kennedy administration did consider it. Having affirmed Eisenhower's response to the first question by underscoring the deterrence of war as the principal political purpose of nuclear weapons, and having set down an operational definition of deterrence in response to the second strategic question – how to deploy the weapons to achieve this purpose – Kennedy, McNamara, and their associates grappled earnestly with the third.

They gave this third question serious attention because war seemed more than remotely possible. Kennedy's thousand days in the White House included one of the most parlous periods of the Cold War. Relations between the United States and the Soviet Union were tenser in 1961 than at any time since the 1940s.[58]

That year there were, in the recollection of one administration official, "a whole series of major foreign policy crises, more than crises, if you think of crisis as a sort of temporary heating up of a normally dormant problem; these involved the most fundamental kinds of matters in East-West relations. Really, it was a period of overt basic testing between the U.S. and the Soviet Union after Kennedy's election."[59] Kennedy's public rhetoric reflected this reading of events. The variations on the theme of the urgency of the Cold War that he had sounded in his campaign cropped up repeatedly during the first months of his presidential term.[60] The newly inaugurated President exchanged friendly greetings with the Chairman of the Council of Ministers and the Chairman of the Presidium of the Supreme Soviet,[61] but the air of cordiality was quickly dissipated by two events. In Laos Communist insurgents pressed an American-supported government to the brink of collapse. And in Cuba an American-sponsored group of refugees launched an invasion, in an attempt to topple the government of Fidel Castro, which failed ignominiously.

In April Kennedy traveled to Vienna to take personal measure of the Soviet leader, moved as much by curiosity as anything else.[62] The meeting turned out badly. Khrushchev harangued Kennedy about the sins of the West. Their conversation wandered off into wrangling over fine points of ideology, intellectual ground where the President was not at home. Kennedy tried to persuade Khrushchev to disavow guerilla wars. The Soviet leader rebuffed him. The encounter left a grave impression on the young President.[63] Upon his return to the United States he reported to the nation that "it was a very somber two days."[64]

In 1961 as in the late 1940s the tension between the United States and the Soviet Union came to center on the city of

Berlin. The Western powers clung to the portion of the city they had occupied in 1945, despite various forms of Soviet encouragement to abandon it. One hundred ten miles inside East Germany, West Berlin was a small island in a red sea, with the tide constantly lapping at its shores. At Vienna Khrushchev threatened to sign a separate peace treaty with East Germany. This, he claimed, would void the occupation rights of the Western powers, including access to the city and the corridor connecting it to the Federal Republic.[65]

Kennedy termed the exchanges on Berlin "our most somber talks." He made it clear that the United States would not budge there. He did decide to ask Congress for special authority to call troops from the reserves to active duty.[66] And he announced the request in a televised address to the nation on July 26, 1961.

This was one of the most alarming speeches by an American President in the whole, nerve-wracking course of the Cold War. In making public the number of additional men for the armed forces he was requesting, he said that the addition was to be permanent, since the request was "based on our needs to meet a worldwide threat...a basis which stretches far beyond the present Berlin crisis."[67] And he reiterated, in ringing terms, the commitment of the United States to keeping Berlin out of the Communist orbit, whatever the cost: "I hear it said that West Berlin is militarily untenable. And so was Bastogne. And so, in fact, was Stalingrad. Any dangerous spot is tenable if men—brave men—will make it so."[68] The effect of the speech was to frighten his American listeners. The President revealed the grimmest imaginable outlook on the world situation: "When I ran for this office," he said, "I knew that this country faced serious challenges, but I could not realize—nor could any man realize who does not bear the burdens of this office—how heavy and constant would be those burdens.[69]

In Berlin the abstract possibility of war with the Soviet Union took concrete form. Kennedy declared that the city had become "the greatest testing place of Western courage and will."[70] But if the West were tested there, if the Soviet Union and her allies did attempt to take control of the city by force, courage and will and all the heroic examples of World War II would not suffice to protect it. No commander would have chosen to make a stand in Berlin, given any say in the matter. NATO's military position was extraordinarily weak. The conventional forces stationed there were unlikely to be able to stand off a determined assault for long. If the Soviet Union were bent on seizing Berlin, and if the United States were resolved to try to stop this, the two sides might find themselves swept along into a war that neither wanted, but that neither could avert.

As the tension there mounted, as both sides advertised their tenacity by rushing troops to the area, dispatching commanders to the scene who had been in Germany during past crises, and conducting military maneuvers in and around the city, the spark of war seemed on the point of igniting central Europe.[71] "If fighting should break out over Berlin," the President was asked at a press conference in August, "do you believe it can be limited to conventional war or would it lead to the use of nuclear weapons?" Kennedy begged the question: "Well, we are hopeful that we would be able to reach peaceful solutions to these problems."[72] But the question was a good one, and the answer was by no means clear.

And because it was not clear, because the President could not be certain that fighting would not break out over Berlin, and that if it did that the level of violence could be kept below the nuclear threshold, he and his associates felt obliged to consider what would happen in the event that nuclear weapons were used.

The sustained and serious attention that the problem of fighting a nuclear war received from the Kennedy administration was also due to the style of governance that Kennedy and his men brought to the conduct of the nation's affairs. They took upon themselves the responsibility for exploring every contingency of national policy from all possible angles. They were inclined by temperament to probe as deeply as possible into the workings of the nuclear age. The Eisenhower administration had not approached the question in as thorough or systematic a way. It had placed its faith in deterrence. It was

willing to go to the brink of war to deter the Soviets. It gave
little thought to what would happen if it should be forced over
the brink. "If deterrence does fail, and war does come," the
Kennedy men believed, by contrast, "we cannot simply abandon ourselves to whatever the terrible consequences might
be."[73] They felt obliged to make such preparations as were
feasible for nuclear war before it took place.[74]

How could a nuclear war be fought? There was no way to
answer the question fully without staging such a war. And
however curious the Kennedy administration was about the
possibilities of the nuclear age, its curiosity did not extend
that far. So the investigation of nuclear tactics was an exercise
in educated guessing; in games, simulations, and dry runs.
Nor did the investigation proceed in a deliberate, purposeful,
coordinated fashion. This episode in the history of nuclear
weapons policy and of the Kennedy administration has to be
pieced together after the fact. McNamara and his associates did
not consciously address themselves to the third question of
nuclear strategy. What they did do was scrutinize closely military programs that had been under way before Kennedy came
to the White House, and which, in most cases, would survive
his departure.

Clausewitz's general thoughts on war drew these disparate
programs together, for together they constituted an exercise of
the sort that all commanders, in Clausewitz's day and before,
had attempted, and for which Clausewitz had conceived an
analytic framework. The Kennedy administration's search for
a way to use nuclear force fits into that framework. But this
search differed from all previous such undertakings in two
ways.

First, commanders in the past had relied on their own experience, and the experience of others as recorded by military
historians and taught in military academies. But there was no
experience of nuclear combat on which Kennedy and his associates could draw. Hiroshima and Nagasaki were useful only
as foretastes of the destruction that the vastly more powerful
nuclear explosives of the 1960s could produce.

Second – and this illustrates perhaps more vividly than anything else the radical difference between nuclear weapons and all other armaments – the fundamental premise of the exercise was the opposite of the central assumption that Clausewitz and all other strategic planners of the past had made. Whereas their task had been to find ways to *increase* the force that they could bring to bear upon the enemy, Kennedy and his men sought to *restrict* the violence of warfare.

For Clausewitz war was not only a duel between two combatants, but, for each of them, a struggle against the natural limits of force as well. Those limits always kept actual wars short of "absolute" extremes. But nuclear weapons were not governed by those limits. Nuclear war would not be fragmented, as previous wars had been. One state could bring upon another "in the twinkling of an eye" the kind of devastation that was previously possible only through the drawn-out process of defeating its army and then slaughtering its citizens wholesale. "Friction" – the numerous annoyances and uncertainties that keep military plans from being flawlessly carried out – which was the other natural barrier to "absolute war," was irrelevant to nuclear combat. Even with the normal quota of mishaps, a nuclear strike could wreak far more destruction than any war of the past.

Clausewitz had seen Napoleonic France create a military juggernaut of unprecedented power by mobilizing for battle the resources of an entire society. But even the "Grande Armée," mighty and terrible though it was, did not challenge the natural limits to war; the physical power of nuclear armaments, however, had the capacity to obliterate them. Whereas for Clausewitz absolute war, war as a sweeping, senseless, uncontrolled spasm of destruction, had been not only absurd but impossible, for the Kennedy administration it had become all too dangerously plausible. It was no longer an abstract category but a reality. Addressing the third question of strategy for nuclear weapons meant searching for a way to draw back from it, to keep nuclear war short of a holocaust.

So instead of chipping away at the barriers to the expansion of force that Clausewitz had noted, the administration tried to fortify one of them. Clausewitz had deemed the defensive mode of warfare intrinsically superior to the offense. Nuclear weapons had tilted the balance between attack and defense decisively in favor of the offense. To redress the balance Kennedy and his associates tried to develop a system for defending the United States against ballistic missile attack. And instead of trying to enlarge the three components of military violence that Clausewitz had identified, the Kennedy administration attempted to restrict them.

For the first component, physical force, they studied the uses of "tactical" nuclear weapons. They attempted to call upon the second, the tactical virtuosity of the commander, to diminish rather than expand the force expended on the battlefield, through a targetting policy designed to spare populated areas during a nuclear exchange. And they tried to employ the third component, morale, for the opposite of its customary purpose, through a program of civil defense whose success depended ultimately not on the willingness of soldiers to fight – the importance of morale in the past – but on the willingness of the American people to suffer nuclear punishment.

Together these programs amounted, in effect, to an effort to stand Clausewitz on his head; an exercise akin to working out the principles of an economics based on abundance, not scarcity, or positing the physical laws of a universe in which the force of gravity pulls away from, rather than toward the earth. And it was an effort to reverse the "certainty" that Kennedy and McNamara had achieved. They had given the United States the certain capacity to bring more damage to the Soviet Union in response to a provocation than the accomplishment of any political goal could plausibly justify incurring. Now they were searching for a way to keep nuclear destruction within politically acceptable limits, so that nuclear war could be, as Clausewitz had said all war must be, an act of policy. They could wage "absolute war" if they chose to do so. But answering the third strategic question for nuclear weapons involved searching for a way not to wage it if they chose not to do so.

The Rise and Fall of Nuclear War

When barriers which in fact consisted only in ignorance of what was possible are broken down it is not easy to build them up again.   Clausewitz[1]

Tactical nuclear weapons

The revolutionary character of nuclear weapons stemmed, of course, from the dramatic expansion of physical force. Ironically, in Clausewitz's day the other two of the three ingredients of violence that he identified — a commander's cleverness and an army's morale — were thought to offer greater opportunities for enlargement. The European powers of the early part of the nineteenth century assiduously cultivated the "genius" — the tactical adroitness — of their commanders. And the wars of the French Revolution showed how a cause or ideology could engage the energies and kindle the enthusiasm for war of an entire society. The "ignorance" to which Clausewitz referred was the ignorance of the potential for warfare of full-scale social mobilization, not ignorance of the laws of nature whose discovery made possible atomic weapons. Those were undreamed of at the beginning of the nineteenth century. Physical force then seemed firmly tied to the number of men a state could put into the field, and thus, ultimately, to its population.

The industrial revolution changed the calculus of military
might. Weapons of greater and greater destructive power were
produced. Physical force became elastic. The harnessing of
nuclear energy made it almost infinitely elastic. The first war-
fighting program that the Kennedy administration explored
attempted to constrict rather than expand force by scaling
down the power of nuclear weapons in order to make them
manageable instruments of warfare. As Kennedy assumed office, several thousand "tactical" nuclear weapons were on station in Europe. Unlike the "strategic" weapons based in the
United States, which formed the core of the nation's deterrent
force, these tactical warheads could be delivered by artillery
and short-range aircraft as well as missiles and huge long-
range bombers like the B-52. They were designed not to pulverize cities but to win battles – to check opposing forces and
support conventional forces in seizing and holding territory.
They were aimed at the same kinds of targets as nonnuclear
arms – "artillery battalions, aircraft squadrons, and the
like" – and were integrated into the conventional forces.[2]
They seemed "very much like conventional weapons, only
with a bigger punch."[3]

Tactical nuclear weapons were born at the beginning of the
1950s, when techniques of miniaturization that permitted the
mating of nuclear explosives with battlefield weapons became
available. The political impetus for producing small-scale nuclear weapons came from the debate over whether to make the
hydrogen bomb. J. Robert Oppenheimer and others were horrified at the prospect of adding to the American arsenal a
weapon capable of causing such colossal destruction. They
suggested miniaturized nuclear weapons as an alternative, to
"return nuclear weapons to the battlefield," where the hydrogen bomb, which was suitable only for crushing cities, was of
no apparent use.

The Eisenhower administration adopted both weapons.
Both fitted into the New Look. The threat of low-level nuclear
strikes by small atomic explosives supplemented the threat of
massive retaliation to deter the Soviets. In 1953 the first tactical nuclear armaments arrived in Europe, and the American

government made clear its intention to use them to repulse a Soviet attack there.

From the beginning there were doubts about how different tactical nuclear weapons were from the strategic varieties of nuclear hardware. They were smaller, but many were comparable in power to the bombs that had laid waste to Hiroshima and Nagasaki. The tactical armaments were distinguished also by their locations and the targets thay they could strike. They were deployed outside the boundaries of the United States and the Soviet Union, and in general could not reach the cities of either country. But they could bring vast destruction to the central and eastern European countries that would be the battlegrounds of a "tactical" nuclear war. It would scarcely console a German, whether he lived east or west of the Elbe, to know that the weapons that had demolished his city were more properly called "tactical" than "strategic." And there was no guarantee that a nuclear war begun in Central Europe would not spread. It might grow until it brought strategic weapons into play and engulfed the United States and the Soviet Union as well.

These issues did not weigh particularly heavily on the highest officials of the Eisenhower administration, who were mainly interested in deterring war, not fighting it. But they became controversial in the circle of strategic thinkers outside the government. In 1957 one of the nuclear strategists, Henry Kissinger, published a book called *Nuclear Weapons and Foreign Policy*,[4] in which he argued that nuclear warfare could remain limited and that limited nuclear war was an appropriate way to defend Western Europe against the Soviet Union. The book aroused skepticism, anger, and some lively rebuttals.[5] Such studies as could be made of how "tactical" nuclear war would be fought did cast doubt on the feasibility of limiting its destructiveness to tolerable levels of damage. These simulations were known as "war games" and two of them, conducted in 1955 and called "Sagebrush" and "Carte Blanche," indicated that Central Europe, which would serve as the battlefield, would suffer devastation far beyond what World War II had brought.[6] And Carte Blanche assumed that only the United States would use tactical nuclear weapons, although the Soviets were also beginning to deploy them. As the Soviet tactical nuclear force grew, and further studies were made, what faith there was in the potential for a nuclear defense of Europe waned. Kissinger revised his view, placing greater emphasis upon the need to prepare for nonnuclear combat.[7]

The Kennedy administration came to office skeptical that nuclear weapons, no matter how small, could be kept within "acceptable" limits once introduced. The strategy of defending Western Europe with tactical nuclear weapons seemed as shortsighted and dangerous as deterrence through the threat of massive retaliation. Indeed, it seemed, in the eyes of the new custodians of American security, to amount to the same thing. Early in his campaign President Kennedy had avowed that small atomic weapons "suffer from the same handicaps as large ones."[8] A small-scale "tactical" battle would inevitably erupt, he felt, into a strategic exchange of terrifying scope. The thrust of the Kennedy defense program was therefore away from the use of nuclear armaments of any caliber. The requested increase in the administration's first year in office was designed to obviate the need to rely on the tactical nuclear force in case of invasion of Western Europe. To underscore its reluctance to bring nuclear arms of any kind into use, the administration gave conspicuous emphasis in its defense planning to the dividing line between conventional and nuclear force. The doctrine of the "pause" or "firebreak" stressed that the United States would go to some lengths to keep from firing a nuclear shot – perhaps even to the extent of relinquishing territory in a European conflict with the Soviet Union.[9]

Despite the President's skepticism, the Kennedy administration continued the investigation of "limited" nuclear war. In the early 1960s the Defense Department undertook to discover how tactical nuclear warfare might unfold. The results of their studies depended to a very great extent upon the governing assumptions that were laid down beforehand. But even the most optimistic guidelines led to disastrous consequences: "Even under the most favorable assumptions," according to two of McNamara's aides, "it appeared that between 2 and 20 million Europeans would be killed, with wide-spread damage to the economy of the affected area and a high risk of 100 million dead if the war escalated to attacks on cities."[10]

This was so, they reflected, because "no weapon of any kind, nuclear or conventional, can consistently be delivered precisely and accurately on military targets and *only* military targets."[11] Accuracy would be a particular problem in a tactical nuclear battle because of likely damage to target-acquisition and communications facilities. Moreover, "where both sides have soft and concentrated forces, as is the case in Europe, enormous advantages accrue to the side that strikes first. The side that is losing at one level of conflict may thus be tempted to preempt to a higher level in order to improve his prospects, especially if he fears a sudden escalation on the part of his opponent." The chances for restricting the damage of a tactical nuclear exchange were further diminished by the design of the Soviet arsenal, which was useful chiefly for "blanketing" fire rather than precision strikes. This raised doubts about the Soviets' "*capability* to fight a limited tactical nuclear war, much less one in which collateral damage and civilian casualties are to be kept to low levels."[12]

McNamara acknowledged that "tactical" models did not necessarily bring nuclear weapons back within the bounds of traditional war that Clausewitz had outlined. He told a Congressional committee:

Nuclear weapons, even in the lower kiloton range, are extremely destructive devices and hardly the preferred weapons to defend such heavily populated areas as Europe. Furthermore, while it does not necessarily follow that the use of tactical nuclear weapons must inevitably escalate into global nuclear war, it does present a very definite threshold, beyond which we enter a vast unknown.[13]

He also said that "the civil damage resulting from large-scale use of tactical nuclear weapons would be catastrophic to Europe."[14] And he himself was "inclined to think that there is very little chance of limiting a conflict that has already seen the rather widespread use of tactical nuclear weapons to tactical nuclear weapons. I think that such a conflict would almost

certainly evolve very rapidly into a full nuclear exchange between the Communist bloc and the West."[15]

Tactical nuclear weapons did not provide a way to use nuclear armaments in battle. And because their use was not
compatible with any meaningful limits to warfare, tactical nuclear weapons had no place in the American arsenal. Logically
they should have been uprooted from their stations in Western
Europe and discarded. But they remained in place. Kennedy
and McNamara could not afford to jettison them until NATO
had brought its nonnuclear forces to a higher plateau of
strength. In 1961, with the new doctrine of flexible response
only recently unveiled and far from implemented, and the
estimate of the strength of the Warsaw Pact forces greater than
the figures that intelligence evaluations would ultimately
produce, the Soviets seemed on the verge of moving against
Berlin. The administration could not be certain that a wholly
conventional military defense of the city, and of the central
front, would stop them.

But as the estimate of the size of the Eastern bloc forces was
lowered, the Kennedy administration not only did not remove
the tactical nuclear weapons from Europe, it put more of them
there. The increase was due to the same kinds of pressures that
hindered the implementation of the strategic principles of deterrence.

Once again "friction" came between theory and practice,
and influenced the deployment of tactical nuclear weapons,
just as it had helped to shape the long-range "strategic" arsenal and as it affected the other war-fighting programs that
were explored between 1961 and 1963. In the case of tactical
nuclear weapons, pressure came from the European members
of NATO, who opposed their withdrawal for the same reasons
that they were reluctant to supply more troops to resist the
Soviets. The Europeans relied upon deterrence for their safety
and believed that the greater the likelihood that Soviet aggression would bring on Armageddon, the smaller the chance that
the Soviets would behave aggressively. It was precisely the
explosive power of the weapons and their potential for trigger-
ing a full-scale thermonuclear exchange, the qualities that

made them poor candidates for fighting a war within Clausewitz's definition of the term, that commended tactical nuclear weapons to the European members of NATO.

The Europeans worried, too, about the firmness of the American promise to come to their aid in time of danger. The Soviets had accumulated a formidable strategic arsenal, which made the continental United States vulnerable to enormous destruction. The Europeans wondered how anxious the Americans would be to interject themselves into a quarrel in Europe that might bring on such destruction. They could not help suspecting that the Kennedy administration's fondness for conventional warfare was a way of sacrificing Europe's cities in order to spare America's. The French expressed their suspicions publicly. The administration was at great pains to avoid giving this impression, fearing the political damage to the alliance that might ensue. Nightmares of Germany and even France, stricken with doubts about the worth of the American deterrent, rushing into the arms of the Soviet Union, prompted administration spokesmen to emphasize that the United States remained quite willing to drop atomic bombs on Russian soldiers or even Russian cities to protect its allies.

Tactical nuclear weapons became symbols of the American resolve to carry out its commitments to its NATO partners. Administration officials felt compelled to keep them in place, to deploy more of them, and to stress publicly that they would be used if the need arose. But the Americans had no illusions that their use would be a neat, clean, "tactical" exercise like the military engagements of the past. The weapons were "tactical" in name only. Scattered throughout Western Europe, they served as a security blanket for their nervous hosts, keeping them from feeling isolated and abandoned. But in case of fire the blanket offered no protection; it would only make the blaze hotter. That prospect might make the Soviet Union more cautious about touching off sparks along the central front. The collection of compact atomic rockets and missiles that the United States had placed overseas might form part of a deterrent force. But the devastation they would bring if fired would make a mockery of any political goal their use had been in-

tended to achieve. They could not, therefore, provide the
United States with a way of fighting a nuclear war.

The counterforce doctrine

Tactical nuclear weapons posed two kinds of problems. The
first was technical. Their explosive power was, for the most
part, if less than that of strategic weapons, still far greater than
any armaments with which wars of the past had been fought.
The other problem was psychological. Even if nuclear
weapons could be made small enough and accurate enough to
be confined to use on the battlefield, there was no assurance
that, in a real war with all its pressures and uncertainties,
commanders would use them only against carefully chosen
military targets. To employ nuclear weapons to fight wars as
well as to deter them required restraints not only on their
power but on how that power was used.

The use of force is the province of the commander. The
outcome of battle depends, as well as on the firepower available to each side, upon his ingenuity and courage in maneuvering his troops, which Clausewitz termed his "genius" for
war. In its search for a way to keep a nuclear conflict within
acceptable limits of damage the Kennedy administration
called upon the skills of the commander, but to restrain rather
than to expand battlefield violence.

The policy that enlisted these skills for the converse of the
purpose that they had served in Clausewitz's day applied not
to the tactical nuclear arsenal but to the American strategic
weapons, the warheads carried in the bays of huge bombers
and inside submarines, and poised on the tips of long-range
ballistic missiles, all aimed at the heart of the Soviet Union.
These were, in the eyes of the officials responsible for them,
instruments of deterrence almost from their inception. The
United States would fire them only as a very last resort, as a
way of making good on the threat that deterrence implied.
Few believed that a strategic nuclear exchange would resemble any of the rounds of organized violence that the world had
experienced. Still, a strategic exchange was not inconceivable.

An accident, a surprise attack, a mushrooming clash over Europe beginning with conventional forces, spilling over into the use of tactical nuclear weapons, and growing in intensity might send the heart of each nation's nuclear arsenal hurtling toward the territory of the other.

Careful rationing of force in such circumstances would not be easy. But the administration sought to limit damage in the event of strategic nuclear war by making provisions for concentrating its fire upon military installations and avoiding populated areas.

By mustering the qualities of the commander in the service of diminishing rather than augmenting military violence, this reversed normal military practice. But in another sense it carried forward an old tradition. The policy of avoiding civilian casualties as far as possible was part of the Christian rules of war in force in Europe during the Middle Ages. And concentration upon the destruction of the enemy's military force had been no more than tactical common sense for centuries. Clausewitz himself recommended it.

The emphasis in the nuclear age on the bombardment of cities was exceptional in military history. It came about because nuclear weapons made possible for the first time the destruction of a society without the defeat of its armed forces, which nuclear-tipped missiles could simply bypass. It came about, as well, because it was believed that in order to deter the Soviet Union from causing trouble in Europe and elsewhere, the United States had to threaten destruction and not simply defeat. And it was further believed that a nuclear attack could not discriminate between civil and military targets.

From the moment it assumed power the Kennedy administration began to revise the nation's plans for nuclear war. It drew on studies that had already been made. In late 1959 the RAND Corporation, in association with the Air Force, had begun to investigate ways that the American strategic force could be directed initially at enemy military installations, with reserve power to devastate populated areas if that became necessary.[16] In his first week in office McNamara received a briefing on target selection and its implications from William Kaufmann, who had headed the RAND study, and he quickly set about incorporating its findings into American strategic policy.

His special task force on general war, one of the four he set up, recommended consideration of the option of avoiding densely populated parts of the Soviet Union during a strategic exchange.[17] In March work began on redrawing the nation's "Basic National Security Plan." Kennedy did not formally adopt the document that was produced, but McNamara used it as the basis for a series of guidelines for the nation's war plan, which was called by the acronym – bringing to mind some sort of mythical giant – "SIOP (or Single Integrated Operations Plan).[18]

The plan the administration had inherited from its predecessors assumed that, upon the outbreak of nuclear war with the Soviet Union, the United States would release all of its thermonuclear hardware in a single, awful "spasm." The new guidelines stressed that the nation would hold strategic forces in reserve even after the shooting began. They emphasized the distinction between military and nonmilitary targets for American bombs and missiles. They made provision for sparing Soviet command and control systems, to give the other side the chance to maintain that distinction even as a nuclear exchange was taking place. And concurrently, McNamara ordered studies to find ways to preserve the American command-and-control apparatus. This involved both protecting the commanders, especially the Commander-in-Chief, and giving them tighter control over their weapons. For the first, the Defense Department developed both airborne command systems and a deep underground support center; for the second, it refined the guidance system in the Minuteman missile.[19]

McNamara started to give public hints of the change in American war-fighting plans in early 1962.[20] But it was on June 16, in a commencement address at the University of Michigan, that he spelled out, in the words of a high administration official, "the American doctrine of the nature of nuclear war with a depth and authority that had no public precedent."[21] McNamara announced publicly what he had told the foreign ministers of the member nations of NATO in private two weeks before: "Principal military objectives, in the event of a nuclear war stemming from a major attack on the alliance, should be the destruction of the enemy's military forces, not of his civilian population."[22] The new policy was an attempt to approach nuclear conflict "in much the same way that more conventional military operations have been regarded in the past."[23] The military forces to be destroyed would presumably include, in the case of the Soviet Union, the nuclear striking force.

McNamara delivered this message with several important qualifications. He emphasized that the policy was not one that the United States looked forward to carrying out, and that however it was conducted "all of us would suffer deeply in the event of major nuclear war."[24] He stressed that the new doctrine was not to be taken as a way of avoiding the need to build up NATO's nonnuclear strength. And the speech was intended not only — perhaps not even primarily — to introduce a new refinement in American military policy. It was also given to discourage America's military partners from going into the nuclear business themselves. McNamara cited the new targeting policy as evidence of the increasing complexity of nuclear strategy, which made small independent nuclear arsenals, of the kind that the French were building and, it was feared, the Germans might want, obsolete and possibly dangerous.[25]

The speech was greeted as a sharp departure from the strategic policies of the past. And it became controversial — more controversial even than the question of the proper disposition and use of tactical nuclear weapons. Its manner of presentation especially distressed the Western Europeans.[26] The French did not receive enthusiastically the suggestion that they abandon their small nuclear force. The British did not appreciate the minimal worth McNamara assigned to their nuclear arsenal. And the abrupt and public way that the doctrine was announced exposed the distribution of power within the alliance, to the chagrin of both the British and French who found themselves branded for all the world to see as very junior partners.[27]

The doctrine itself attracted criticism on strategic grounds. The plan McNamara had outlined risked provoking the Soviets, it was charged, for it looked like preparation for a preemptive American strike. Aiming the American arsenal at Soviet weapons could give the impression that the United States would try to eliminate them in a surprise attack, which was precisely the impression that Kennedy and McNamara had been trying to avoid in shaping a strategic force suitable for a "second" rather than a "first" strike. The Soviets had particular cause to worry about a disarming first strike because the additions to the American thermonuclear arsenal that Kennedy had ordered put the Soviet strategic force, at least for a few years, in a position of uncomfortable inferiority. A "successful" American first strike, given the dimensions of its strategic stockpile, was not unthinkable.

It was, in fact, never made wholly clear whether the new war plan did or did not anticipate that the United States might initiate a nuclear attack in response to the "massive Soviet conventional assault" on Western Europe that haunted American defense officials. Whatever the true intent, the possibility had the potential for making Soviet leaders extremely nervous. In a moment of international tension, critics suggested, they might decide to unleash their weapons to prevent the United States from knocking out their arsenal with a "counterforce" blow.[28]

The new targeting policy had two names. As the "no-cities" doctrine, it appeared a humanitarian effort to spare as many lives as possible in the terrible event of a nuclear exchange. As a policy of "counterforce," it seemed to presage a dangerous predisposition to attack the retaliatory force of the other side. But the two names referred to the same policy.

The potentially provocative character of the doctrine was related to a difficulty that it shared with the other damage-limiting programs that the Kennedy administration explored: To the extent that they were successful they ran the risk of weakening deterrence. If the damage to be suffered in a nuclear war came to seem bearable, one side or the other might not draw back from adventures that could ignite one. What made war less brutal once it broke out might, because deterrence depended upon the certain horrors a nuclear exchange would bring, make it more likely to break out in the first place.

The no-cities doctrine as a damage-limiting program had another difficulty. It required Soviet cooperation. It was, in effect, an invitation to observe certain ground rules during a nuclear conflict. But there was no way, in advance of the event, of being certain that the Soviets would accept these rules. They said that they would not. A month after the Ann Arbor speech, the Soviet Prime Minister termed the plan "monstrous" and declared that his country would have no part of it.[29] He had little incentive for keeping to the counterforce guidelines. For they favored the side with the larger supply of weapons, which could plaster the presumably well-protected arms installations of its adversary and still retain some forces in reserve. It was, McNamara said, the sizable thermonuclear stockpile that the United States had accumulated that made the new doctrine feasible.[30] In the future, as the margin of American nuclear superiority diminished, a city-avoidance protocol would become less unattractive to the Soviet Union. But the very growth of the Soviet arsenal that might predispose cooperation in sparing population centers would undercut the American capacity to "limit damage" by knocking out Soviet striking power—which was, in McNamara's view, one of the advantages of the doctrine. To keep that advantage the United States would have to augment its strategic forces perpetually. This posed yet another problem; the logic of counterforce led to an accelerated arms race.[31]

A final question hung over the counterforce doctrine; whether the United States and the Soviet Union would be able to follow it even if they so desired. Even if both sides intended to observe counterforce rules, they might find themselves, in the blazing heat of battle, unable to do so. With unprecedented devastation taking place, with huge bombs exploding within their borders, would even the incarnation of Clausewitz's ideal commander, with a cool head and a steady nerve, be able to keep a tight rein on his military forces, and apply them in measured and careful fashion? And even assuming the strongest will to keep damage limited, a further problem remained. Even if each side made a strenuous effort to avoid laying waste to the others' cities, would the technology of nuclear warfare permit them to do so? "Even if a war should begin as a counterforce war," one skeptic with experience in defense affairs predicted,

it would quickly expand into a war against cities and people. Because many cities are close to missile bases and airfields, it has been estimated that some 30 million Americans would be killed in a first counterforce-type strike. The first bombs to fall would knock out most communications and reconnaissance facilities. Neither government could know whether the other was 'playing the game,' which forces were still in existence, and what its own men were doing. In such confusion, total war would be almost inescapable.[32]

Counterforce proponents could respond that none of the nation's largest cities was close to missile bases. But airports in these cities qualified as military targets – and important ones – because the strategic bomber fleet could be dispersed to them and could refuel and perhaps even reload bombs from Air Force transports there.[33] A thermonuclear bomb falling on the airport of a major American city would not be able to distinguish between airplanes and adjacent population centers.

And even if a heroic display of mutual self-restraint kept bombs away from cities during a nuclear war, both the United States and the Soviet Union would suffer grievously. The Department of Defense estimated that between 30 and 150 million Americans would die, depending on what kind of civil defense arrangements were available. The strictest adherence to counterforce guidelines would not prevent the greatest bloodletting the world had ever seen – a slaughter that would far outweigh any conceivable political objective.

McNamara did not explicitly repudiate counterforce. But he gave it little emphasis after the Ann Arbor address. Asked about the doctrine a month later, he told his interviewer that he thought that "in some ways the press overplayed that part of the speech."[34] He rejected a "full" counterforce capability (that would also have given the United States the capacity for a preemptive attack on the Soviet Union's nuclear striking force) on the grounds that it would not be feasible to destroy any large portion of the Soviet ICBMs. He doubted publicly that the Soviets could be counted on to abide by counterforce rules, telling the Senate Armed Services Committee in 1963 that Soviet rockets would probably be directed "primarily against our cities and our urban society."[35] And as he described it, the counterforce doctrine came to appear less a program for fighting nuclear war than a rationale for the size of the American strategic force.[36]

The counterforce mission was invoked to justify an arsenal whose size had been pushed higher by "friction" than purely strategic considerations warranted. The list of targets for American bombers and missiles continued to include Soviet military installations as well as cities.[37] But this did not give either side the assurance that counterforce guidelines could keep a nuclear war from reaching "absolute" extremes.

Ballistic missile defense

Scenarios of tactical nuclear warfare and the doctrine of counterforce depended upon mutual self-restraint and tacit cooperation to restrict damage during a nuclear exchange. The Kennedy administration investigated another approach to limiting the destruction of nuclear conflict, which did not require Soviet cooperation for success. It attempted to devise a system of active defenses against nuclear attack. This was an exercise in applied technology, not crisis diplomacy. It had far less to do with the psychological strength of the political leaders of the two nations than with the ingenuity of their scientists and engineers. And whereas the first two damage-limiting programs of the Kennedy administration endeavored to "reverse" the components of military violence, this third one sought to reimpose one of the barriers to absolute war that Clausewitz had identified and that the fearsome power of nuclear weapons had struck down – the superiority of the defense over the offense.

The search for some way to fend off assaults from the sky began when airplanes first appeared in combat roles, in World War I. They were challenged in the air by interceptor aircraft, sometimes called "fighter" planes. And they were attacked from the ground by antiaircraft batteries. The contest between the offense and defense that runs through military history from the first recorded battle runs as well through the early decades of the air age, and it continued in the first years of the nuclear age.

NSC-68, the founding document of American defense policy in the Cold War, recommended that the United States deploy an active air defense to foil a Soviet bomber attack without having to resort to nuclear weapons.[38] An air defense system was, in fact, built in the 1950s. In his Special Defense Message of 1961 President Kennedy stressed its importance and requested additional funds to reconstitute the back-up control mechanism for the American "Semi-Automatic Ground Environment System" (SAGE). But SAGE did not give the United States real protection against nuclear attack. For one thing, much of it was designed to shield strategic weapons, not cities. By safeguarding the "survivability" of the nation's long-range bombers, the air defense mechanisms contributed to deterrence, not defense. They would not limit damage to American society in any significant way. For another, the threat SAGE had been constructed to meet turned out not to be the principal danger facing the United States. The Soviet Union never developed a large complement of strategic bombers. Instead, the Russians invested heavily in long-range ballistic missiles.[39]

But ballistic missiles, when armed with nuclear explosives, presented special problems. A marching column of soldiers was always relatively easy to intercept, if not to defeat. Airplanes were more difficult to track down and repulse, but the task was still manageable. But missiles could arrive far more swiftly, and with much less warning than airplanes, even airplanes powered by jet engines. And they could arrive accompanied by "decoys" to complicate further the task of defense. President Kennedy compared this task with "hitting a bullet with another bullet."[40]

There was a further problem. A defensive system would have to work perfectly to be effective, because each nuclear warhead mounted on an incoming missile was powerful enough to level a large city. The antiaircraft batteries and interceptor planes of World War II seldom fought off all the attacking aircraft. At least a few bombs always managed to strike even well defended cities. But the cities could withstand the effects of these strikes. They would not, however, be able to weather a nuclear attack without grave damage, even if only one warhead found its mark.

The first American ballistic missile system, the Nike-Zeus, began life as a surface-to-air missile designed to counter supersonic manned bombers. In 1956 the Secretary of Defense ordered that attention be given to missile defense, but divided responsibility for it. He charged the Air Force with developing area defenses. The Army undertook to devise a point defense system, and the Zeus was its candidate for the role.[41] The Army nursed the system along for five years, and Kennedy and McNamara inherited it. Along with it the new administration inherited an attitude toward missile defense that was an odd mixture of grave doubts about whether an effective system could ever be built and firm resolve to keep trying to build one.

The attitude dated back to the first appearance of the guided missile. In 1945 General H. H. Arnold had written, "although there now appear to be insurmountable difficulties in an active defense against future atomic projectiles similar to the V-2 but armed with atomic explosives, this condition should only intensify our efforts to discover an effective means of defense."[42] Hitting a bullet with a bullet, deflecting or destroying each and every incoming projectile, seemed a task beyond the capacity of even the most sophisticated machinery that human ingenuity could devise. Yet the United States could not afford to discontinue trying to devise one, since if the machine could be built the nation that first set one up would have a decisive military advantage over its rivals.[43]

Thus successive Secretaries of Defense, beginning in 1958, pressed Congress for funds for the Zeus and its successors to "accelerate development of this system's readiness for production," funds that were to be "devoted primarily to research and engineering aspects instead of actual production and development which, in our judgement, would at this time be premature."[44]

In his first brush with the Zeus system McNamara took precisely that position. "A practical and effective system of active defense against the ICBM" was an urgent priority, he told the House Committee on Defense Appropriations in April of 1961. The Nike-Zeus was "well along in development and progress has been quite satisfactory." There was much to be said for starting to produce it.[45] On the other hand, there remained "widespread doubts as to whether the NIKE-ZEUS system should ever be deployed. There is still considerable uncertainty as to its technical feasibility and, even if successfully developed, there are many serious operating problems yet to be solved."[46] The most serious problems were the susceptibility of the system to deception by decoys and to saturation by a barrage of incoming warheads. "Weighing all the pros and cons," McNamara summed up, "it is our conclusion that we should continue the development, testing, and evaluation phase of this program on an urgent basis, but we should not at this time take any steps for the production and deployment of the system."[47] Like his predecessors in the Eisenhower administration, McNamara felt that he could not afford to spend the money necessary to manufacture and deploy a system that might not work, but neither could he afford not to continue to invest in the search for one that might. "We recognize that this decision will delay the date by which the system could be operational – if later it should be decided to put it into production" he continued. "But we simply do not have a sound basis now to make such a decision."[48]

The next year he was even less sanguine about the prospects for effective missile defense. He warned of the need to counter the threat of missiles launched from submarines as well as from land-based pads and silos, and raised the possibility "farther out in the future of a satellite-born threat."[49] He proposed that the Congress deal with the problem exactly as before: money for more research, but not for deployment.[50]

In 1963 the Pentagon modified the design of the Zeus system. It was to be equipped with more sophisticated radar and a swifter missile that could intercept enemy warheads at shorter range, and thus with greater reliability, than the one it then employed.[51] But, as with the Zeus, the Secretary declined to give the signal to commence building the "Nike-X." It was premature to do so, he said.[52] He repeated for the Senate Committee the customary rationale for the decision. Asked when all the resources being ploughed into research would produce a system worth deploying, he replied,

I think the answer to that is we can't look ahead with great accuracy, but the problem is so severe, so serious, the danger so great, were the Soviets to find a defense and we not, that I would strongly urge that we continue to spend at least the sum we are talking about on the development of a NIKE-X type anti-ballistic missile defense.[53]

But even as he authorized further research on missile defense apparatus, McNamara's hopes that a worthwhile system would ever be perfected seemed to grow fainter. Asked point-blank, "Do you think we will ever develop a successful anti-intercontinental ballistic missile system?" he replied, "We will certainly develop an anti-intercontinental ballistic system that will be able to destroy certain kinds of intercontinental ballistic missiles — the kind that attack the defensive system without sophisticated decoys or countermeasures. Whether we will ever be able to advance the art of the defense as rapidly as the art of the offensive developments in intercontinental ballistic missiles I don't know. At the moment it doesn't look at all likely."[54]

Pentagon analysts studied the problem of ballistic missile defense in conjunction with the development of American offensive nuclear weapons. Their findings gave them more confidence in their capacity to break through Soviet defenses than in the possibility either side could acquire the capacity to ward off enemy attacks. Asked about Prime Minister Khrushchev's boast that the Soviet Union had a defensive capability that could "hit a fly in the sky," the President replied in a way that summed up the reasons why even the most intricate system of ballistic missile defense could not reason-

ably hope to give the United States, or the Soviet Union, the
means to fight a nuclear war without suffering unjustifiable
extremes of destruction:

He might hit a fly, but whether he could hit a thousand flies with decoys —
you see, every missile that comes might have four or five missiles in it, or
[what] would appear to be missiles, and the radar screen has to pick those
out, and hit them going thousands of miles an hour, and select which one is
the real missile and which are the decoys, when there might be hundreds of
objects coming through the air. That is a terribly difficult task.... The offensive has the advantage.[55]

The idea of missile defense did not fade away during Kennedy's term of office as did the doctrine of counterforce. Powerful political forces gathered in support of it, and in 1967
McNamara announced that the United States would begin to
deploy an anti-ballistic missile system (ABM). But the announcement was made in a way that made clear that the familiar "friction," in the form of political pressure, not strategic
conviction, had prompted it. In his speech McNamara first set
out the reasons why it was not sensible to deploy the ABM.
The system he authorized was modest, aimed at the infant
Chinese nuclear force and not at the Soviet arsenal. And he
made plain his hope that it would grow no larger. The political power of the armed services, who wanted to build an ABM,
had forced him to agree — against his wishes and his judgement. But he conceded as little as possible.[56] In 1970 the Congress approved an ABM system. But the design had changed
drastically from McNamara's proposal. The "Safeguard"
would protect American missiles, not cities. It would reinforce
the deterrence of war by reducing the vulnerability of the nation's retaliatory force, rather than limiting damage once war
broke out, as the original model was designed to do. Its
strategic purpose was the same as the concrete siloes in which
the Minuteman missiles were encased, not the antiaircraft
systems from which it was distantly descended. And even this
modest system was coveted by the Nixon adminstration not
for its own sake but as a bargaining counter to use in the
strategic arms limitation negotiations that had begun with the
Soviet Union. As a result of these negotiations, both sides
subsequently relinquished the right to construct ABM sys-

tems. Extensive ballistic missile defense systems would be effectively banned for both sides by treaty in 1972.[57]

Civil defense

Even when his meager enthusiasm for a ballistic missile defense system was at its height, Secretary McNamara insisted that such a system could not stand alone. "Even with effective active defense systems for all of the major targets in the United States," he said in 1961, "an enemy attack could produce enormous fallout casualties unless shelter were available."[58] In his 1963 Posture Statement he said flatly: "The effectiveness of an active ballistic missile defense system in saving lives depends in large part upon the existence of an adequate civil defense system. Indeed, he went on, "in the absence of adequate fallout shelters, an active defense might not significantly increase the proportion of the population surviving an all-out nuclear attack."[59]

Civil defense — the provision of shelters where the civilian population could take cover during and after an atomic attack — like tactical nuclear weapons, the doctrine of counterforce, and a ballistic missile defense system, offered a way of limiting damage to the United States in the event of a nuclear war.

Civil defense reversed Clausewitz's third component of military violence, which has been variously called "spirit," "will," and "morale." The best weapons and the most ingenious commander could not bring victory if the troops who wielded those weapons under his command would not stand and fight with them. The propensity to fight is the third part of the "trinity" of warfare. In the nuclear age the ability to fight a nuclear war came to depend not on the capacity of soldiers to inflict punishment, as had been true in the past, but on the willingness of citizens to absorb it. Morale meant not the will of the soldier to fight but the capacity of ordinary people simply to survive.

The importance of civilian morale in warfare did not begin in 1945. Civilians took part in both world wars of the twentieth century by manning the factories that produced the weapons and ammunition that were used up in enormous quantities in the battle zones. And in both wars civilians ceased to be as completely insulated from the violence of battle as they had ordinarily been in the nineteenth century. The airplane punctured the barrier that separated soldier from citizen, because it could fly over the troops that had heretofore defended their countrymen from the armies of the opposing state. Accordingly, the first efforts at civil defense began in World War I, and the protection of civilians took on even greater importance between 1939 and 1945. The British took special measures to protect their citizens from German bombing. In London, subway stations served as shelters. The Germans, too, built large communal shelters in their major cities. But civil defense received fitful attention from the American government in the early years of the nuclear age. Only a few members of the House of Representatives took an interest in it.[60]

In 1955 shelters replaced evacuation as the principal way of protecting Americans against nuclear attack. Several semiofficial studies recommended extensive shelter programs. The Gaither Report of 1956, although giving priority to bolstering the nuclear striking force, also suggested the expenditure of about five billion dollars over a five-year period[61] for civil defense. But the Eisenhower administration did not bestir itself to carry out these recommendations.

Of all the war-fighting measures that his administration explored, President Kennedy himself had the greatest personal enthusiasm for civil defense.

With the changes in the strategic forces in motion in the first half of 1961, he turned his attention to the protection of civilians. He commissioned "an intensive study of the whole subject of emergency planning"[62] that concluded that the nation ought either to invest more resources in the protection of the civilian population during and after an enemy attack, or abandon any hope of trying to do so.[63] The study sketched the outlines of a serious civil defense program, which included federal subsidies for converting space in existing structures into fallout shelters and incentives for including shelters in new ones. It also allotted funds for stocking the shelters with

food and medicine. Three billion dollars was the rough estimate of the cost of the program over four years.[64]

A program of civil defense appealed to Kennedy for several
reasons. The technical difficulties seemed manageable. It
might not be possible to assemble machinery that could bat
away incoming Soviet nuclear "bullets" like a flawless skeet
shooter, but it was certainly feasible to construct or reinforce
buildings that would afford at least some measure of protection from the lingering poisons that the bullets that struck
their targets would leave behind. And he felt responsible for
providing "insurance for the civilian population in case of an
enemy miscalculation. It is insurance we trust will never be
needed — but insurance which we could never forgive ourselves for foregoing in the event of catastrophe."[65] He felt, as
well, political pressure — again the "friction" that bears on
American strategic policy in the nuclear age. The pressure this
time came not from within the executive branch of the federal
government or from the allied nations of Western Europe, but
from his political rivals, and especially from his likeliest opponent in the presidential election of 1964, Governor Nelson
Rockefeller of New York, who was an energetic champion of
building shelters.[66] So Kennedy put his personal prestige behind civil defense.

He signalled his seriousness in his special congressional
message on "Urgent National Needs." He promised to submit
in short order a request for more funds for civil defense, which
he said would probably be triple the pending budget proposal.
And in July Kennedy announced the specifics of his new program.

It generally followed the lines that the initial report had
suggested. Almost half the new appropriation would "cover
the cost of a national program for identification and marking
of available community shelter space in existing buildings."[67]
The bulk of the rest of the request was for stocking the newly identified and designated shelters with "the minimum essentials for survival during a 1- to 2-week period."[68]

Despite his personal support, however, civil defense as an
experiment in conducting a nuclear war short of absolute extremes proved, like tactical nuclear weapons, the doctrine of

counterforce, and the ABM, a failure. The experiment was
modest from the beginning. It always aimed at mitigating the
secondary effects of a thermonuclear attack, not at shielding
people from the blows themselves. Kennedy was candid about
this. Civil defense, he admitted, "cannot give an assurance of
blast protection that will be proof against surprise attack or
guaranteed against obsolescence or destruction."[69] The administration had no plans to try to provide such protection.
McNamara estimated that that might cost "as much as perhaps
$20 or $50 or $100 billion"[70] and would involve building
heavily fortified bunkers deep underground for every
American — a staggering project. "It is not practical," he told
the House Armed Services committee, "to think of protecting
our population against thermal effects and blast effects for all
conceivable forms of nuclear attack."[71]

And the chances for approval and support for the civil defense program that the Kennedy administration did propose
were hurt by the way they were first presented to the public.
Kennedy chose to include a strong endorsement of civil defense in his July 1961 television message on the Berlin crisis.
Set in that grim context, with fears of war running high, it
touched off what was almost a wave of hysteria in the country.
As they had been when Sputnik went aloft, the American
people were agitated. The excitement, according to the President's closest aide, "got out of hand. People were talking
about barring their neighbors from their shelter, do-it-yourself
shelter kits were being sold, and all kinds of articles were
written speculating about how many or how few lives would
be saved."[72] The President became disturbed. He "felt that
there was too much misinformation — too much fear being inspired by some, and too much confidence [in shelters] being
inspired by others."[73] He partly blamed himself "for having
included a general civil defense shelter plea in a very somber
speech about how we would have to meet the Berlin pressure
from the Soviet Union."[74]

The response to the Berlin address called into question the
political wisdom of giving visible and unreserved support to
civil defense. In the speech Kennedy had promised "to let

every citizen know what steps he can take without delay in case of attack."[75] The Defense Department prepared a booklet that advised each family to construct its own shelter, and gave instructions on how to do so.[76] Defense officials proposed to mail one to every household in the land, over the President's signature. Kennedy vetted it carefully. He decided to place the emphasis on communal rather than individual shelters. More important, he toned down the text of the pamphlet, declined to sign it himself (it finally bore McNamara's name), and directed that it merely be made available in post offices rather than sent to everyone. He had not entirely abandoned civil defense, nor did he ever cease to believe that it provided valuable insurance for the nation. But by Thanksgiving of 1961 he had decided not to place the full weight of his personal authority behind the program he was recommending. And without the authority his program languished in Congress. In 1962 the administration requested $582 million, but only $113 million was authorized. In 1963 Congress was even more skeptical of civil defense. One member expressed the doubts that troubled many of them:

I would like to say, further, Mr. Secretary in regard to this shelter program, that while I wish you all possible success, if a bomb hit at night, the District that I represent – with which you are quite well acquainted, I am sure – the people would be from 8 to 15 miles from a shelter, any kind of a shelter. There is not one building in my district that in my opinion would be an adequate shelter. And I have listened for a long time to these programs. And I doubt if you could get those people back down into a shelter, or if anybody in his right mind would be willing to try for the interior of Detroit. So I think the shelter marking program, while it might have some real advantages, in the long run can be both an illusion and a snare if you think that you are going to save anybody with it.[77]

And the members of Congress reflected the doubts of their constituents. Americans were not willing to make elaborate preparations to withstand a nuclear attack. They paid with few complaints for the huge, complicated, and deadly machinery necessary for deterrence. This was deployed where few would ever see it. But a serious civil defense program would reach directly into their everyday lives. And this they did not want. On the battlefield the test of an army's morale is its willingness to fight. When morale collapses soldiers often lay down their arms and flee. This is sometimes called "voting with their feet." The American people, by failing to support civil defense, were in effect "voting with their feet" — against nuclear war.

"We are all dead . . . "

Since the Kennedy administration's search for a way to fight a nuclear war was never formally begun — indeed it was not consciously a policy — no official conclusion was ever announced. The goal of keeping the damage of a nuclear exchange within tolerable limits was not publicly repudiated. And the programs that McNamara and the Defense Department explored between 1961 and 1963 did not end abruptly with the Kennedy presidency. New approaches were tried, new weapons were introduced, fresh doctrinal twists were offered. But the old problems remained.

This was true not only of ballistic missile defense, whose demise in 1972 was a landmark in the nuclear age. The refinement of tactical nuclear weapons continued also. The American weapons laboratories produced warheads of smaller and smaller explosive power coupled with delivery systems of increasing accuracy. A decade later their role in the defense of NATO was still controversial. The same uncertainties surrounded them. The commander of NATO forces in Europe, testifying in favor of the deployment of a new generation of tactical nuclear weapons before a Senate committee, was asked for his estimate of the chances that the United States could use nuclear weapons in Europe without provoking a Soviet response in kind. "I would not go so far as to say in all probability...but I think there is an appreciable probability that they would not," he replied. "What percent?" he was pressed. "I wouldn't be able to make such an estimate," he responded.'[78] A civilian Pentagon official, asked how much damage a tactical nuclear exchange would do, admitted that "there is very little understanding of these types of problems."[79]

The counterforce doctrine was revived in 1973 by another Secretary of Defense, but once again there was less to it than at first appeared. It was advanced as a means of making the strategic war plan more flexible, not as a way to brink nuclear war into line with the conflicts or the past.[80] And the civil defense program continued, without substantial resources or great presidential interest, for the balance of the Democrats' term of office.[81]

But if the verdict at which the administration had arrived by the end of 1963 was not final, it was definitive. The American government could find no plausible, reliable way to keep the damage the United States would suffer in a nuclear exchange with the Soviet Union within limits that could make nuclear war a continuation of policy. George Bernard Shaw once remarked that Christianity could not be said to have failed because it had never been tried. This was not quite the case for nuclear war. It did have a trial, of sorts. No full-fledged nuclear war — in which both sides make extensive use of thermonuclear weapons — has ever been fought. But between 1961 and 1964 the government of the United States went as far as it could in exploring its possibilities without actually touching one off. The Kennedy administration's examination of the prospects for tactical nuclear weapons, its efforts to devise a ballistic missile defense system and build a civil defense network across the country, and its attempt to establish the principle of city-avoidance as the protocol for a nuclear exchange, these together added up to a quest for a way to keep a conflict in which thermonuclear weapons came into play from crossing the boundary that separates war from holocaust.

The quest arrived at a dead end. The hope of building a defense against enemy attack by air fell victim to the permanent advantage of the offense over the defense in the missile age. Plans for sheltering the civil population of the United States bumped up against the indifference of the American people and perhaps the notion that the costs of a nuclear war would inevitably outweigh any of the benefits that it might bring, no matter what precautions the nation took to protect itself. The doctrine of counterforce seemed doomed to be smothered in the chaos of an actual war, and preparations to abide by it aroused fears of a surprise attack. And tactical nuclear weapons appeared, from the simulated battles that the Pentagon conducted, to have all the drawbacks of their strategic counterparts.

McNamara came to recognize the implications of this dead end. He laid greater and greater emphasis on the deterrent role of the nation's nuclear arsenal, with the intricacies of trying to fight a nuclear war fading into the background.[82] Asked to speculate about the condition of American strategic forces after a full-blown nuclear exchange, which none of the damage-limiting measures could guarantee to prevent once nuclear weapons had been used, he said:

Now when you consider on the order of 300 million people dead in those areas, it is very difficult to conceive of what kind of military weapons, even if provided ahead of time, would continue to exist or if they existed how they might be used.

We have nonetheless faced that issue, and we have systems provided that we believe would survive. For example, certain elements of our Navy almost certainly would survive, and we have other elements of our forces that we believe would survive.

But it exceeds the extent of my imagination to conceive of how those forces might be used and of what benefit they would be to our Nation at that point.[83]

But what was perhaps the ultimate pronouncement on nuclear warfare had come a few minutes before, in a colloquy involving two Congressmen:

Mr. *Chamberlain* "Now, Mr. Chairman, if I may, I would like to address one further question to the Secretary.

This is just in a very general framework. We hear of this tremendous nuclear exchange, that we are talking of, that their numbers of missiles that they have, that they could fire at us in hardened sites or beneath the seas, and ours that we are going to fire at them, and we seem to talk to the total number of missiles that we are going to shoot off.

But I have often wanted to hear from someone a projection of what is going to happen after we fire all our missiles and we have not any more in the silos, or they fire all theirs.

And then it is a question of getting some more for the second round. And what is the situation we are going to be confronted with at that time. And so that we will know the facet of the problem that prompts the question.

It is for the need at that time for maybe aircraft or to get our forces to where they are going to be to take over whatever may be left. What are we going — what is the military situation after we have had this tremendous exchange? *Mr. Wilson* "We are all dead."[84]

The barriers to absolute war that Clausewitz had cited could not be put back up. The vectors of military violence could not be reversed to limit rather than expand the intensity of nuclear war. War as an instrument of policy could not be kept alive once the nuclear threshold was breached.

This meant that there was no answer, for nuclear weapons, to the third question of strategy. Or rather, it meant that to the question of how to fight a nuclear war, the answer was that there was no way to do so and be certain of being consistent with the traditional definition of warfare. Nuclear war was absolute war. It was, to use Clausewitz's phrase, "something pointless and devoid of sense."[85] And that meant that the American response to the first strategic question, which the Kennedy administration had confirmed, was all the more important. If it was impossible to fight a nuclear war, it became all the more important to carry out the political purpose of nuclear force – to deter one.[86] And this, in turn, inflated the significance of the American response to the *second* strategic question. It was all the more important for the United States to deploy its forces in a way that deterred the Soviet Union.

Kennedy and McNamara could feel confident that they had solved one part of the problem of deterrence. The extraordinarily powerful striking force that they had authorized gave the United States the capacity to deal a death blow to the Soviet Union even after the most terrible Soviet attack imaginable. This permitted them to feel "quite certain" of deterring the Soviets from launching a direct nuclear attack. But the "graduated" concept of deterrence to which they both subscribed required more than an assured nuclear retaliatory capacity to keep the Soviets at bay. To discourage the array of provocations and challenges that fall between peace and nuclear war on the scale of military violence, the United States needed, according to this concept, a varied and versatile military arsenal. The doctrine that the administration embraced

gave cause to doubt that the great deterrent would deter everything.

Deterrence of aggression short of a nuclear strike fell into a
kind of grey area. It did not lend itself to precise calculation,
like assured destruction. The question of what forces were
necessary to deter what forms of Soviet provocation, and the
related question of how much of the range of provocations the
forces that the United States deployed would actually deter,
were difficult to answer in concrete fashion. But here, as with
the question of how to fight a nuclear war, events did give an
answer. It was an answer, in effect, to the questions raised by
the graduated view of deterrence. It therefore completed the
American response to the problem of strategy in the nuclear
age. And it emerged dramatically, out of the gravest crisis of
the nuclear period, the confrontation between the United
States and the Soviet Union in the fall of 1962 in the Caribbean.

The Great Fright: The Cuban Missile Crisis

The Chinese say I was scared. Of course I was scared. It would have been insane not to have been scared. I was frightened about what could happen to my country – or your country and all the other countries that would be devastated by a nuclear war. If being frightened meant that I helped avert such insanity then I'm glad I was frightened.   Nikita Khrushchev[1]

The greatest danger was not that Khrushchev would deliberately launch nuclear war, but that the situation might have gotten out of control.
                                          Robert McNamara[2]

The crisis

On the morning of October 16, 1962, President Kennedy learned that Soviet technicians were busy installing, in western Cuba, medium and intermediate range ballistic missiles that were capable of carrying nuclear warheads to American cities as far west as Chicago. Thus began the Cuban missile crisis, "the most dangerous issue," in British Prime Minister Harold Macmillan's judgement, "which the world has had to face since the end of the Second World War."[3] It was a time when, in the words of Soviet Party Chairman Khrushchev, "the smell of burning" hung in the air, when the United States and the Soviet Union arrived at "the first direct nuclear confrontation, unlike any in the history of our planet."[4]

The details of the crisis, especially on the American side, are largely on the public record. In memoirs, interviews, and public statements, the American participants have given an unusually thorough and clear account of what they did and why, and what they thought and felt during the two tense weeks

129

between the first discovery of the missiles and Chairman Khrushchev's decision to remove them.[5]

The news of the missiles, it is clear, shocked the President, and dismayed him. Rumors that nuclear arms were being sent to Cuba had floated around Washington for several weeks. Large shipments of military equipment from the Soviet Union had indeed been arriving on the island since the beginning of September, although none had been positively identified as being nuclear. In a statement on September 4, and again at a press conference on September 13, Kennedy had said that the United States would not tolerate the transformation of Cuba into "an offensive military base of significant capacity for the Soviet Union."[6] The Soviet government had exerted itself to persuade the administration that it had no such plans. On September 6 Moscow's ambassador in Washington, Anatoly Dobrynin, sought out Theodore Sorensen and told him that his government had done "nothing new or extraordinary in Cuba."[7] He said the same thing to the President's brother, Attorney General Robert Kennedy,[8] and other Russian officials circulated a similar message.[9] Administration officials, with the notable exception of the Director of the Central Intelligence Agency, John McCone, accepted those assurances. They had in hand no reliable information to the contrary.[10] In his September 13 statement, under the presumption that they contained no nuclear cargo, Kennedy reported that the shipments arriving in Cuba did "not constitute a serious threat to any other part of this Hemisphere."[11]

As soon as he learned that medium range ballistic missiles (MRBMs), launch facilities for intermediate missiles (IRBMs), and IL-28 aircraft, all capable of nuclear attacks against the United States, were in Cuba, the President decided that, somehow, they would have to be removed. "He knew," Robert Kennedy wrote later, "he would have to act. The U.S. could not accept what the Russians had done. What that action would be was still to be determined, but he was convinced from the beginning that he would have to do something."[12] He summoned a group of fifteen men, "who had little in common except the President's desire for their judgement,"[13] and charged them with devising the American response to the emplacement of the missiles.[14] The group, which was subsequently christened the "Executive Committee of the National Security Council," met at least daily thereafter for a week. While the President kept to his planned schedule so as not to alert the Soviets that the weapons had been discovered, the Committee reviewed the courses of action available to him. These ranged from doing nothing at all to invading Cuba, seizing the missiles, and taking control of the island. Debate was lively and extended. Individual preferences skipped from one alternative to another. By the weekend sentiment had crystallized in favor of throwing a naval blockade around the island to intercept military supplies but not other shipments. A blockade had the virture of emphasizing to the Russians how seriously the United States regarded the situation in Cuba, and hampering the military fortification of the island, without actually initiating hostilities.

On Monday evening, October 22, Kennedy made a televised address announcing the presence of the missiles and his decision to impose a "strict quarantine on all offensive military equipment under shipment to Cuba."[15] He placed the blame for the sudden crisis squarely on the Soviet Union. He denounced Soviet perfidy in deploying their mightiest weapons ninety miles from the United States while insisting that no such undertaking was contemplated.[16] He appealed directly to Chairman Khrushchev "to halt and eliminate this clandestine, reckless, and provocative threat to world peace and to stable relations between our two countries."[17] And he warned that:

Should these offensive military preparations continue, thus increasing the threat to the Hemisphere, further action would be justified. I have directed the Armed Forces to prepare for any eventualities; and I trust that in the interests of both the Cuban people and the Soviet technicians at the sites, the hazards to all concerned of continuing this threat will be recognized.[18]

The President's speech inaugurated a long week of wrenching suspense and high drama, the most nerve-wracking in the history of the Cold War. The next day the Soviet government issued an indignant statement charging the United States with unwarranted provocation. But almost immediately a flurry of diplomatic activity began. It took place through a variety of channels — by unofficial contacts between Soviet officials and American private citizens as well as in direct messages between Kennedy and Khrushchev. The blockade succeeded in halting the supply of arms to Cuba by sea. On October 24, two days after the President ordered the quarantine, a number of Soviet ships on course for Cuba stopped dead in the water. Ultimately, they turned back. And two days after that, on the twenty-sixth, as an earnest of the administration's resolve to enforce the blockade strictly, a ship headed for Cuba was stopped, boarded, searched, and, when no nuclear contraband turned up, allowed to continue.

In Cuba, however, work continued on the missile sites and by Saturday, October 27, the President was convinced that the moment of truth was near. Over two hundred thousand troops were massing in Florida, preparing to assault Cuba. Squadrons of tactical fighter planes moved to within striking distance of the island.[19] Kennedy got word that a U-2 plane carrying out a reconnaissance mission over the island had been shot down, and the pilot lost. In the previous twenty-four hours he had received two letters from Khrushchev: the first conciliatory, although rambling and disjointed; the second more to the point, but harsher. He decided to dispatch a message to Moscow accepting the terms of a settlement hinted at in the first letter as a final stab at resolving the crisis before it erupted in violence. But he was not optimistic that he would succeed in doing so. That somber Saturday, according to his brother, "...he had not abandoned hope, but what hope there was now rested with Khrushchev's revising his course within the next few hours. It was a hope, not an expectation. The expectation was a military confrontation by Tuesday, and possibly tomorrow..."[20]

But the next morning the clouds of war suddenly lifted. A message from Chairman Khrushchev informed Kennedy that "in order to eliminate as rapidly as possible the conflict which endangers the cause of peace....the Soviet government,....in addition to earlier instructions on the discontinuation of further work on weapons construction site, has given a new order to dismantle the arms which you describe as offensive, and to crate and return them to the Soviet Union."[21]

The Soviet leader reiterated that he had provided military assistance to Cuba solely for the purpose of protecting the island from American invasion, noted "with respect and trust" the pledge to leave Cuba alone that the President had made in his letter the day before, and revealed that he was dispatching the Deputy Foreign Minister, V. V. Kuznetsov, to New York to work out the details of the liquidation of "this dangerous situation."[22]

Its passing was the most important feature of what came to be known as the Cuban missile crisis, which is significant above all for what did not happen. The United States and the Soviet Union had a close brush with war in the fall of 1962 in the Caribbean — or so it seemed to those who guided the destinies of the two countries. The felt closeness of war accounts for the celebrity of the missile crisis. The participants set down their versions of what had happened because, like Thucydides with the Peloponnesian War, and the dozens of men who fought in the Battle of Waterloo and later wrote about it, they sensed that they had taken part in something of monumental importance, about which people would be eager to read. Students of international politics have turned their attention to the missile crisis not only for its own sake, but for what it might teach them about the management of conflict and relations between the United States and the Soviet Union in the nuclear age.[23]

What did happen during those two tense weeks is significant also. The missile crisis was an event of consequence in the histories of both nuclear strategy and nuclear diplomacy. Its significance for strategy lies in the glimpse it offers of the way deterrence between the United States and the Soviet Union has actually worked in the age of nuclear weapons. The doctrine of deterrence that Kennedy and McNamara had embraced posited what kinds of threats would discourage which sorts of challenges. But this doctrine was hypothetical. The missile crisis involved real challenges and actual threats. It showed that deterrence did not operate in precisely the way that the Kennedy administration, and the nuclear strategists who influenced it, had supposed.

The events of October 1962 constitute a landmark also in the evolution of nuclear diplomacy. The resolution of the crisis short of war was an example, albeit a highly unorthodox one, of successful nuclear diplomacy. And it marked the beginning of successful nuclear diplomacy of a more formal sort. Their close brush with war instilled in the leaders of both the United States and the Soviet Union the determination to reach formal agreements on nuclear matters; and the following year, after political twists and turns, they managed to do so for the first time.

The nuclear shadow

The Cuban missile crisis showed that the Kennedy view of deterrence was not entirely accurate. The crisis began with a challenge of the sort that the administration had expected, and feared, and for which it believed Eisenhower and his associates had not adequately prepared the United States. But events unfolded, and the crisis ended, differently than their response to the second question of strategy in the nuclear age – the question of how to deploy force to secure the overriding political goal of deterrence – had anticipated. Deterrence in practice turned out to be less graduated, and more "absolute" in character than the nuclear strategists and the Kennedy administration had imagined.

The emplacement of missiles capable of striking American cities with nuclear explosives was a challenge of the sort that Kennedy and McNamara believed nonnuclear rather than nuclear weapons were necessary to meet. It was not a nuclear attack, upon the United States or an American ally. It was not the kind of step that has historically triggered wars most frequently; it was not a direct attack. Neither was it a clear violation of international law. The Cuban government, whatever its feelings about playing host to them, had certainly given permission for the missiles to be set up.[24] President Kennedy compared their sudden and unexpected deployment to the German *démarches* of the 1930s. The political lesson that he cited in defense of his decision to force their removal of the missiles may have been germane: "Aggressive conduct, if allowed to grow unchecked and unchallenged, ultimately leads to war."[25] But Hitler's aggressive conduct overturned international agreements. Khrushchev's did not. The shipment of the missiles was not even an unambiguous violation of the warnings that the President had issued about the kinds of military shipments to Cuba that the United States would tolerate. He had gone on record as objecting to "the presence of offensive ground-to-ground missiles; or of other significant offensive capability either in Cuban hands or under Soviet direction and guidance."[26] But the practical distinction between "offensive" and "defensive" armaments is difficult to draw, and the principle of deterrence further blurs the line between the two.[27]

The Cubans certainly could have used the planes and boats that the Russians had been sending, without American interference, for "offensive" purposes – to harass the mainland. The important distinction for Kennedy was between nuclear and nonnuclear arms.[28] The transfer of control over nuclear weapons to the Cubans would have been cause for alarm in Washington, where the Cuban government was regarded as both reckless and implacably hostile to the United States. A draft statement for the President's September 13 news conference, which he did not deliver, said in part: "We are not prepared to permit a nuclear weapons capability to be delivered into hostile hands in this hemisphere."[29] But the Russians took pains to retain control of the missiles in Cuba – they dispatched as many as 20,000 troops to guard and operate them – and they were careful to make this clear to the Americans.[30]

If it did not fit into the most familiar, or logical categories of clear and menacing aggression, why did Kennedy conclude on the spot that the shipment of missiles to Cuba would have to be reversed? He gave his reason in his televised address to the nation: the missiles represented "a deliberately provocative and unjustified change in the status quo which cannot be accepted by this country if our courage and commitments are ever to be trusted again by either friend or foe."[31] But it was not as powerful, momentous, or drastic a change in the status quo as the gravity of the crisis would at first suggest. The weapons did not, in the opinion of the Secretary of Defense, alter the purely military balance between the United States and the Soviet Union. "A missile is a missile," McNamara is reported to have said. "It makes no great difference whether you are killed by a missile fired from the Soviet Union or from Cuba."[32] There was disagreement within the ranks of the administration about the military value of the missiles that were being deployed. According to his Deputy, Roswell Gilpatric, McNamara "didn't have the apocalyptic view that some of the others had that the whole security equation had been changed overnight if these missiles were in there."[33] On the other hand Paul Nitze, the Assistant Secretary of Defense for International Security, "felt that the presence of missiles in Cuba exposed a large part of the American strategic bomber force, based in the Southeastern states, to sudden attack from the ground. The warning time would be cut from fifteen minutes to two or three minutes."[34]

But if the missiles shifted the overall political balance between the two great powers in a direction unfavorable to the United States, they did not do so in the most dramatic possible fashion. They did not move Cuba from the camp of one to the sphere of the other. Both the United States and the Soviet Union have used force since 1945 to try to prevent this from occurring, the United States at the Bay of Pigs in 1961 and in the Dominican Republic in 1965, the Soviet Union in Hungary in 1956 and in Czechoslovakia in 1968. But by October 1962 Cuba had already passed into the Soviet orbit. Fidel Castro had declared himself a "Marxist–Leninist." Military, political, and economic ties between Havana and Moscow had been firmly established.

In sum, the violation that set the missile crisis in motion was not a mortal threat to the security, or even, by the standards of postwar international politics, to the power and prestige of the

United States. It was precisely the sort of challenge that the American nuclear arsenal could not deter, according to the Kennedy deterrence doctrine. "An eye for an eye" had to be the guiding principle in issuing threats. A threat to take two eyes, or more, would not be credible. The Soviets did not, however, behave as this theory of deterrence predicted they would, nor did the Americans.

The Cuban missile crisis was a nuclear crisis. What drove it, what lay behind the calculations of both sides, and what ultimately forced its resolution was the fear—held by both the United States and the Soviet Union—that it would explode into a nuclear exchange. The graduated theory of deterrence that Kennedy and McNamara had adopted presumed that in a confrontation between the two great powers each would raise the level of force gradually, cautiously, and in controlled fashion up to the nuclear threshold. "Escalation," in this view, was like climbing a ladder; each side would take one rung at a time, and each could stop anywhere. The events of October 1962, however, were governed by the presumption, or at least the terrifying absence of the confident presumption to the contrary, that once fighting between the United States and the Soviet Union began, it would slide down a slippery slope of mounting violence into the nuclear abyss, without either side being able to stop .

McNamara told a congressional committee a few months later that, "Krushchev knew without any question whatsoever that he faced the full military power of the United States, including its nuclear weapons.... And that is the reason, and the only reason why he withdrew those weapons."[35] Khrushchev's subsequent statements confirm this assessment.[36] His public statements might be dismissed as rationalization after the fact for having pulled back. But the Soviet leader's private communications to Kennedy during the crisis were dotted with apocalyptic forebodings. "I hope that the Government of the United States will show prudence and renounce the actions pursued by you, which could lead to catastrophic consequences for peace throughout the world."[37] "The Soviet Government considers that violation of freedom of the use of international waters and international air space is an act of aggression, pushing mankind towards the abyss of a world missile-nuclear war."[38] ". . . . If indeed war should break out then it would not be in our power to stop it, for such is the logic of war."[39]

His alarms were in keeping with the public Soviet interpretation of the "laws of war." Soviet military commentators had proclaimed that war between the great powers would inevitably become nuclear war. They gave no credence to the concepts of graduated deterrence, limited war, and nuclear "firebreak" that were popular with their American counterparts.

And in the moment of truth, the Americans themselves had little confidence in these concepts. They, too, feared – even expected – that the laws of war would operate according to the Soviet rather than the American interpretation. They feared an unstoppable slide into the abyss, despite the pains they had taken in devising their initial response to the emplacement of the missiles, despite the doctrine of deterrence to which they subscribed and in conformity with which they had tried to assemble their military forces, and despite the substantial American nuclear superiority of the moment, which gave the United States genuine hope – and it was one of the rare moments in the nuclear age when either side could have had such a hope – of launching a successful preemptive strike against the Soviet Union.[40] "It isn't the first step that concerns me," the President said midway through the decisive week, "but both sides escalating to the fourth and fifth step – and we don't go to the sixth because there is no one around to do so."[41] In his initial private letter to Khrushchev he said that he had "not assumed that you or any other sane man would, in this nuclear age, deliberately plunge the whole world into war which it is crystal clear no country could win and which could only result in catastrophic consequences to the whole world."[42] The next day he expressed concern "that we both show prudence and do nothing to allow events to make the situation more difficult than it already is."[43] And in his final message, sent on October 28 before the agreement to remove the missiles, he observed that "developments were approaching a point where events could have become unmanageable."[44]

What he did even more than what he said underlined Kennedy's fear that either side could set in motion a sequence of events that would end in disaster. The overriding principle of American policy during the missile crisis was to avoid using force directly against the Soviets. This was the reason for throwing a blockade (or, as Kennedy preferred to call it, a quarantine) around Cuba. The blockade had a great disadvantage. It permitted work on the missile sites to continue.[45] But the alternative approach, an air strike, which did not suffer from that drawback, had an even more perilous shortcoming: It could, Kennedy and his associates feared, set off a chain reaction that would ignite the nuclear arsenals of both sides.

"I will always remember," Theodore Sorensen recalled two years later, "Dean Acheson coming into our meeting and saying that he felt that we should knock out Soviet missiles in Cuba by an air strike. Someone asked him, 'If we do that, what do you think the Soviet Union will do?' He said, 'I think I know the Soviet Union well. I know what they are required to do in the light of their history and their posture around the world. I think they will knock out our missiles in Turkey.' And then the question came again. 'Well, what do we do?' 'Well,' he said, 'I believe under our NATO treaty with which I was associated, we would be required to respond by knocking out a missile based inside the Soviet Union.' 'Well, then what do they do?' 'Well,' he said, 'then that's when we hope cooler heads will prevail and they'll stop and talk.' "Well," Sorensen adds, "that was a rather chilling conversation for all of us."[46]

Having put the blockade in place, the President used the greatest possible restraint in enforcing it. His televised speech of October 22 announcing it set no precise deadline for removing the missiles, and did not specify what the United States would do if they remained, thus avoiding a public commitment to use force. He changed the radius of the blockade from eight hundred to five hundred miles, and then permitted a ship of uncertain cargo to reach Cuba, in order to afford the Soviet leaders more time to come to a decision on whether to contest it.[47] When he decided to intercept a vessel bound for the island, he nominated the target, the *Marucla*, with great care. Kennedy was "demonstrating to Khrushchev that we were going to enforce the quarantine, and yet, because it was not a Soviet-owned vessel, it did not represent a direct affront to the Soviets, requiring a direct response from them. It gave them more time, but simultaneously demonstrated that the U.S. meant business."[48]

Reconnaissance flights over Cuba continued after the blockade had gone into effect, and the Executive Committee labored over the question of what to do if enemy fire brought one down. The President decided that "bomber and fighter planes would destroy one site."[49] But when, on Saturday, October 17, word reached him that a surface-to-air missile had indeed knocked a U-2 out of the sky, killing its pilot, he deferred retaliation. By that Saturday, October 27, however, despite this deferral, the United States seemed on the point of attacking Cuba. The troops that had assembed in Florida, the naval flotilla moored off its coast, and the harassment of Soviet submarines in the Caribbean by the American navy no doubt conveyed this impression to the Soviets and contributed to the decision to withdraw the missiles. If the decision had not been made, the attack might well have taken place.

But it might not have. The point is, of course, ultimately moot. Robert Kennedy expected war within a few days. And yet it might not have come.[50] The Executive Committee was divided and uncertain about what the next step after the blockade should be.[51] On the Sunday when Khrushchev's decisive note arrived, McNamara had risen early and made a list of measures short of invasion that the United States could take to put more pressure on the Soviets.[52] The reluctance to use force was extremely powerful.

Asked in retrospect to characterize American policy during the missile crisis, McNamara chose the term "controlled response." And in deploying their forces the Americans had acted in careful, artful, and restrained fashion. The blockade they imposed represented a triumph of painstaking calculation. But once the blockade was in place the American motto became "don't shoot." Once the die had been cast, the administration was interested not in applying force in a controlled way but in doing everything possible to avoid applying force at all. A French general before World War I was asked how many British troops would have to be stationed in France to commit Britain to France's cause in case of war with Germany. "A single British soldier," he is said to have replied, "and we will see to it that he is killed." Kennedy and his advisors similarly believed, or feared, that one casualty would lead inexorably to thousands, even millions more. And so they did everything possible to have no casualties at all.[53]

The Executive Committee spent hours, at the President's behest, pondering the consequences of possible American action, asking "What response could we anticipate? What were the implications for us?"[54] But they could not be certain that, once the shooting began, events would stop short of catastrophe. During the crisis, Barbara Tuchman's account of the outbreak of World War I, *The Guns of August*, was on the President's mind. The book portrays governments helpless to stop the execution of war plans once they have given the signal to begin; the military machines on both sides rumble on beyond the control of national leaders, toward a horrible bloodletting. Kennedy told his brother that he did not want some historian of the future to write a book with a similar theme called "The Missiles of October."[55]

The Cuban missile crisis clarified the workings of deterrence in the nuclear age. It began, it is true, with the failure of deterrence. The Soviets violated the status quo, and were then forced to return to it. And the outcome of the crisis cannot properly be termed "deterrence," either. It belongs to a different category of relations among states — "compellence."[56] A threat induced the Soviet Union to do rather than to refrain from doing something. But an act of compellence was necessary to define the reach of deterrence. For when it is successful deterrence is, in effect, invisible. It is impossible to say with assurance why acts of aggression do not take place. To ascertain that a provocation will summon a response, there must be a response. To fix the limits of deterrence, these limits must be breached. The missile crisis was like a warning light on the dashboard of a car, which flashes when the engine is over-

heated but before it has become so hot that the vehicle comes
to a stop. It signalled that the Soviets had upset the status quo
seriously enough to start a war, but did not actually bring on
war.

A nuclear threat caused the Soviets to withdraw their missiles. Kennedy and McNamara had believed that a nuclear
threat would not be credible in such circumstances if it were
issued. It proved, in the event, to have sufficient credibility
despite the fact that it was not explicitly issued. The reason for
its credibility was a property of the crisis that was precisely
the opposite of what Kennedy and McNamara had deemed
essential for effective deterrence. They had worked to endow
the American deterrence policy with certainty. "Assured destruction" prevented a nuclear assault on the United States
because it permitted absolute confidence that the United
States could make an annihilating reply, if it so desired, no
matter how powerful the attack. During the missile crisis the
Soviets (and the Americans) felt the pressure of uncertainty.
The Soviets withdrew a challenge far less formidable than a
nuclear attack because they were uncertain that, if war broke
out, it could be kept from expanding into just such a devastating nuclear assault, by and against both sides, even if neither
desired this.

The emplacement of missiles in Cuba may have been part of
a deliberate series of Soviet provocations that were designed
to test how far the young American President could be
pushed.[57] Khrushchev may have put his finger nearer and
nearer the fire to see how close he could come without being
burned. If so, he found that the heat became intolerable sooner
rather than later, and earlier than the Kennedy deterrence doctrine suggested.

This was the lesson of the missile crisis. The leaders of both
countries acted on the presumption that a wide range of provocations might start a war between them, that a war begun as
"conventional" might become a mutually disastrous nuclear
exchange, and that it was therefore incumbent upon them to
avoid starting a war of any kind. This lesson corresponds to a
rule of Jewish religious practice known as the principle of

"fences."[58] The principle enjoins the erection of barriers —
"fences" — between man and error to prevent even accidental
violations of the law. It is, for example, forbidden to work after
sundown on the Sabbath. The pious man ceases his labors an
hour before sundown, or two, or even three, to make absolutely certain that no unintentional transgressions take place.
Similarly, by avoiding war of any kind in the Cuban missile
crisis, the United States and the Soviet Union put extra distance between themselves and nuclear war.

Any reasonably alert man can tell when sundown is approaching and stop work before it comes. And similarly, it is
not at all clear that a shooting war between the United States
and the Soviet Union would turn, precipitately and automatically, into a nuclear war. The two might well prove capable of
restraining their hostilities at the brink of nuclear use. But the
consequences of stepping over the brink, in both cases, have
seemed too awful to justify running even a small risk of doing
so.[59]

The principle of "fences" meant, in the Cuban missile crisis,
that since war of any kind might become nuclear war, war of
any kind had to be avoided at all costs. And carried one step
further, it has meant that the United States and the Soviet
Union have scrupulously sought to avoid political conflicts
that could raise the specter of war, which in turn could raise
the specter of nuclear war.

This nuclear-induced caution has had its limits. It has not
affected everyone, everywhere. The threat that nuclear
weapons might be used did not prevent the North Koreans
from moving south in 1950, or the Vietminh from challenging
and defeating the French in Indochina, or their successors, the
National Liberation Front and North Vietnam, from battling
the government of South Vietnam and its American ally, with
help from the Soviets.

The avoidance of conflict of any sort between the United
States and the Soviet Union would have required the resolution of the fundamental political differences between them
that lay at the heart of the Cold War and were, and continue to
be, rooted ultimately in the radically dissimilar domestic sys-

tems of the two states. And to have removed all possibility of all conflict among all states would have meant, of course, doing away with separate national sovereignties, which even the power of nuclear weapons has never accomplished.

But in the spheres of direct concern to the United States, where a direct clash between their forces growing out of a conflict could (and can) be easily imagined – the "industrial circumference"[60] that includes Europe, Japan, and North and South America – each great power has conducted its foreign policy with extreme delicacy where the interests of the other were involved.

If they left room for conflict, the "fences" that the nuclear threat erected were more extensive than the doctrine of graduated deterrence had implied. Nuclear weapons cast a broader shadow over international politics than the nuclear strategists of the 1950s had believed. The reach of nuclear deterrence was not infinite, but it was longer than Kennedy and McNamara had supposed. The deterrence that the Cuban missile crisis revealed bore a striking resemblance to the policy to which Kennedy's Republican predecessors had committed themselves.

This was the deterrence of the New Look. For economic reasons, because of the weaponry available in the early 1950s, and on the basis of a particular interpretation of the way wars begin, Eisenhower and Dulles had relied chiefly on nuclear threats to keep the Communists at bay, Kennedy and McNamara wished to minimize the role of nuclear weapons in American policy. But that role turned out to be larger than they had initially believed, and it could not easily be reduced. The Eisenhower administration had carried out a policy of deterrence through the threat of massive retaliation out of conviction; the Cuban missile crisis showed that the Kennedy administration was carrying out the same policy *despite* its convictions.

Gunpoint diplomacy

The missile crisis was not only a strategic exercise. It changed the course of nuclear diplomacy as well. The settlement that ended the crisis was a nuclear accord. It was, to be sure, a rather unusual diplomatic settlement. It was arranged, literally, at gunpoint. But the guns pointed in both directions; neither side dictated terms to the other. No official of either government ever affixed his name to a formal document. But each understood that an agreement had been made. The way the United States and the Soviet Union argued, bluffed, threatened, and finally agreed during the last two weeks of October in 1962 corresponded in its essentials to the working out of a diplomatic accord. Debate about the appropriate response to the missiles took place within the American government, just as it had before every major disarmament negotiation. With the blockade in place, negotiations proceeded in a variety of forums between the two great powers. Finally they struck a bargain — the first involving nuclear weapons that the United States and the Soviet Union had ever concluded.

Khrushchev behaved like a negotiator seeking the best terms he could get. He shifted positions several times during the crucial week. His first response to the American demand that the missiles be removed was belligerent and unyielding. He and other Soviet officials put about the impression that their ships bound for Cuba would not stop, and that the sinking of one would trigger the sinking of American ships in retaliation.[61] He told Kennedy that the weapons were "destined exclusively for defensive purposes."[62] And he indignantly accused the United States of "grossly violating the United Nations Charter," of interfering with freedom of the seas, and of taking "the path of aggression against both Cuba and against the Soviet Union."[63] Later he endorsed a suggestion by the then Acting UN Secretary-General U Thant that the blockade be suspended for several weeks and a summit conference convened to try to hammer out an arrangement that would satisfy both sides.[64] Kennedy turned down the proposal. Finally, he sent a letter to Kennedy on October 26 that contained the seeds of the eventual settlement.

The outcome of the missile crisis is sometimes seen as a victory for the United States, in which superior American firepower and a steady nerve forced Khrushchev to back down; a confrontation in which the two sides were "eyeball to eyeball" and the Russians blinked.[65] In fact it was more a negotiation between equals. The Americans were as fearful as the Soviets of the consequences if no solution were found. Accordingly they made concessions to the Soviets in exchange for the withdrawal of the missiles.

Kennedy understood from the beginning of the crisis that he would have to pay a price to get what he wanted.[66] The administration canvassed a number of bargaining approaches. The State Department drafted a message to Fidel Castro suggesting that he get rid of the Soviet weapons himself, and holding out the possibility that "many changes in the relations between Cuba and the OAS [the Organization of the American States, which had condemned the deployment of the missiles and endorsed the blockade] countries, including the U.S." could follow if he did.[67] Harold Macmillan offered to immobilize British missiles temporarily in return for taking the weapons out of Cuba.[68]

Finally the President settled on two concessions. The first was a pledge that the United States would not invade Cuba. In a long and rambling letter received in Washington on October 26 Khrushchev proposed that "We, for our part, will declare that our ships bound for Cuba will not carry any kind of armaments. You would declare that the United States will not invade Cuba with its forces and will not support any sort of forces which might intend to carry out an invasion of Cuba. Then the necessity for our military specialists in Cuba would disappear."[69] In response Kennedy wrote:

The key elements of your proposals, which seem generally acceptable as I understand them — are as follows:

(1) You would agree to remove these weapons from Cuba under appropriate United Nations observation and supervision; and undertake, with suitable safeguards, to halt the further introduction of such weapons systems into Cuba.

(2) We, on our part, would agree — upon the establishment of adequate arrangements through the United Nations to ensure the carrying out and continuation of these commitments — (a) to remove promptly the quarantine measures now in effect and (b) to give assurances against an invasion of Cuba.[70]

The next day the message from Moscow arrived sealing the bargain; removal of the missiles in exchange for "the statement you made in your message of 27 October 1962 that there would be no attack, no invasion of Cuba...."[71] Three weeks later, when the last of the IL-28 bombers had left the island, the President issued a statement acknowledging that, in return for carting the strategic weapons away and providing the opportunity to check to see that this was happening, the United States had promised the Soviet Union to "remove our naval quarantine and give assurances against invasion of Cuba."[72] Although wrangling about the means of verification that the Soviets and Cubans would allow made the administration reluctant to stand foursquare behind the no-invasion pledge in public, Kennedy in fact remained faithful to his part of what UN Ambassador Adlai Stevenson termed "the contract" between the two countries.[73]

Kennedy made another concession. He agreed to dismantle the Jupiter missiles that the United States had stationed in Turkey, and that stood as close to the borders of the Soviet Union as the weapons in Cuba were to American soil. Before the President's televised address, Stevenson raised the possibility of trading the withdrawal of the Soviet missiles in Cuba for the elimination of the Jupiters in Turkey.[74] Several members of the Executive Committee developed a contingency plan for withdrawing the Turkish weapons.[75] And in the frantic correspondence between the two leaders in the last days of October, Khrushchev demanded their withdrawal.

Kennedy was chagrined and angry to learn that the missiles were still in Turkey. He had instructed the State Department to arrange for their removal with the Turkish government that summer, and had assumed that his orders had been carried out. Failure to do so had, in his view, "permitted the...obsolete Turkish missiles to become hostages of the Soviet Union."[76] The President did not want to make such a trade, at least not publicly. It would imply, he felt, that the Soviets had some right to station missiles in Cuba. And it would also, he feared, sow uncertainty in the ranks of NATO about America's reliability, since it would amount to acceptance of a "specious

Russian offer of a face-saving accommodation at the expense of America's allies."[77]

The letter from Chairman Khrushchev to President Kennedy of October 26 offered to bring back the weapons in the Caribbean on condition that the United States "evacuate its analogous weapons from Turkey."[78] This has come to be known as the "second letter," because another had arrived the previous day that did not mention the Turkish installations. Kennedy decided to ignore the second message and respond to the terms of the first with a proposal that the Soviet leader eventually accepted, thereby avoiding war without risking shaking the alliance. But if the American government never explicitly tied the departure of the Jupiters to the lifting of the blockade, they were tacitly included in the bargain. In this Saturday meeting with Ambassador Dobrynin, Robert Kennedy heard the removal of the Turkish missiles raised. He later reported his reply as follows:

I said that there could be no quid pro quo or any arrangement made under this kind of threat or pressure, and that in the last analysis this was a decision that would have to be made by NATO. However, I said, President Kennedy had been anxious to remove these missiles from Turkey for a long period of time. He had ordered their removal some time ago, and it was our judgement that, within a short time after this crisis was over, those missiles would be gone.[79]

Six months later the Jupiters had all come down, although the President was careful to note that Polaris submarines had taken over their duties.[80]

The agreement that ended the missile crisis fulfilled the three requirements of successful diplomacy.[81] The first of them, the political will to agree, grew as the crisis wore on. Its source was plain: the danger that without agreement war would break out. The accord was negotiated under duress, but it was not simply a surrender. Both the United States and the Soviet Union felt the pressure of impending disaster. It may not have conferred benefits evenly upon the two. Although he later trumpeted the outcome of the crisis as a triumph for Soviet foreign policy, Khrushchev may not have accomplished all or any of what he had set out to achieve by placing missiles in Cuba.[82] But the terms of settlement respected the principle of reciprocity, which is the second requirement for successful diplomacy.

The final requirement – a common frame of reference – was also met. The United States and the Soviet Union resolved the crisis along traditional rather than liberal lines. The negotiating procedures and the substance of the final accord followed the recommendations that Henry Stimson had made seventeen years before. In the thirteen years between 1946 and 1959, the two sides had drifted away from the liberal principles that had underlain the Baruch Plan and toward the more traditional approach that the efforts to agree upon a mutual cessation of nuclear testing represented. Under the threat of war in 1962 they arranged an accord, which was far more traditional than liberal, in thirteen days.

Unlike the Baruch Plan, but like the proposals for a test ban, the terms on which the crisis was resolved were limited. There was no time to make the international system over in a liberal image. What was urgently required was to take steps to keep it in one piece. Kennedy deliberately restricted American aims to the removal of the missiles. He was advised to seek wider goals – the removal of Castro, for example. This he refused to do.[83] Nor did he try to wring further concessions from the Soviets. He wanted to restore the status quo – the status quo before the missile crisis, not before Castro came to power and pledged his allegiance to the Soviet Union – not to change it.

The array of channels through which the negotiations to end the crisis took place illustrates the shift from the liberal to the traditional pattern of diplomacy. Both nations initially took their complaints against the other to the United Nations, where the Baruch Plan and its successors had been presented and discussed. The American representative there, Adlai Stevenson, requested an emergency meeting of the Security Council on October 22, and presented a resolution calling upon the Soviet Union to dismantle and withdraw "all missiles and offensive weapons from Cuba."[84] The next day the Soviet representative handed in an angry letter in reply, charging the United States with "piracy."[85] The Council became a

verbal battleground, as it had been during the debate over the
Baruch Plan. The two principals in the crisis hurled angry
accusations across the meeting room, while their allies echoed
them. The political warfare reached its zenith on October 25,
when Stevenson dramatically wheeled blown-up photographs
of the missile sites into a crowded Council chamber, demanded an explanation from the Soviet delegate, Valerian Zorin, and declared that he was "prepared to wait until hell
freezes over" for it.[86]

The United States and the Soviet Union made occasional
use of the UN Secretary-General to carry messages back and
forth.[87] But when coming to grips with serious issues they
spurned the international organization.[88] Communications
passed through irregular channels. On October 24 Khrushchev
summoned to his office William Knox, the President of Wes-
tinghouse International, who was on a visit to Moscow, and
lectured him for three hours on the precariousness of the situation. The Chairman urged Knox to relay this information to the
proper authorities in Washington, where the fact of the meeting, and several similar incidents, were taken as encouraging
signs that the Soviet leader was anxious to avoid a clash.[89] On
Friday, the 28th, two other unofficial contacts took place that
appeared to form part of an effort by the Soviet Union to find a
way out of the crisis. That morning Yuri Zhukov, a confidante
of Khrushchev who happened to be attending a conference in
Maine – by coincidence on the subject of communications –
approached members of the American delegation and asked
whether, if the Russians withdrew the missiles, the United
States would boast of its triumph all over the world and follow
it with "more aggressive action against the Soviet Union." He
received assurances to the contrary.[90]

And that afternoon John Scali, the State Department Corre-
spondent for the American Broadcasting Company, got a tele-
phone call from Aleksander Fomin, a counselor at the Soviet
Embassy who was thought to be an intelligence agent, and
hence a person of greater importance than his formal rank
suggested.[91] Fomin arranged to meet Scali in a Washington
restaurant, and there outlined a plan for settling the crisis: The

missile sites would be dismantled and sent back to the Soviet Union under the supervision of the United Nations, and Fidel Castro would promise not to accept such weapons in the future, if the United States would pledge not to invade Cuba. Fomin asked whether the American government would find such terms attractive.[92] Scali carried the suggestion to the State Department, where Secretary Rusk authorized him to relay an official expression of interest.[93] The terms of Fomin's proposal turned out, of course, to be the basis for settling the crisis.

The most important "informal" discussions during the missile crisis took place between Soviet Ambassador Dobrynin and Robert Kennedy. It was safe to presume that the Attorney General had the ear of the President. In September Dobrynin had used him as a conduit for a new test ban proposal.[94] On Tuesday evening, a day after the President's televised speech, Robert Kennedy called on the Ambassador to try to learn what the Soviets would do about the blockade, but came away with no further information.[95] A second encounter, four days later, at the moment of greatest tension, however, may have had some effect on the outcome of the affair. Kennedy strongly emphasized the gravity of the situation. He pointed out the steady drift toward war that was taking place, and went over with Dobrynin the possible grounds for halting it.[96] The next day, with Khrushchev's letter, the danger subsided. In his remembrances Khrushchev notes Dobrynin's report of the conversation, and indicates that it had an important bearing on the deliberations of the Soviet government.[97]

Either Dobrynin's account of the conversation, or Khrushchev's account of it may, of course, be distorted. Still, it seems plausible that, as Khrushchev notes, "We could sense from the tone of the message that tension in the United States was indeed reaching a critical point."[98] And Khrushchev emphasizes the avenues of communication he used when timely contact with the United States became vital: "As tensions rose to the point where war might break out, our countries resorted to secret diplomacy. We maintained contact with President Kennedy through his brother Robert."[99] When the two great

powers had urgent business to transact, multilateral diplomacy disappeared, and the ritual of the UN became at best a
luxury, at worst a hindrance.

As well as bypassing, for serious business, international organizations, they ignored other countries. Although the crisis
threatened others as well, its outcome depended wholly on the
maneuvers of the United States and the Soviet Union. The
NATO allies played a decidedly supporting role in the drama.
Charles de Gaulle grasped this immediately. President Kennedy sent Dean Acheson to apprise him of the blockade
shortly before the public announcement was made. "May we
be clear before you start," de Gaulle said when Acheson offered to provide him with details of the situation, "are you
consulting or informing me?" Acheson admitted that his mission was not one of consultation.[100]

The pact that removed Soviet strategic weapons from the
western hemisphere was traditional also in that it overcame
the largest single barrier to arms control accords in the past,
the vestige of liberal insistence on breaking down national
sovereignties – inspection. The United States made certain
through aerial surveillance that all of the MRBMs, IRBMs, and
IL-28 bomber aircraft left the Caribbean. Reconnaissance
flights by U-2 planes had played a critical role in the origins
and development of the crisis. A sortie over western Cuba on
October 14 had produced the pictures that gave the first reliable evidence of the burgeoning missile complex. Those pictures prompted Kennedy's initial decision to force the removal
of the missiles, and the formation of the Executive Committee
to consider how to accommplish this. During the thirteen days
between the discovery of the weapons and the Soviet promise
to dismantle them, the U-2's powerful camera recorded the
progress at the sites in preparing the launchers to receive nuclear warheads. The pace of these preparations infused the
American government's deliberations, and its actions, with a
strong sense of urgency.

The Soviets made no secret that their distaste for inspection
extended even to monitors thousands of feet above the earth's
surface. They had managed to bring down a U-2 over Siberia
in 1960, and Khrushchev had used the incident to torpedo the

summit conference scheduled for that year. On October 26 Soviet surface-to-air missiles claimed another of the planes, this one over the western part of Cuba.[101] The Soviets' reluctance to expose their most powerful arms to Western eyes may have helped to make the blockade effective. The President, according to Theodore Sorensen, surmised that they were unwilling "to have us stop ships which carried...highly secret and sensitive material. The Soviet military, he reasoned, long obsessed with secrecy, could not risk letting their missiles, warheads, and electronic equipment fall into our hands."[102] From the American point of view, the "adequate arrangements through the United Nations to ensure the carrying out and continuation" of the Soviet promise not to station strategic weapons systems in Cuba was a crucial part of the bargain that ended the crisis.[103] The Soviet leadership seemed prepared to cooperate. In his decisive communication of October 28 Khrushchev reiterated the willingness expressed in the note sent the previous day "to reach agreement and to enable UN representatives to verify the dismantling of the strategic weapons in Cuba.[104]

But if the Russians were amenable to permitting teams of United Nations officials to visit the missile sites, the Cubans were not. Fidel Castro refused to accept the terms of an arrangement that the two great powers had made over his head. "Whoever comes to inspect Cuba," he declared, "must come in battle array." U Thant tried to soften his objections, but failed. No observers ever set foot in Cuba.[105] This disturbed the Americans. They had, after all, received assurances that no strategic weapons had come to Cuba in the first place, and these assurances had turned out to be false. The President withheld a formal guarantee against invasion of the island for the rest of 1962 and into the first months of 1963 on the grounds that it could be issued only when adequate means of verification and safeguards against the return of weapons became available.[106] Until then, the other side had not fulfilled its contractual obligations.[107]

But aerial surveillance did continue, and, in the end, it proved satisfactory. On November 4, just four days after Khrushchev's decisive letter, President Kennedy felt able to

assure the American public "on the basis of yesterday's aerial
photographs...as well as other indications" that "the Soviet
missile bases in Cuba are being dismantled, their missiles and
related equipment are being crated, and the fixed installations
at these sites are being destroyed."[108] A briefing paper for his
November 20 press conference noted that while air surveillance could not "detect hidden missiles, it can detect any
movement of these missiles necessary for their use; you cannot
fire a missile in a cave."[109] The Soviets may well have accepted the need for the reconnaissance flights. A CIA report of
a conversation between a Soviet general and U Thant and one
of his UN aides described the Soviet officer as "showing little
concern over the prospect of continued U.S. surveillance of
the missile sites."[110] Khrushchev reflected in retrospect:

I won't deny that we were obliged to make some big concessions in the
interests of peace. We even consented to the inspection of our ships – but
only from the air. We never let the Americans actually set foot on our decks,
though we did let them satisfy themselves that we were really removing our
missiles.[111]

Although on-site inspection had not taken place, on January
30, 1963, Secretary McNamara gave the House Armed Services
Committee an extensive briefing on the Cuban situation, including a comprehensive summary, drawn from photographs
of the military hardware the Russians had transported to the
island, and the news that aerial reconnaissance had permitted
the American government to verify the dismantling of
medium- and intermediate-range ballistic missiles, and the
dispatch of the IL-28 bombers.[112] For the first time the
standards for policing a nuclear accord on *both* sides were
met. The United States could monitor Soviet compliance; the
Soviets could keep foreign observers off their soil and away
from their military equipment.

The crisis in perspective

The Cuban missile crisis illustrates the truth of Raymond
Aron's observation that in the nuclear age crises have taken
the place of war. Before 1945 wars were the earthquakes of

international politics. States and empires rose and fell in the
crucible of battle. And wars provided the raw materials of the
military art. Strategy was nothing more than the perceived
lessons of the best remembered or most recently fought conflicts of the day. War was the forcing-house of diplomacy as
well, where bargains were struck and new combinations
formed. The close brush with war in the Caribbean in 1962
had the same effects. It rivaled the bombings of Hiroshima and
Nagasaki in its impact on nuclear strategy and diplomacy.

By proving for all the world to see the stupendous destructive potential of atomic energy, Hiroshima shaped the answer
to the first question of strategy in the nuclear age, the question
of the proper political goals of force. So great was the explosive power of the first two bombs, and so much greater was the
power of those that would follow, that the prevention of aggression by the threat to use these armaments became their
logical – and ultimately their only – political purpose. The
vivid demonstration of that power that Hiroshima and
Nagasaki offered gave such threats considerable weight.

The outcome of the missile crisis addressed the second and
third strategic questions – how to deploy force to achieve the
designated political goals, and how to use it. The two sides
were guided during the crisis by the answer to the third question at which the Kennedy administration, through the fail-
ures of its various damage-limitation programs, eventually arrived: There was no way to fight a nuclear war. Such a war
would be a natural calamity, like a flood or an earthquake or
plague, not an act of policy. In striving to avoid having to fight
a nuclear war they took great care not to start a war of any
kind, which they feared would become nuclear. And in so
doing they showed that the nuclear deployments on both
sides, which were designed (at least in the American case) to
prevent preemptive nuclear attacks, would serve to deter a
wide variety of other provocations as well. The answer to the
second strategic question that emerged from the missile crisis
was that a large invulnerable nuclear arsenal would discourage a great deal of political mischief by the Soviet Union.[113]

Hiroshima and Nagasaki also inspired the first flurry of nuclear diplomacy. They galvanized scientists and horrified

civic and political leaders in the United States, who felt that
something had to be done about the bomb, to save the world
from destruction. Out of that feeling came the Baruch Plan,
The destruction of the two Japanese cities persuaded the
Plan's proponents that nuclear weapons had to be abolished.
The moral that the United States and the Soviet Union drew
from the missile crisis was similar, although more modest. It
was that in the nuclear age strategy, even a strategy of mutual
deterrence, was not enough by itself to ensure peace. Diplomacy was needed as well.

The shock of the crisis made compelling the need to take
steps to keep such dangerous situations from arising again.
The accord that settled the affair did not entirely serve this
purpose. It was too irregular, jerry-built, and narrow. It provided neither the substance of a new, less contentious (or at
least more cautious) relationship between the two thermonuclear giants, nor an adequate symbol of their mutual resolve to
create one. From the commencement of the crisis, in fact, to its
conclusion, Kennedy and Khrushchev recognized that they
would have to find firmer ground for dealing with each other.

As he announced the imposition of the quarantine, Kennedy
expressed his willingness to "discuss new proposals for the
removal of tensions on both sides."[114] Khrushchev's correspondence included similar overtures. The terms for settlement he proposed on October 27, he said,

...possibly would serve as a good impetus to searching for mutually acceptable agreements on other disputed issues, too, on which there is an exchange of opinion between us. These problems have not been solved, but
they wait for an urgent solution which would clear the international atmosphere. We are ready for this.[115]

Among the problems he mentioned were the "great dangers in
our age of thermonuclear weapons, rocketry, spaceships,
global rockets and other deadly weapons."[116] To improve the
international atmosphere he turned to the substance of nuclear
diplomacy, which seemed the most potent symbol of
American-Soviet relations. Successful nuclear diplomacy
might serve as an additional "fence" between the two countries and a nuclear conflict. Kennedy agreed. In reply he
wrote,

We must devote urgent attention to the problem of disarmament, as it relates to the whole world and also to critical areas. Perhaps, now, as we step back from danger, we can together make real progress in this vital field.[117]

And among the issues to which he suggested they give priority was the test ban. Two weeks after the danger of war had been lifted, the President said that it had produced "a turning point, possibly in the history of the relations between East and West."[118] The crisis had created the possibility for a change in the shape of international politics. It had not, quite, brought that change about.

The First Step: The Limited Test Ban Treaty of 1963

A journey of a thousand miles must begin with a single step.
John F. Kennedy, 1963[1]

Nuclear diplomacy before the missile crisis

The Kennedy administration's interest in nuclear diplomacy rose dramatically in October 1962. But it did not begin then. The President entered office proclaiming the same determination to press for nuclear accommodation with the Soviet Union that he brought to what he saw as the task of reshaping American nuclear strategy. He declared that the two tasks were equally urgent.[2] He included appeals for progress in nuclear diplomacy in his public statements. He appointed a special disarmament advisor (as Eisenhower had). He won congressional approval for a new "peace agency," which he had promised during his campaign. The Arms Control and Disarmament Agency was set up as an adjunct of the State Department, but its duties were vague and it had little to do with the nuclear diplomacy that the Kennedy administration did subsequently conduct.

Kennedy's efforts to find common ground with the Soviets fared no better than had those of his predecessor. And they failed for the same reason; his proposals were tainted by traces of liberal diplomacy that were descended from the Baruch Plan, and that the Soviets would not accept. Kennedy's special disarmament advisor, John McCloy, met with the Soviet Deputy Foreign Minister Valerian Zorin to try to work out a broad statement of principles that could then guide more specific discussions. The document that they issued, on September 29, 1961, had a distinctly liberal flavor. It called for a "program which will ensure that disarmament is general and complete and war is no longer an instrument for settling international problems."[3] It envisioned a supranational organization, to preside over a disarmed international system. Obtaining Soviet acceptance of this principle was an achievement, but the document skirted, because McCloy and Zorin had not been able to resolve the issue, the perennial bugaboo of disarmament discussions between the United States and the Soviet Union – "inspection."

The McCloy–Zorin agreement, like other schemes for the reduction of armaments in the nuclear era, foresaw the destruction of instruments of warfare ranging from stockpiles of hydrogen bombs to the furniture of army bases not being converted to peaceful uses.[4] The Soviets were willing to permit foreigners to observe the destruction of their military hardware, but not to check to make certain that everything they had pledged to destroy was in fact done away with. In an exchange of letters McCloy insisted upon verification machinery to make certain that Soviet forces did not exceed agreed-upon levels of weaponry.[5] Zorin replied with the familiar Soviet objection that such inspection would amount to "an international system of legalized espionage, which, of course cannot be accepted by any state which is interested in its security and in the maintenance of world peace."[6] The joint statement thus neither avoided nor overcame the thorny problem of inspection.

The major nuclear negotiating proposal that the Kennedy administration offered, the result of a review within the government as sweeping as the reappraisal of strategy over which McNamara presided, had a similarly liberal cast. The President unveiled it in a speech before the United Nations General Assembly on September 25, 1961, just five days after the release of the McCloy–Zorin protocol.

It was not a modest proposal.[7] Debate had taken place within the administration about whether the United States should aim ultimately at a fully disarmed world.[8] The President decided that this should be the American goal. So the proposal called for the creation of an International Disarmament Organization, to perform much the same duties as the "International Atomic Development Authority" that the Baruch Plan had proposed fifteen years before. The Disarmament Organization would take custody of fissionable materials, and supervise the destruction of weapons by setting the timetable to see whether all nations were keeping to it. When the plan was fully implemented only the United Nations would have military forces, and so the UN would serve, if not as a world government, at least as a kind of world policeman.

But Kennedy also followed the other, more traditional diplomatic course that Eisenhower had opened. He too sought an agreement to prohibit the testing of nuclear weapons. He inherited a voluntary moratorium on explosions in the atmosphere, which the United States and the Soviet Union had begun in 1958, and he continued to observe it. He subscribed to the "first step" philosophy that lay behind the American push for a test ban, believing that one agreement, no matter how narrow its scope, might clear the way for others of greater substance. And a test ban appealed to Kennedy as a measure to restrict a development that he found particularly menacing – the spread of nuclear weapons beyond the four states that possessed them as he took office.

In the early years of the nuclear age the United States was more or less indifferent to the prospect of "nuclear proliferation."[9] But in 1958 the American attitude began to shift. The Eisenhower administration requested from Congress the right to share more nuclear information with Great Britain than the McMahon Act, which governed the dissemination of atomic energy data, permitted. Congress refused it. And the French made plain their intention to acquire nuclear weapons, with or without American assistance. By 1959 the United States was supporting a United Nations resolution, introduced by Ireland, which prohibited the transfer of control of nuclear weapons to countries that did not already have them.[10]

What were doubts in one administration became an "obsession" in the next.[11] In an article published two months before his election, Kennedy noted the need to place the dispersal of nuclear armaments within an international framework. In his Inaugural Address he was blunter. Both the United States and the Soviet Union, he declared, were "rightly alarmed by the steady spread of the deadly atom."[12] The President had a "basic conviction" that it would be in the interest of neither the United States nor world peace for atomic arms to pass into the hands of national leaders who did not already have them, and opposition to proliferation became a fundamental tenet of his foreign policy.[13]

Proliferation would make nuclear war likelier, Kennedy and others feared, because the further the bomb spread the greater would be the likelihood that it would fall into the hands of men prepared to use it. Even without nuclear war, proliferation was bound, they believed, to have unsettling effects. A nation's acquisition of nuclear weapons would alarm its neighbors. And proliferation was thought to be highly contagious. If one nonnuclear nation equipped itself with atomic or hydrogen bombs, others would surely follow. Finally, the spread of nuclear weapons would complicate nuclear strategy. The rules that had been laboriously worked out during the first decade and a half of the nuclear age might have to be scrapped if it became necessary to take into account countries other than the United States and the Soviet Union.

These general dangers were raised by the spread of nuclear weapons anywhere. Two candidates for the status of nuclear power in particular preoccupied the Kennedy administration; France and Germany. The quarrel between France and the United States over the French "force de frappe" was partly strategic; the complement of the dispute over the utility of conventional forces and the character of deterrence. The Americans claimed that a small, weak nuclear force would dilute NATO's deterrent by tempting a preemptive Soviet strike against France, and would complicate matters if nuclear war did break out. The French insisted that the ability to "tear the arm off the bear," to inflict painful, if not mortal damage to the Soviet Union, provided insurance against Soviet aggression. The French doubted that, in the moment of truth, the United States would risk nuclear destruction to protect France. French motives were political as well. President de Gaulle said that the bomb seemed to him a purely political instrument. A great power had to have nuclear weapons. France, he assumed, had to be a great power. Thus France needed an independent nuclear arsenal. Whatever the logic of this chain of reasoning, it evoked little sympathy in Washington.[14] France's trajectory toward nuclear status was particularly disturbing because it had the potential, the Americans feared, to stir support for a similar course in Germany. And a German bomb would send waves of anxiety through the ruling circles of the Soviet Union. Nor would it sit well with other Western Europeans, whose recollections of World War II were as fresh and vivid as the memories in the Eastern bloc. Yet to attempt to stifle completely German nuclear yearnings once they were born might strain the Federal Republic's still-fragile parliamentary political system, and turn it away from NATO toward either an accommodation with the East or dangerous adventures on its own.[15] A test ban would not be proof against nuclear proliferation, with all its perils. But it could help to retard the spread of nuclear weapons if widely observed, because it would make the fabrication of a bomb more difficult than if testing were freely allowed. And it might lead to other, further-reaching agreements to contain the "deadly atom."

Like the attempts that the Eisenhower administration had made, Kennedy's efforts to secure a test ban bumped up against the American insistence on the right to inspect earth shocks of uncertain origin on Soviet soil, and the Soviet resistance to this on the grounds that it was nothing other than spying. In the course of the wrangling over inspection, Kennedy made a proposal that was to have, ultimately, major importance. On August 27, 1962, along with yet another slightly altered version of a pledge to discontinue all tests and an elaborate organization to monitor it, the United States put forward the draft of a treaty obliging the signatories not to explode nuclear devices "in the atmosphere, above the atmosphere, or in territorial or high seas."[16] This "three-environment" test ban did not cover tests underground, and made no reference to any international control system.

Twice before the United States had put similar propositions to the Soviet Union. In a letter to Chairman Khrushchev on April 13, 1959, President Eisenhower had suggested an atmospheric test ban, to apply only to tests in the atmosphere up to fifty kilometers. But this scheme had included some international control features.[17] The offer that President Kennedy and Prime Minister Harold Macmillan, his partner in seeking a test ban, made in a letter to the Soviet leader on September 3, 1961, was never translated into a formal proposal, and involved only tests in the atmosphere, not under water or in outer space.

Kennedy preferred a comprehensive to a partial agreement on test cessation. But if Soviet objections to inspection ruled out the first, he was prepared to try for the second. Nothing came of the "three-environment" test ban when the United States first broached it. Ultimately, however, it became the basis for agreement. And agreement on this limited test ban was assisted by a technical development that began in the 1950s and that came to fruition just as Kennedy assumed office – the reconnaissance satellite. In early 1961 the United States began to send vehicles into orbit around the earth equipped with cameras of extraordinary sensitivity and with other monitoring devices. These satellites gave each great power – for the Soviet Union soon sent its own aloft – a far greater capacity to monitor the activities of each other than either had previously enjoyed. The idea of permitting each side to observe the other from the air went back at least as far as Eisenhower's "Open Skies" proposal of 1953. But the Soviets rejected that proposal, and showed how strongly they felt about proprietary rights in their own air space by shooting down an American U-2 airplane on one of its missions to photograph Soviet military installations in 1960.

But technical advance put American reconaissance vehicles beyond the reach of Soviet antiaircraft missiles. The same missiles that could carry nuclear warheads from one continent to another through space could hurl satellites into orbit around the earth. And the satellites proved useful almost immediately. The photographs the first ones made in 1961 fixed the total of Soviet missiles, and revealed that no missile gap existed after all.[18] During the Cuban missile crisis, Soviet satellites recorded the assembly of a large American force in Florida, and this may have helped to persuade the Soviet leaders to withdraw the missiles. These same satellites had the capacity to detect a wide range of activities in space, including nuclear explosions. And so they made it impossible for the Soviet Union or the United States to violate an agreement by conducting tests there without the other knowing of them.

Reconaissance satellites made it possible to overcome the perennial sticking point of nuclear negotiations – inspection. They permitted the United States to monitor the Soviet Union, and the Soviet Union to keep foreign inspectors from its soil, at one and the same time. And having circumvented this problem the effort to achieve a cessation of nuclear testing had fulfilled the first requirement of successful diplomacy, a common frame of reference. The three-environment prohibition met the second criterion – equal terms – as well. But the third requirement, the requisite political will to agree, was present on neither side before the missile crisis. Pressures within the United States hindered the conclusion of any sort of formal agreement with the Soviet Union, on nuclear weapons or anything else. Fifteen years of the Cold War had coated American public opinion with a layer of distrust for the Soviets. Since no concrete nuclear agreement was ever reached before October 1962, the public support for nuclear diplomacy was never put to the test. But Kennedy worried that support was sparse, and that winning approval for any nuclear accord would be difficult.

He had cause for concern. Unlike Eisenhower he had entered office with a tiny margin of victory, the winner of the closest Presidential election of the century. Nor did he have the enormous prestige of a former supreme commander that gave Eisenhower singular authority on military matters. Kennedy's Democratic Party felt vulnerable to the charge that it was insufficiently vigilant in opposing the purposes of world communism, a charge that had hurt the Democrats particularly in 1952, and that energetic nuclear diplomacy risked reviving. And Kennedy's presidential campaign and his first two years in office had probably inflamed rather than reduced American wariness of the Soviets. Military preparedness was his main campaign theme, and upon taking office he expanded the nation's armed forces and its nuclear arsenal. The Berlin and Cuban crises, finally, served to confirm the bellicose image of the Soviets that many Americans held, and probably seemed to confirm also that firmness was the proper approach to them.

Kennedy's sensitivity to public suspicion of any dealings with the Soviets lay behind his major appointments in the field of nuclear diplomacy. In addition to John McCloy as his special disarmament aid, he selected Arthur Dean as his representative to the Geneva test ban discussions. Both were Wall Street lawyers, Republicans, and veterans of national security affairs. McCloy had served as High Commissioner in Germany immediately after World War II; Dean was the principal negotiator in the Korean armistice talks of 1953. Kennedy hoped that their reputations would mute partisan criticism of whatever diplomatic initiatives he decided to take.[19] His regard for public opinion on nuclear matters shaped, as well, his response when the Soviets broke the moratorium on testing at the beginning of September, 1961. He felt immediate pressure to follow suit.

Even while the moratorium had been in effect, he had received vigorous counsel in favor of resumption from the Joint Chiefs and from the Chairman of the Atomic Energy Commission, who believed that the Soviets were conducting nuclear tests in secret. To ward off these demands the President appointed a special panel, headed by physicist Wolfgang

Panofsky, to consider the problem. The Panofsky Panel reported that "there was no urgent technical need for immediate resumption by the United States."[20] The Joint Chiefs of Staff dissented, and appealed for permission to commence a new series of tests, but the President turned them down. Still, he was pessimistic that he could observe the moratorium much longer without some sort of formal agreement with the Soviet Union.[21]

And once the Soviets resumed, Kennedy felt that he could not hold the American apparatus for conducting tests in abeyance, and pursue patiently the search for a test ban — "for reasons of the American Congress and the American public," among others.[22] So on September 5 he announced that the United States would resume testing, but in the laboratory and underground, so that there would be no fallout.[23] Even this, however, did not restrain the political pressure to follow the Soviet lead in conducting atmospheric tests. Finally, in March of 1962, despite his great reluctance to do so, Kennedy authorized them.

The decision to settle the Cuban missile crisis rested ultimately with Kennedy and Khrushchev, and with them alone.[24] In moments of crisis, when nations stand poised on the edge of war, when decisions must be made swiftly and action taken decisively, power concentrates and congeals in the hands of the state's foremost political leader. But in less pressured circumstances, in most political systems, power tends to be more diffused. Out of the missile crisis both Kennedy and Khrushchev brought a resolve to find further, more formal agreements. But their personal inclinations were not sufficient to achieve a test ban. A wider consensus was needed in both countries, which the better part of a year was required to assemble.

The politics of a test ban

Kennedy and Khrushchev picked up the search for a test ban both publicly and privately following the missile crisis. Less than a month after its dénouement, Kennedy noted that "the crucial developments within recent weeks have served to con-

firm both the need and the urgency" for some kind of disarmament measures, and asked that "high priority...be given to
the conclusion of an effective agreement which would end
once and for all tests of nuclear weapons."[25] The private correspondence they had begun under the threat of war continued
after the threat had eased. On December 19 the Soviet leader
made a major concession. He declared that, since the realities
of American politics demanded it, he was prepared to concede
two or three on-site inspections each year on Soviet soil. He
said that Ambassador Arthur Dean, in a meeting with Deputy
Foreign Minister Kuznetsov on October 30, had stated that "in
the opinion of the United States government 2–4 on-site inspections" would be sufficient. He also wrote that he would
permit three automatic recording stations — known as "black
boxes" — to be set up in seismic areas inside the Soviet Union.

But he had not conceded enough. The United States, Kennedy responded, would entertain a quota of eight to ten annual inspections, but not two or three. And the American government would insist that these take place in aseismic, as well
as seismic areas.[26] Kennedy also found the three locations that
Khrushchev had suggested for the unmanned detection stations inadequate. He refused to come down from the figure of
eight to ten that had been set as the minimum acceptable
number of on-site inspections. The Russians declined to
budge from their adherence to a lesser number, and
Khrushchev let it be known that he felt "betrayed" by American intransigence. He had believed that the concession he had
offered in volunteering any inspections at all would seal the
bargain, and had run some political risk to make it.[27] A dispute also continued about the number of "black boxes" to be
located in the Soviet Union.[28] And although the Soviets had
agreed to the principle of the on-site inspections, when it
came to working out the details of how these visits would be
conducted, their representatives were evasive.[29]

As 1963 wore on Kennedy's hopes for a test ban, which
Khrushchev's proposal of December 19, 1962, had sent soaring, began to sag. At a news conference in February the President said that the chances for an agreement would be clear by

the spring.[30] A month later, he confessed, "my hopes are somewhat dimmed, but nevertheless I still hope."[31] On April 15 he and Macmillan sent a joint letter to Khrushchev in an attempt to break the deadlock. They held themselves ready, they said, "to send in due course very senior representatives who would be empowered to speak for us and talk in Moscow directly to you."[32] But they had written the letter, Kennedy explained, because "we feel time is running out." He was not "overly sanguine about the prospects for an accord."[33] And by May he was "not hopeful at all."[34] Despite Kennedy's gloom, progress was being made toward a test ban in the first part of 1963. But it was taking place within the Soviet government.

In the last part of 1962 and for much of 1963, a conflict apparently occurred within the ranks of the Soviet leadership, involving the proper policy toward the United States toward China, and toward nuclear weapons, as well as the personal authority of Nikita Sergeievitch Khrushchev. By the beginning of August 1963, a political consensus existed, however precariously, in favor of a different foreign policy than the one the Soviets had been following in the fall of 1962.[35] This new Soviet foreign policy included agreement on a test ban.

The initial policy had two important strains: an aggressive, and, as it turned out, provocative stance toward the West — centered on Berlin and then Cuba; and a simmering dispute with China — worrisome and growing in seriousness but for the most part kept secret.[36] The Sino-Soviet dispute had several sources. It was an ethnic and national conflict between two great peoples whose relations had not always been tranquil. It involved territorial grievances; the Chinese insisted that a large swatch of land on the Soviet side of the thousand-mile border between the two countries rightfully belonged to them. And the conflict had bitter ideological overtones, which recalled the religious conflicts in Europe in the sixteenth and seventeenth centuries. For it pitted rival claimants to the throne of world communism. The Chinese decried what they regarded as the stultifying grip of the bureaucracy on Soviet society, and the Soviet leadership's undue timidity in confronting the imperialist camp. For their part, the Soviets considered the Chinese temerity in questioning their authority and policies a species of heresy.

At the heart of the Sino-Soviet rift lay the problem of nuclear weapons. The USSR gave substantial assistance to the Chinese nuclear program between 1957 and 1959, and then, abruptly, terminated it.[37] Evidently the prospect of their giant neighbor equipped with a full complement of thermonuclear armaments began to alarm the Soviet leaders, and they started an ultimately futile campaign to keep the weapon out of Chinese hands.[38] This did not please the Chinese. They feared Soviet collusion with the United States to keep them from joining the "club" of nuclear nations, and, after it had been signed, interpreted the aim of the test ban treaty as precisely that.[39] The Chinese themselves advocated "a complete ban of nuclear weapons and the unconditional destruction of all nuclear weapons."[40] Like the Soviets in the 1940s and intermittently in the 1950s, and like the French in the 1960s, they claimed to be willing to forsake their nuclear ambitions if the nations that had already fulfilled their own would divest themselves of the prize the challengers were seeking.

The Cuban missile crisis touched both strands of Soviet foreign policy. It brought the diplomatic and political offensive against the West to a sharp halt. It underscored the futility of trying to bully the United States. And it raised the danger of pushing the tactic of bullying too far. The Soviets, too, were shaken by the events of October. Khrushchev's confidant, the *Pravda* columnist Yuri Zhukov, pronounced it "the most difficult week since World War II."[41] It added, in addition, fuel to the burgeoning quarrel with the other great communist power. The attempt to station missiles in the Caribbean, the Chinese jibed, had not only been reckless; it had failed.[42] It proved the incompetence of the Soviet leadership.

Khrushchev took up these issues when he reported to the Supreme Soviet of the USSR on December 12, 1962, less than six weeks after he had agreed to withdraw the weapons from Cuba. He stoutly defended his conduct during the crisis. He took the Chinese to task for their dangerous bellicosity in a franker way than any Soviet leader had previously ventured.[43]

Most important, he made a powerful plea on behalf of his policy of "peaceful coexistence." Had he acted as aggressively during the missile crisis as the Chinese now demanded, he said "it would have been like the tale in which two goats met on a small bridge over an abyss and, both of them refusing to make way, butted one another. As you know, both of them crashed into the abyss." "Is it sensible," he asked, "for men to behave like that?"[44] The missile crisis had ended in a victory not for either side but for "the cause of peace and of the security of nations."[45] It deserved to serve as a precedent for the "sensible norms of international relations" that nations ought to follow. The December 12 speech sent a signal to both domestic and foreign audiences that the search for some form of accommodation between the two great nuclear powers had the wholehearted support of the highest authority of one of them.

Soviet policy between the end of October and the beginning of July appeared to alternate between, on the one hand, a conciliatory attitude toward the West, a cooperative approach to the cessation of nuclear tests, and the personal ascendance of Chairman Khrushchev, and on the other hand, overtures to China, disinterest in a test ban, and an upswing in the fortunes of the First Secretary's political rivals. In December and January the first pattern seemed to hold sway. After Khrushchev's December 9 letter to Kennedy that raised hopes for a test ban, and his speech three days later, came an address in East Berlin in January, where he declared that the need for a separate German peace treaty had become less pressing.[46]

In February and March the pendulum appeared to swing back in the other direction. Khrushchev evidently came under attack within the party hierarchy.[47] On February 27 he made a gloomy speech, forecasting a shift in resources from consumer goods to military needs. His assessment of the state of foreign affairs betrayed, according to the American Ambassador in Moscow, Foy Kohler, an "air of pessimism."[48] He himself seemed subdued. Shortly afterward feelers went out from Moscow to Peking about patching up their quarrel. The test ban discussions bogged down.

In late April and May, however, a shift back toward the initial pattern occurred. Kennedy wanted to encourage it. He had done what he could, from the beginning of the year on, to coax the Soviets into friendlier relations with the United States. The 1963 State of the Union message, for example, stands in vivid contrast to the same report of two years before. The emphasis rests chiefly on domestic rather than foreign affairs. And the cadenced battle cries of 1961 had given way, two years later, to the recognition that national ambitions had splintered the monolith of world communism, and to the message that "if all these trends and developments can persuade the Soviet Union to walk the path of peace, then let her know that all free nations will join with her."[49] The President's attitude towards the Soviet Union had mellowed considerably.[50]

In an otherwise gruff and exasperated reply to a Kennedy—Macmillan proposal of April 15 Khrushchev had agreed to receive the senior representatives of the two men in Moscow.[51] Kennedy decided to make the most of the opportunity. He had been contemplating a major address on the Cold War for some time. Norman Cousins, the editor of the magazine *The Saturday Review*, who had important contacts in the Soviet Union and who traveled to Moscow frequently, had advised him that the Soviet leadership had reached a crucial juncture. Khrushchev, Cousins surmised,

...would be required to take one of two courses: either denouncing the United States as imperialist warmongers who failed to respond to his peaceful initiatives; or, if possible, pointing with pride to the growing success of a policy of peaceful coexistance, listing concrete results achieved since the withdrawal of the missiles from Cuba.[52]

The President wanted to nudge the Soviets forward toward coexistence. He had his principal assistant, Theodore Sorensen, draft a speech on the subject of peace, and delivered it at Commencement exercises at the American University on June 10.

The address was a landmark in the history of relations between the United States and the Soviet Union. It had, perhaps, more influence on them than any speech since the one Harry Truman gave in 1947 announcing the Truman Doctrine and,

as it turned out, formally inaugurating the Cold War. Kennedy
asserted that in the age of thermonuclear weapons "total war
makes no sense." He asked his listeners, and the American
people, to reexamine their own attitudes toward the Soviet
Union and the Cold War. He warned against believing that
conflict between the two great powers was inevitable; and he
asked for a moratorium on the polemics between them.[53] Although the Soviet system held no appeal for Americans, he
said, "we can still hail the Russian people for their many
achievements – in science and space, in economic and industrial growth, in culture and in acts of courage."[54] He mentioned their terrible suffering during the Second World War,
and emphasized that they shared with Americans an abhor-
rence of another global conflict.

He called, too, for a new attitude toward peace. He explicitly
set aside the liberal approach to international politics that had
gripped American foreign policy in the postwar period, that
had been at the center of the evolving suspicion and hostility
toward the Soviet Union during the 1940s, and that had inspired so much of the American policy on the control of nuclear weapons. "I am not referring to the absolute, infinite
concept of universal peace and good will of which some fan-
tasies and some fanatics dream," he said. "I do not deny the
value of hopes and dreams, but we merely invite discourage-
ment and incredulity by making that our only and immediate
goal." And he invited the Soviets to join in the search for
peace, "a more practical, more attainable peace, based not on a
sudden revolution in human nature but on a gradual evolution
in human institutions – on a series of concrete actions and
effective agreements which are in the interest of all concerned."[55] Kennedy disclosed that the high-level discussions
on which he, Macmillan, and Khrushchev had agreed would
soon begin in Moscow, and announced that the United States
would refrain from conducting nuclear tests in the atmosphere
as long as other nations also abstained.

The American University speech found an almost unprecedentedly favorable reception in the Soviet Union. Ambassador
Kohler reported that a Russian translation of the text came

through "clear and unjammed" on the Voice of America, giving Russian listeners an "unusual chance to hear [a] major U.S. policy statement."[56] The next day the official party newspaper *Pravda* devoted thirteen column inches to the speech, and portrayed it in a generally favorable light. Its article was the "most extensive Soviet press coverage of remarks by [a] U.S. official in many months."[57] The President's remarks had, in the estimation of the British Ambassador in Moscow, "a very marked effect upon Soviet official opinion."[58] Privately, Khrushchev was full of praise for the talk,[59] and in an interview a year later he called it "courageous and more realistic than what the Soviet Union and other countries of the socialist world often heard from American shores."[60]

The American University address came at a crucial moment in the history of Soviet foreign policy, when the dispute with China was coming to a head. On June 6, Peking warned the Soviet leaders, in a private memorandum subsequently made public, "against any agreement with the United States that would amount to depriving China of the right to equip itself with nuclear weapons."[61] On June 14 the Chinese released a letter that openly and harshly criticized the Soviet Communist Party for the first time.[62] And in July, delegations from both China and the United States were in Moscow for negotiations with the Soviet government, recalling the summer of 1939, when both the democratic and fascist governments sent representatives to the Soviet capital to woo Stalin, who decided to throw in his lot with Hitler. This time his heirs chose the United States, and their dispute with the Chinese burst out of the confines of private channels in which it had been conducted, into the public arena of world politics.[63]

It is difficult to judge whether the test ban treaty "was the cause or consequence of the break with China."[64] Certainly the two were closely bound up with each other. American officials believed that concern about the budding Chinese nuclear capacity pushed the Soviets toward an agreement to limit testing.[65] But it was not the only incentive for a test ban. The Soviet leaders desperately wanted to keep nuclear weapons out of German hands, as well.[66] More generally, they were undoubtedly eager to take steps to avoid war. Their horror of nuclear conflict was certainly genuine. They may have "calculated that it would be politically advantageous to them to take an initiative which would give them the sympathy and support of practically the whole of the developing countries,"[67] especially since the Chinese would receive neither, and they were certainly aware that the arms race extracted a huge slice from the nation's yearly economic output. Finally, the policy of mending fences with the West seems to have been associated with Nikita Khrushchev's personal fate.[68]

Whatever the mixture of motives that lay behind it, the foreign policy that emerged from Moscow in the early summer of 1963 had a clear and portentous theme: the will to move toward some form of nuclear accommodation with the United States. In a speech in East Berlin on July 2 Khrushchev praised the American University address as "notable for its sober appraisal of the international situation" and responded to Kennedy's summons to negotiate seriously with the special representatives that the American and British governments were dispatching to Moscow by offering a limited test ban, to prohibit nuclear explosions in the atmosphere, in outer space, and under water.[69] His offer signalled that the Soviets, at least, had mustered the third requirement for diplomatic agreement, political will, and set the stage for a brief, intensive, and successful round of negotiations.

The Moscow negotiations

The American and British delegations arrived in Moscow in mid-July in a spirit of confidence. Despite disappointments in the past, Western officials had "no real doubt that a treaty would be obtained."[70] President Kennedy, once persuaded of the sincerity of Khrushchev's July 2 declaration, "was determined to have a treaty, and arguments over language and wording, and all the other dangers and disadvantages which might be pointed out, could not deter him...."[71] The most potent symbol of his determination was the man he chose to lead the American team of negotiators, W. Averell Harriman.

Harriman was ideal for the task. He had had more experience in high-level diplomacy than any other American. His dealings with Russia had begun in the 1920s, when he had arranged business contracts with the infant Soviet government. He had served as Roosevelt's Ambassador to Moscow in the period when Soviet-American contact had been most intimate and vital — during the Second World War. And he had earned a formidable reputation as an effective negotiator in unpromising circumstances. He had, in fact, conducted the most fruitful parley with the communist nations that the Kennedy administration had undertaken. He had represented the United States at meetings in Geneva that had worked out an accord to put a stop (temporarily, as it it turned out) to the civil war that was raging between communist insurgents and the established government in the sleepy principality of Laos.

His experience and his stature gave Harriman enough independence to be able to seize upon a promising initiative without wasting time cabling back to his capital for instructions. But he retained the trust of the men behind the desks in Washington, especially the President. His word counted for a great deal and his counsel had encouraged Kennedy to deliver the American University speech.[72] His credentials as an opponent of communism were sound enough to allay the suspicions, felt by the military and many Republicans, of trafficking of any sort with the Soviet Union.[73] Yet his long association with the Soviets had given him the reputation in Moscow of a serious and forthcoming partner. "As soon as I heard that Harriman was going," one Soviet official is reported to have told an American counterpart, "I knew you were serious."[74]

The Soviets were serious also. The two sides worked out a treaty that committed its signatories "to prohibit, to prevent and not to carry out any nuclear weapon test explosion or any other nuclear explosion, at any place under its jurisdiction or control. . .in the atmosphere, beyond its limits, including outer space or underwater, including territorial waters or high seas. . .."[75]

Both the President and the Secretary of State, in putting the case for the treaty before the American people, described it as a step toward the goal envisioned by the Baruch Plan seventeen years before.[76] And the negotiating team for each was led by a man of considerable national stature, whom the President had brought in from outside the ranks of the professional bureaucracy to lay the American case before the Soviet Union. But their respective provisions and their implications differed dramatically, and confirmed the shift in the American approach to the problem of nuclear weapons that those seventeen years had brought.

The Test Ban Treaty did pay lip service to what had been the core of the Baruch Plan; the formation of a supranational organization to take charge of nuclear weapons, and to regulate international politics. The preamble proclaimed that the parties' principal aim was "the speediest possible achievement of an agreement on general and complete disarmament under strict international control in accordance with the objectives of the United Nations which would put an end to the armaments race and eliminate the incentive to the production and testing of all kinds of weapons, including other nuclear weapons."[77] But the treaty set no schedule for such an achievement, and its provisions represented no real progress toward it. And in fact the provisions and implications of the two measures differed dramatically, and their differences reflected the shift in the American approach to nuclear diplomacy that the intervening seventeen years had brought. The test ban treaty, unlike the Baruch Plan and its offspring, was narrow and specific in its terms. The Soviets expressed interest in combining it with a nonaggression pact between NATO and the Warsaw Pact. The Americans and the British replied that they could not commit the entire alliance to anything, and urged that the issue not be allowed to stand in the way of an agreement to end nuclear tests. The Soviets settled for a paragraph in the communiqué prefacing the treaty that announced that such a pact had been discussed, and that the three parties had "agreed fully to inform their respective allies in the two organizations concerning these talks and to consult with them about continuing discussion on this question. . . ."[78] The American side made a minor concession by dropping a clause that had been a part of draft treaties it had previously submitted permitting "peaceful" explosions above ground in certain narrowly defined circumstances. The Soviets objected to this, and Kennedy acceded to their wishes.[79]

In fact, the final version of the treaty, which was initialed on July 25 and signed by the foreign ministers of the three participating nations on August 5 in Moscow, made careful detours around any issue with the potential for controversy or misinterpretation. Along with the promise of a nonaggression pact and the provision for "peaceful" explosions in the atmosphere, the understanding that an unpoliced moratorium on underground testing would accompany a formal injunction against nuclear experiments in other environments (which the Soviets had demanded in the fall of 1962) was missing from the accord of 1963. The legal experts in the delegations even managed to concoct a way for states not maintaining diplomatic relations with each other to join in signing the treaty without thereby according formal recognition.[80] This attested to the determination on both sides not to permit the tangle of political disagreements that stood between them to block a limited accord on nuclear weapons.

And the treaty was the product of direct negotiations between the two great powers, the United States and the Soviet Union. They took place in private meetings in Moscow, far from the multifarious political interests and passions and the penetrating gaze of the media at the United Nations, where the Baruch Plan and its successors had made their debuts and then invariably had collapsed or faded away. The British were represented — but as the junior partner of the principal western party, the United States. Ultimately over one hundred nations signed the document. But what they signed was what the Americans and Soviets had decided upon.

Both the President and Chairman took an active interest in the progress of the talks. Kennedy made arrangements for only six top officials to read the cables from Moscow reporting on the discussions.[81] He met with them each evening to review the day's messages: "All communications to the delegation in Moscow were cleared through Kennedy. Frequently he altered or rewrote completely the daily cable of instructions prepared in the Department. He confidently granted considerable leeway to the initiative of his negotiators. But he made certain that overall direction remained in his hands."[82] Khrushchev for his part put his own personal imprimatur on the negotiations by presiding over the first meeting of the two teams in the Kremlin, and he obviously kept close track of the ongoing talks.[83]

The Baruch Plan and the Test Ban Treaty differed because, ultimately, they reflected the perceived lessons of two equally monumental but quite different episodes in the history of American foreign policy. The Baruch Plan expressed the conviction of American leaders that another conflict like World War II, and especially more Hiroshimas and Nagasakis, could only be prevented by transforming the anarchy of international politics into the liberal order of a world governed by an international organization, according to the principles of international law. The Test Ban Treaty stemmed from the recognition by a different generation of American officials, in the wake of the missile crisis, that they could not wait for the distant and uncertain arrival of a liberal world order to limit the competition between the United States and the Soviet Union. Since they could not, in the foreseeable future, reform it, they would have to do what they could to make tolerable and stable an "anarchic" international system, in which states would have nuclear weapons and in which no supreme authority would exist to prohibit their use. The high hopes that had lain behind liberal diplomacy had been replaced by the more modest expectations that underpinned the traditional principles of international negotiation that the United States had come, willy-nilly, to adopt. "I think it is a very dangerous, untidy world," the President said. "I think we will have to live with it."[84]

The Senate ratification

Having signed it, the administration still had to make good on its signature by persuading the rest of the American government, and the American people, that the Limited Test Ban Treaty was an appropriate step in coming to terms with the untidy world in which they were fated to live. However they arrived at it, once the ranking members of the Soviet Politbureau took a decision, Soviet policy was fixed. No other body could block it. Public opinion, such as it was, counted for nothing. But the President could not act for the United States with equal authority. Custom, political wisdom, and the most common understanding of the Constitution required him to submit the Moscow treaty to the Senate for ratification.

Ratification was, in the President's judgement, far from assured. Pockets of real resistance to making common cause with the Soviet Union in any form existed in the country and in the Congress. He feared that a coalition of Republicans and southern Democrats would block the agreement.[85] He would not have his treaty, he believed, without a hard fight.

Kennedy took every opportunity to advertise his own enthusiasm for a test ban. And some opponents of the accord may have been caught off guard by the relatively swift conclusion of business in Moscow in July, especially since so many other rounds of negotiations had come to nothing.[86] The signing of the treaty presented the Senate with a fait accompli. To reverse a decision, in effect already taken by the administration, risked damaging the nation's international reputation, especially since over ninety other nations had ratified the treaty by the time the Senate voted on it. And Kennedy tried to reinforce the Senate's commitment to the accord by sending a bipartisan delegation of legislators with the Secretary of State to the formal signing ceremony in Moscow, on August 5.[87]

Once signed the treaty became the focus of a large-scale campaign on behalf of ratification, spearheaded by the President. He took his case before the public a number of times between July and September. He delivered nationally televised addresses on July 26 and September 8. He gave two extensive interviews that dealt with the test ban; one to the representative of a group of magazine editors on August 1; and the other to a television newsman on September 2. He devoted considerable parts of his news conferences of August 20 and

September 12 to the importance of approving the treaty. He oversaw the creation of a number of citizens' groups that worked for passage of the accord, and he helped direct their activities. And he supervised lobbying in Congress. All in all Kennedy fully committed the resources of his office, and his personal prestige, to the Limited Test Ban Treaty.[88] Wary of the possible interference of political "friction" with his diplomatic as well as his strategic plans, he took special care to get the consent of those departments of the executive branch whose opposition would carry greatest weight in Congress and in the country; the Atomic Energy Commission, the Central Intelligence Agency, and especially the Joint Chiefs of Staff of the armed forces.[89] To win the support of the Joint Chiefs, he pledged that the United States would maintain an active program of nuclear testing underground, which the treaty did not prohibit, after it went into effect. Even so, the head of the Air Force, General Curtis Lemay, said that if the pact had been simply a hypothetical possibility, and not something to which the American government had provisionally committed itself and that so many nations had already agreed to, he might well not have supported it.[90]

Kennedy won his fight. The Senate ratified the Test Ban Treaty on September 24 by eighty votes to nineteen, a margin safely above the two-thirds majority needed. The importance of the debate that preceded the vote, which centered upon the hearings held by the Senate in which administration witnesses argued for the treaty and others made the case against it, goes beyond the vote's result. The hearings, and the President's statements on behalf of the test ban, served something like the same purpose for negotiations that McNamara's annual "posture statements" and his extensive congressional testimony did for strategy: They revealed the general principles that underlay specific policies. They set forth the aims of, and the rationale for, nuclear diplomacy.

The test ban debate brought into focus the relationship of nuclear diplomacy to nuclear strategy. The terms of the treaty made plain that diplomacy would supplement, not replace strategy. Nuclear weapons would not be abolished. The

United States would continue to rely upon a large and growing stockpile of nuclear armaments to deter the Soviet Union. Throughout the hearings administration spokesmen warned against feelings of "euphoria" that might lull the American public into a false sense of complacency about the Soviet threat. The debate affirmed not only the continuing relevance of strategy in general but the validity of the particular strategic principles on which the Kennedy administration had settled. The defense of the treaty showed that its terms were compatible with the answers to the three questions of strategy in the nuclear age at which the Kennedy administration had arrived.

The answer to the first question, the proper political purpose of nuclear weapons, was deterrence. The opponents of the treaty, notably Edward Teller, a physicist who had made a large contribution to the fabrication of the first American hydrogen bomb, maintained that the parade of revolutionary technical developments that the first decade of the nuclear age had seen, and that had made deterrence the chief (and the only) political purpose of nuclear weapons, would continue. As it continued, opponents asserted, the political uses of the bomb might conceivably alter. But a test ban would, Teller feared, give the Soviet Union, which would be prone to cheat, an advantage over the United States in making and exploiting technical advances in nuclear weaponry. The treaty, Teller testified, would "prohibit future science" and was "directed against knowledge."[91]

The test ban's defenders did not share Teller's fears. Harold Brown, the Defense Department's Director of Research and Engineering, declared that under the terms of the treaty "in the worst possible case — that is assuming as much cheating as I can possibly believe would go undetected with any confidence — I do not believe that the Soviets could obtain any substantial military gain relative to the United States compared with the situation in which both sides test without restriction."[92] The proponents of the treaty doubted that any revolution in strategy comparable to those triggered by the harnessing of atomic energy and the advent of intercontinental ballistic missiles was likely in the future.[93]

The defense of the treaty also affirmed part of the administration's responses to the second strategic question, the question of how to deploy military forces in the nuclear age. To deter the Soviet Union the United States needed a striking force so mighty and so resilient that it could deliver a devastating retaliatory blow even after absorbing the full weight of a Soviet surprise attack. Such a "survivable" arsenal would assure that a Soviet attack on the United States would be an act of suicide, and so prevent one. Critics of the treaty pointed out that the prohibition of atmospheric explosions would make it difficult for the United States to match the bombs of colossal power that the Soviets had tested, bombs equivalent in destructive force to fifty megatons, or fifty million tons of TNT. The administration replied that it could test warheads that large, but that an arsenal composed of many smaller weapons, of the order of one or two megatons in power, was better suited to weather an attack than a stockpile of fewer, larger warheads, and could do just as much damage to the attacker in retaliation.[94] Neither side, Harold Brown testified, could destroy the retaliatory force of the other.[95] And this, the defenders of the treaty believed, was not at all likely to change. "I am convinced," Robert McNamara told the Senate, "that even undetected clandestine tests will not alter the basic military balance."[96]

The treaty's opponents, especially Edward Teller, disputed this. They did not believe that the condition of mutual assured destruction that, in the Kennedy administration's view, the United States and the Soviet Union had reached, was as sturdy as was claimed. Atmospheric testing, the critics maintained, could perfect a system of ballistic missile defense, which would radically change nuclear strategy. An optimistic view of the prospects for making a viable ABM contradicted the administration's answer to the third strategic question in the nuclear age, the question of how to fight a nuclear war. There was no way to fight a nuclear war, McNamara and his associates had decided, because there was no way to be certain of keeping such a war from inflicting destruction on a catastrophic scale. But if an ABM system could defend successfully against a nuclear attack, it could keep damage within tolerable limits, and make nuclear war an act of policy rather than a senseless spasm of violence. And this would cast doubt on the administration's response to the second strategic question. For one side could not be sure of delivering a crippling retaliatory blow against an adversary well protected by an ABM system. Teller suggested that the experimental explosions that the Soviets had broken the testing moratorium to conduct in 1961 and 1962 had brought them closer than the United States to a workable system of missile defense.

Administration spokesmen responded that perfecting an ABM did not require atmospheric testing. What needed improvement was not the nuclear warhead that would destroy the incoming missile but the radar and guidance systems that would track, sort out, and intercept the attacking weapons. And for the upgrading of these components of an ABM, setting off nuclear explosions anywhere was irrelevant. McNamara's attitude toward the ABM during the test ban hearings was cautious, as it was whenever he discussed the subject in 1963. He did not stress then, as he would later, his doubts that ballistic missile defenses would ever be worth building. But he was considerably less sanguine about the ABM than Teller.[97] And other witnesses favoring the treaty said flatly that the task of defending against a missile attack was hopeless.[98]

The Test Ban Treaty and the debate surrounding it also set out the main lines of nuclear diplomacy, which, like the principles of strategy, were to last beyond the Kennedy presidency. The treaty showed that a shift from liberal to traditional diplomacy could make for successful negotiation. It was traditional in that its terms were narrowly drawn, it was negotiated directly and privately between the United States and the Soviet Union, and it left intact the sovereignty of both. It thus fulfilled the first and second requirements for successful negotiation – a common frame of reference and provisions that affected the parties more or less equally.

The Test Ban Treaty was as well an exemplar of the fulfillment of the third condition of successful diplomacy, the political will to agree. Like the accords that were to follow, the treaty did not follow automatically once its terms were framed. A political consensus had to be formed within both countries, and this was easy in neither case. The leadership of the American President and, probably, of the First Secretary of the Soviet Communist Party, was crucial in forging this consensus in 1963, as they would be again.

The task of mustering the political will to agree was in one sense more difficult for the test ban than for subsequent successful rounds of nuclear diplomacy. For the test ban was the first such agreement, and some of the arguments that its opponents used against it could not easily be recycled. One such argument was that the Soviets would not adhere to any treaty that they signed. It was not, according to the treaty's most vehement critics, safe to take the Russians' word on any matter. Senator John Sparkman of Alabama told Secretary Rusk during the Foreign Relations Committee Hearings: "Most of the mail that I get which is critical of the treaty brings up certain points....The principal point is that Russia cannot be trusted."[99] Another skeptical Senator read into the record of the hearings a document compiled in the Pentagon in 1962 entitled "Soviet Treaty Violations," which listed a long series of agreements that the Soviet Union had signed, and then allegedly violated, between 1920 and 1960.[100] The administration stressed, in response, that it was unnecessary to take Soviet compliance with the treaty on faith, since any illegal nuclear explosion would almost certainly be detected. Once the agreement was in force, and the Soviets observed it, this objection lost its force.

The existence of a working agreement also took the wind out of a second criticism, namely that any agreement the Soviets were willing to sign must necessarily be harmful to the United States. Kennedy met this criticism squarely: "I know that there are some people who believe that the mere fact that the Soviet Union signs it must mean that there is something ominous to it," he said of the treaty. But he insisted that "there are occasions when interests of countries, even though they may be ideologically hostile, may coincide."[101]

The Test Ban Treaty paved the way for further nuclear diplomatic initiatives, not just by clearing away skepticism about any dealings with the Russians, but by revealing a reservoir of positive enthusiasm for them. This appeared when the President made an ostensibly "nonpolitical" tour through several western states in the latter part of September. The official theme of the trip was conservation, but Kennedy also wanted to take soundings for the 1964 presidential campaign. As he moved through Wyoming, Montana, Washington, and Utah, he began incorporating remarks about the test ban into his appreciations of dams and power plants.[102] To his surprise, his audiences responded warmly. Kennedy had fretted about the impact of the test ban on public opinion in the United States. Now he found that it had become, a year before he would stand for reelection, a potent political issue that counted in his favor. With this recognition the politics of the Kennedy nuclear policy had made a 180 degree turn. In 1960 the President had ridden to victory as a dynamic and unyielding nuclear strategist. In 1964 he would be prepared to campaign for another term as an experienced nuclear diplomat.

The next decade was to show that the Test Ban Treaty was, as President Kennedy had advertised it, "the first step" in a long journey. But the nuclear diplomacy that it inaugurated was not the journey that Bernard Baruch, in 1946, and later the original enthusiasts of a test ban as a "first step," had envisioned. They had conceived nuclear diplomacy as leading, rapidly in the first case and gradually in the second, to disarmament and the transformation of international politics. It had instead turned out to entail a series of limited accommodations between the two nuclear giants, who remained nonetheless determined and sometimes bitter rivals.

Because it was the first, the test ban was a modest step. Subsequent negotiations were longer and more complicated. Later agreements relied more heavily upon satellite reconnaissance for verification. And the accords that followed advanced further the common interests of the United States and the Soviet Union, to which Kennedy had referred. The treaty was important less for what it did than for what it was. It did not serve these common interests so much as it signaled that they existed. It was a kind of preface to arms control, which set forth its major themes without extensively developing them. Three themes, three shared interests, were and continued to be important.

The first of them was the restraint of the arms competition between the United States and the Soviet Union. The Test Ban Treaty, Kennedy said, would "inhibit, though it does not prohibit, the nuclear arms race."[103] In truth it scarcely inhibited either side at all. The American Joint Chiefs of Staff were persuaded to support the pact by the promise that it would not hinder the development of new weapons, which could be, and were, perfected in laboratories and through underground tests. But the test ban revealed the administration's conviction that the restraint of the competition in armaments was in the interest of both the United States and the Soviet Union, because it was a competition that neither side had a real hope of winning. In the debate McNamara argued that the Soviets would have greater difficulty in overcoming the American advantage in nuclear weaponry with than without a treaty. But he admitted that, when estimating the time it would take for the Soviets to catch up, "at best we are only speaking of a few years."[104] If the arms race continued, neither side could expect to win; each could look forward only to investing heavily in weaponry to stay even with the other.

But if the United States and the Soviet Union were not especially eager to restrain their own accumulation of nuclear weapons in 1963, they both emphatically wanted to restrain others. Nonproliferation was the second common interest that the Test Ban Treaty reflected. Both great powers were interested in keeping nuclear weapons out of the hands of other countries. Both were especially interested in keeping them from the Chinese, although the Soviets could not afford to be explicit about this.[105] And the Soviets were urgently concerned about West Germany's nuclear future. The Test Ban Treaty by itself did not pose insurmountable obstacles to the acquisition of nuclear weapons. Any signatory remained free to assemble a bomb without testing it, or to test underground. As with the first common interest, the restraint of the arms race, the treaty was important for nonproliferation not so much for what it accomplished as for what it signified – and for the subsequent agreements to which it led.

The treaty's third major theme was the avoidance of war. Its actual terms were even more distant from this goal than from the other two. Atmospheric testing was very far from being a potential cause of war between the United States and the Soviet Union. Peace depended, and depends, much more upon the effectiveness of deterrence. Strategy, as embodied by the two nuclear arsenals, was, and is, a greater spur to caution than diplomacy. And among diplomatic accords, the test ban made a less direct contribution to peace than an agreement that was also concluded, with less fanfare, in 1963. This was the establishment of a direct communications link between Washington and Moscow. The idea for the "hot line," as it came to be known, arose from the difficulty that Kennedy and Khrushchev had had during the missile crisis in getting their messages to each other rapidly. "On one or two occasions," Kennedy noted, "it was necessary to rely on open broadcasts of messages, rather than sending them through the coding procedure which took a number of hours."[106]

The relation of the Test Ban Treaty to the prevention of war was symbolic. The treaty was a symbol of the resolve and the capacity of the United States and the Soviet Union to find agreement on nuclear matters despite their deep differences. It was an earnest of their mutual wish to keep their political disputes within bounds. It was a "fence," between them and the nuclear abyss. For this third, symbolic purpose especially, the fact of the agreement was as significant as its substance.

The Test Ban Treaty's significance is in fact related to its distance from the central questions of Soviet – American relations. For these central questions, upon which war and peace rested, were precisely those on which it was not possible, in 1963, for the two great powers to agree. The character of their political systems and those of their allies, the future of Europe, even the dimensions of their nuclear arsenals were not negotiable. But because war would be disastrous for both, it was all the more necessary to find common ground on peripheral matters, like testing, to develop the good will and trust that could cushion the disputes arising from their rivalry.

This third common interest that the Test Ban Treaty reflected connects nuclear diplomacy with the traditional diplomacy of the past. For it is precisely the purpose for which the diplomatic profession came into existence, a purpose that the invention of nuclear weapons made compelling. That centuries-old purpose, into which twentieth century international politics and especially the advent of nuclear explosives had breathed fresh urgency, was to mediate between sovereign states to restrain their quarrels short of war, in an international system in which, because it is "anarchic," because the units are sovereign, war is always possible.

Fencers on a Tightrope

President Kennedy realized that the United States of America should in their own interests and for the improvement of entire international politics look for stands which would ensure peaceful coexistence of states with different social systems. [He came to a] more correct understanding of the fact that unsettled issues between states cannot be solved by means of war, since no sound minded man, especially if he recognizes the other side to be militarily equal to him, would start a war. Nikita Khrushchev, 1963[1]

Nuclear diplomacy, 1963–76

The abbreviated three-year life of the Kennedy administration was a momentous period in the history of the nuclear age. The patterns of nuclear strategy and diplomacy that were ratified, in some case, and introduced in others, remained the basis for American nuclear weapons policy long after November 22, 1963.

Three men of varying personal and political predilections occupied the White House over the next thirteen years. And although his three successors differed from John Kennedy in both personal and political terms, all three followed the broad outlines of policies, for nuclear weapons, that he and Robert McNamara had established. The next thirteen years were, in this sense, a series of footnotes to the Kennedy administration.

Its mark on the nuclear diplomacy that followed was plain. The Limited Test Ban Treaty of 1963 was not only the first, it was the prototype of a series of negotiated agreements on nuclear weapons between the United States and the Soviet Union in the 1960s and 1970s. These successor accords carried forward the interests common to the two great powers that the terms of the Test Ban Treaty had implied.

The Nonproliferation Treaty, or "NPT," which was completed in 1968 and went into effect in 1970, was aimed at a problem that the test ban had addressed indirectly – the spread of nuclear weapons beyond the small circle of nations that possessed them in 1963. The problem seemed all the more urgent after 1964, when the People's Republic of China detonated its first nuclear explosion.[2]

The United States and the Soviet Union also agreed to severe limitations, amounting to a flat prohibition, on the deployment of systems of ballistic missile defense (ABMs). A 1972 treaty restricted each country to two such systems, and an amendment in 1974 reduced the number to one. This, too, represented the development of a theme of the Test Ban Treaty. The treaty's partisans in 1963 had suggested that the cycle of changes in strategy that the first atomic bomb had set in motion had come to an end with the establishment of the permanent superiority of the offensive striking power of nuclear weapons against any conceivable defense, and that no subsequent discovery or innovation would override each great power's capacity to wreak unprecedented destruction on the other. By relinquishing the right even to try to defend themselves against missile attack, both the United States and the Soviet Union conceded – indeed ratified – this superiority.

The year 1972 also saw the beginning of an effort to limit the offensive nuclear weapons of the two great powers.[3] The purpose of this effort was to restrict, and perhaps ultimately to end, their competition in nuclear armaments. The test ban had anticipated this purpose as well. It had been designed to inhibit the development of more and better weapons by eliminating one (as it turned out rather unimportant) step in the weapon development process – environmental testing. In 1972 the United States and the Soviet Union agreed to freeze the number of strategic weapons they deployed for a period of five years. The Soviets had 1,618 land-based missiles and 740 missiles carried by submarines. The American totals for the same "launch vehicles" were 1,054 and 656.[4] In 1974 the leaders of the two countries concurred on a permanent agreement limiting offensive weapons, which allowed each side 2,400 launch vehicles, of which 1,320 could be equipped with multiple, independently targeted warheads.[5]

Like the test ban, and unlike the liberal Baruch Plan and its descendants, the arms control accords of the 1960s and 1970s were emphatically traditional in form. They were, in the first place, produced by direct, private negotiations between representatives of the United States and the Soviet Union. The talks for limiting strategic nuclear armaments (SALT) took place on three levels. Delegations met regularly in Vienna and Helsinki. Messages were passed in Washington between high American officials and the Soviet ambassador. And the 1972 and 1974 agreements were consummated at summit meetings between the American President and the First Secretary of the Soviet Communist Party.

Nuclear negotiations were not only the private business of the great powers, they were the business *only* of those two. While the British had been the junior partners of the Americans in the test ban discussions, in the SALT talks neither they nor any other member of the North Atlantic Treaty Organization had a direct role. Their exclusion troubled America's allies. It aroused the same fear that the doctrinal shifts of the Kennedy administration had provoked, the fear of being adversely affected by a decision made elsewhere. But while the American government was at pains to reassure the Europeans that their interests were not being damaged by the SALT negotiations, it never invited them to join the discussions to see for themselves.

The Nonproliferation Treaty was in theory negotiated under the auspices of the United Nations Eighteen Nation Disarmament Conference, the site of much fruitless nuclear diplomacy in the postwar period. In fact the United States and the Soviet Union worked out its terms between themselves, and then invited other nations to subscribe.[6]

The Nonproliferation Treaty did not simply reflect the hierarchical character of international politics informally; it was explicitly, and officially, an unequal treaty. It distinguished between two different classes of signatories, who incurred different responsibilities. By adhering to the NPT, states without nuclear weapons promised not to acquire them. The nuclear powers that signed — the United States, the Soviet Union, and Great Britain[7] — were forbidden to assist states in the other category from getting these armaments, but were not required to renounce their own.

The arms control agreements that followed the Test Ban Treaty all had a second important feature of traditional diplomacy: All were modest in scope and purpose. This was true of the test ban as well. Although it had enormous symbolic importance as the first nuclear accord between the United States and the Soviet Union, its direct achievements were limited. In substance, it was a kind of environmental protection measure. It did not noticeably retard the accumulation of weaponry by either the United States or the Soviet Union, both of whom continued to conduct nuclear tests underground, where the 1963 prohibition did not reach.

The Nonproliferation Treaty required the great powers to give up nothing — except the right to transfer nuclear armaments to third countries, a right that neither had any intention of exercising.[8] And when the two renounced ballistic missile defense systems, neither had deployed them extensively, and neither, it was clear, had much hope — even after years of costly experimentation — of producing an ABM whose effectiveness would repay the enormous investment required to set it up. No foreseeable technical advance promised to overcome the crushing advantage of the offense in a nuclear exchange.

Finally, the restraints on offensive weapons that were imposed in 1972 and proposed in 1974 left each side extraordinarily heavily armed. Both retained nuclear arsenals with warheads numbering in the thousands. Each had far more nuclear might than was strictly necessary to assure the "destruction" of the other. In fact, neither had to abandon deployed weapons in any number. The limits were high ceilings, placed at the levels that the two nuclear stockpiles had reached. And while the restraints limited the numbers of launch vehicles permitted to each side, they did not prevent either from developing new types of weapons, or refining existing ones.

The accords that followed the test ban respected a third central feature of traditional diplomacy; none infringed upon the sovereign prerogatives of either the United States or the Soviet Union. Each skirted the potential stumbling block of on-site inspection.

The reconnaissance satellites that had played a minor role in the Test Ban Treaty — by rendering almost impossible clandestine tests in outer space — became crucial, indeed indispensable for the agreements limiting both ABMs and offensive strategic weapons. On the satellites were mounted cameras of such power and precision that their pictures gave each side virtually complete information about the other's nuclear deployments. The United States could count the number, and distinguish the types of Soviet missiles, submarines, and bombers, and vice versa. So each could monitor the other's compliance with the terms of the agreements that they had both pledged to observe.

Testimony to the importance of satellite reconnaissance was Article XII of the 1972 ABM treaty, which established "national technical means of verification" (satellites) as the means for providing proof of compliance, and committed both signatories not to obstruct the functioning of these satellites.[9] So important did satellites become for arms control that their powers of observation became the point of departure for nuclear negotiation; what could be inspected from the air could be included in an accord; what could not readily be monitored by satellite came to be regarded as outside the boundaries of serious discussion.[10]

The Nonproliferation Treaty did have a provision for the physical inspection of nuclear equipment. The states lacking nuclear weapons agreed to open their legitimate, "peaceful" nuclear facilities — in almost all cases electric power generating plants — to officials of the International Atomic Energy Agency, an affiliate agency of the United Nations, who would check to make sure that no nuclear material was being diverted to make bombs. But the states with nuclear weapons,

including the United States and the Soviet Union, came under
no such obligation. They were perfectly free to keep any other
nationals away from their nuclear facilities.[11]

The taboo against on-site inspection held so firm that efforts
to halt all nuclear testing by extending the 1963 prohibition to
explosions underground had not, by 1976, succeeded. Despite
increasingly sophisticated means of analyzing distant tremors,
the United States continued to insist upon the need for the
right to examine Soviet territory, to distinguish between earthshocks and nuclear tests. The Soviets were never willing to
agree to this. In 1974 the two countries concluded an accord
prohibiting underground explosions exceeding 150 kilotons
in explosive power. (At this level natural and man-made
events were easily distinguishable.) And in 1976 an agreement
on a protocol covering explosions of the same magnitude, but
detonated for "peaceful" purposes, was announced. This protocol contained what appeared to be a revolutionary provision; it allowed, in certain circumstances, for on-site inspection. But the provision's terms made it unlikely that such inspection would ever take place. To qualify for inspection an
explosion would have had to exceed 150 kilotons in power —
but neither the United States nor the Soviet Union had conducted tests above that level for years. And the explosion
would have to have an avowedly peaceful purpose; but the
Soviets were free to put any questionable tremor in the military category, to which the inspection clause did not apply.
Moreover, by the end of 1976 neither agreement had been
ratified by the United States.[12]

Three decades after the Baruch Plan, the Soviet rationale for
eschewing inspection had necessarily shifted. In 1946 secrecy
had served to conceal military weakness. By 1976 the Soviet
Union was no longer weak, and in any event could not readily
keep the dimensions of its military forces hidden from American satellites. But the Soviet rulers remained allergic to the
principle of openness. Their political system, in 1976 as in
1946, was founded upon secrecy; the Party continued to insist
upon controlling information of all kinds about Soviet society,
and upon limiting strictly what Soviet citizens as well as

foreigners were permitted to know, and see. In 1976 as in 1946, nuclear diplomacy had to accommodate them on this point. But in 1976, as was not the case in 1946, the technical means both to accommodate diplomacy and to monitor nuclear accords were available.

By incorporating the ingredients of traditional diplomacy – direct private talks between the two most powerful nations, agreements of modest scope and purpose, and terms that avoided any violation of national sovereignty – the successors to the Test Ban Treaty fulfilled the first requirement of successful negotiation, a common frame of reference. They fulfilled the second requirement as well. The successor accords affected the United States and the Soviet Union equally. Under the terms of the Nonproliferation Treaty, they gave up the same thing – nothing. And they confined themselves to the same number of ABMs; two, and then one. In both cases, once agreement in principle was reached, hammering out specific terms was easy. Once, that is, the two nuclear giants decided that they had a mutual interest in preventing the spread of nuclear weapons, and in prohibiting the deployment of systems of ballistic missile defense, writing treaties embodying these purposes posed few problems.

This was not the case, however, when it came to restricting the two offensive nuclear arsenals. Agreement on the principle of equality was simple enough; what proved difficult was finding a formula that would leave the two sides, in the eyes of each, evenly matched. The difficulty arose from the differing compositions of the two arsenals. They included missiles of different sizes and capabilities. The missile-bearing submarines of the two sides differed in important characteristics. And the Soviets had no equivalent of the American intercontinental bomber fleet. So balancing the two became an exercise in equating apples and oranges.

Much of the nuclear negotiation after 1963, especially after 1972, was devoted to seeking a point at which the United States and Soviet Union could agree that their arsenals were evenly matched. This was not simply a technical issue. A variety of standards for measuring nuclear strength existed, and so several distributions of strength could be regarded as "equal." The decision of which, if any, to adopt was, for each country, a political choice. So the second requirement for successful diplomacy, equal terms, shaded into the third – the political will to agree.

The politics of the arms control accords that were established after 1963 resembled the political circumstances in which the Test Ban Treaty was forged. International pressures played a role both in 1963 and afterward. In 1972, as in 1963, wariness of China almost certainly encouraged the Soviets to cooperate with the United States. In 1963 the shock of the Cuban missile crisis propelled American leaders toward agreement with the Soviets; in 1972 the rapid expansion of the Soviet nuclear arsenal created an incentive for limiting strategic forces.

The formation of a domestic consensus was a particularly important, and sometimes difficult, process in both countries both in 1963 and afterward.[13] The position of the Soviet First Secretary and the American President was always crucial. The Soviet decision to accept a limited test ban in 1963 came after Nikita Khrushchev had strengthened his own position in the Kremlin.[14] Similarly, just before the May 1972 summit meeting in Moscow that produced the ABM treaty and the five-year "freeze" on offensive weapons, Pyotr Shelest, one of Leonid Brezhnev's rivals, and reportedly an opponent of negotiated agreements with the United States, was expelled from the Politbureau, the highest council of the Soviet government.

On the American side Richard Nixon signed the 1972 accords at the height of his personal popularity, on the eve of his sweeping victory in the November election. By contrast, his successor, Gerald Ford, never submitted the terms of the 1974 agreement on offensive weaponry for congressional ratification, in part because he did not believe that he commanded enough political support to ensure their passage.[15] As an unelected President from the minority political party, faced with a challenge for the 1976 presidential nomination from Republicans who were unenthusiastic about dealings with the Soviets, he felt unable to risk a political battle over the terms that he and his Soviet counterpart had worked out at Vladivostock.

The Nixon administration aspired to make nuclear accords with the Soviet Union the hub of a widening, thickening network of contacts between the two great powers. The wider and denser this connecting web, Nixon and his associates believed, and the more deeply enmeshed the Soviet Union became, the more moderate, and less hostile to American interests would be Soviet policies the world over. This was the policy of "linkage." For a time it seemed to be working. The 1972 agreements on offensive and defensive weaponry were accompanied by the promise of a much closer economic relationship and especially a greater volume of trade between the two.

The rise and fall of the hopes for commercial partnership that the 1972 nuclear accords spawned bears a striking resemblance to what happened after 1963. The Test Ban Treaty also ushered in a brief, heady era of good feelings between the United States and the Soviet Union. Then, too, the seed of limited cooperation seemed on the point of bursting into the bright flower of friendship. A feeler from Soviet officials in 1963 about the possibility of compensating for a poor harvest by purchasing grain from the United States turned into a windfall for American farmers and grain brokers. Kennedy decided to authorize the sale of wheat in quantity to the Russians. In the grain transactions the Soviet Union, he told the Congress, would be "treated like any other customer in the world market who is willing and able to strike a bargain with American merchants."[16] And the Soviet leaders hinted at even bigger bonanzas for American businessmen in early November and spoke of large transaction with American firms.[17]

Nine years later Richard Nixon authorized the sale of much larger quantities of grain to the Soviets, to make up for another disastrous harvest. And the grain sale was advertised as the beginning of a series of renumerative contracts the two countries would sign. But in neither case did the promised transactions come to pass. In neither 1963 nor 1972, as it turned out, was the Soviet Union on the verge of becoming "just another

customer" for the United States. Trade between the two countries remained at modest levels. This was partly because the
two economies were not well matched. While the Soviets coveted American investment and technology, they had little to
offer in exchange that was attractive to American businessmen
or consumers. In addition, political differences inhibited the
growth of commercial ties.

In fact, if there was a "linkage" among the different aspects
of the relationship between the two great nuclear powers, it
worked quite differently from the way that the Nixon administration had intended. Rather than nuclear negotiations shaping relations between the United States and the Soviet Union
in other areas, the reverse took place. Negotiations were affected by what happened elsewhere. Rather than the engine of
Soviet – American relations, arms control proved to be the
weathervane, sensitive to changes in the overall political climate. Thus in 1968 the Soviet invasion of Czechoslovakia
caused the United States to withdraw from the first scheduled
discussions on the limitations of strategic nuclear armaments,
to which the Johnson administration had agreed. In 1975
Soviet involvement in the Angolan civil war diluted American
enthusiasm for ratifying the limits on offensive armaments
that President Ford and Secretary Brezhnev had hammered
out at Vladivostock. And the congressional insistence upon
making the removal of barriers to trade with the Soviet Union
conditional upon changes in the Soviet emigration laws may
have stiffened the Soviet position in the ongoing negotiations
to complete the Vladivostock accords.

The fate of nuclear negotiations rested in the 1970s, as it had
in the 1950s, upon the outcome of the clash of two powerful
forces: on the one hand, the impulse, as Dwight Eisenhower
had put it, "to do something" about the danger that the existence of nuclear weapons posed, that every other American
chief executive has felt since 1945; and on the other hand, the
political differences between the two great nuclear powers,
which have made it difficult to "do" anything that required
their joint assent.

But the diplomacy of the 1970s differed from negotiations
before 1963 in important respects. The Test Ban Treaty pro-

vided a common framework for discussions that made agreement possible when the constellation of political forces, both in the international arena and within the United States and the Soviet Union, was auspicious, as was the case in 1968, 1972, and 1974. The possibility of success gave nuclear diplomacy a larger role in the foreign policies of the two great powers than it had had before the Kennedy years. Arms control considerations began to enter into decisions about the procurement of new nuclear weapons, at least on the American side. And the negotiations themselves took on an air of permanence. Just as the formal apparatus of the General Agreement on Tariffs and Trade signified that free trade had become the international norm, even if national economic policies often violated this norm in practice, so the enduring character of the SALT talks symbolized a Soviet and American presumption in favor of successful nuclear diplomacy,[18] even if actual agreements were seldom easy to achieve. The rise in the status of nuclear diplomacy came about in large measure through the labors of the Kennedy administration.

Nuclear strategy, 1963–76

No monument comparable to the SALT agreements signifies the permanence of the strategic policies of the Kennedy administration. In fact, the evidence of strategic activity seems to call into question the durability of the answers to the three strategic questions, for nuclear weapons, at which Kennedy and McNamara arrived. For the incarnation, albeit imperfect, of strategic principles is nuclear weaponry. And far from keeping their stockpiles of nuclear weapons as they were in 1963, the United States and the Soviet Union increased and diversified their arsenals considerably in the years that followed. At the end of the Kennedy administration the United States deployed 554 intercontinental ballistic missiles, based on land, and about 175 carried on submarines, as well as bomber aircraft capable of striking the Soviet Union from the United States. By the end of 1976 there were 1,054 American land-based and 654 submarine-based missiles.

Similarly, at the end of 1963 the Soviets had fewer than
100 land-based missiles, none carried by submarines, and only a handful of aircraft comparable to the American bomber
fleet.[19] Thirteen years later the numbers for land- and sea-
launched missiles had risen to 1,1618 and 740. The growth of
the Soviet arsenal was more dramatic because by 1964 the increase in the American nuclear stockpile that Kennedy and
McNamara had set in motion at the outset of 1961 was well
under way. But the Americans were the pioneers in producing
technical improvements; hydra-headed bombs known as multiple warheads (or MIRVs), several of which could be mounted
on a single missile and whose separate guidance systems
could steer them to widely separated targets once detached
from their common launch vehicle. and cruise missiles, low-
altitude missiles capable of evading Soviet radar and adapta-
ble for launching from land, sea, and air.

The increase in the two nuclear stockpiles did not, however,
denote a conscious attempt to change the principles of nuclear
strategy on which the Kennedy administration had settled. In
part the new weapons were obtained to reinforce those principles. They added to the capacity of each side to visit crippling
damage upon the other even after absorbing an all-out attack.
And in part the motives for the additions to the two arsenals
had nothing to do with strategic principles at all.

"Friction" drove the levels of nuclear armaments, at least in
the United States, ever higher even after the Kennedy administration had reached its definitive strategic conclusions. The
political pressures that had influenced McNamara and Kennedy's procurement decisions yielded weapons that strategy
did not, strictly speaking, require. After 1963 scientists and
engineers continued to design improved means of packaging
and delivering nuclear warheads. Large industrial firms continued to depend for their existence upon government orders
to manufacture these new armaments. And their allies in Congress continued to press for appropriations to pay for these
orders.

In most cases the weapons that political "friction"
nourished reinforced the Kennedy strategic principles by aug-

menting offensive striking power. In one case, however, a new weapon contradicted the conclusions at which Kennedy and McNamara had arrived. This was the ABM, which had the enthusiastic sponsorship of the Army, the service that was to have charge of it, but which threatened to undercut the answer to the third strategic question – that no way could be found to keep the damage from a nuclear exchange within politically acceptable limits. Not coincidentally the proposal to build an ABM touched off a fierce political controversy in the United States. And in the end the Kennedy principle was vindicated. The Nixon administration switched the ABM's mission from the defense of cities to the protection of ballistic missiles; from fighting a nuclear war, that is, to guarding the retaliatory force in order to deter one.[20] Finally the 1972 treaty with the Soviet Union virtually prohibited the ABM.

If the growth of the two nuclear stockpiles had no particular strategic aim, why did it proceed unchecked? One way to answer the question is to pose a different one: How could this have been stopped? A broad formula for nuclear equality, encompassing all the different varieties of weapons that the two powers deployed, would have been required to stifle the competition completely; and far narrower formulas have proved exceedingly difficult to achieve. Shutting off the production of nuclear weapons altogether would have meant bringing to an end the research, the designing, and the testing that take place before a weapon is finally deployed, since once one side has perfected a weapon the other invariably insists on the right to develop it. And this in turn would require more extensive and intrusive controls than the United States and the Soviet Union managed to devise in the first three decades of the nuclear age. To check the momentum of the development of new weapons would require a degree of cooperation that they have hardly approached since 1946.

And whatever the motives that contributed to it, the growth of the American (and the Soviet) nuclear stockpile after 1963 did not undercut the strategic principles upon which Kennedy and McNamara had decided. More and more of the "iceberg" of nuclear weaponry rose into view in the succeeding thirteen years. But its contours, the crucial physical properties of those weapons, were precisely those that Kennedy and McNamara had anticipated. So the strategy that they had devised to accommodate those characteristics remained intact. The numbers of weapons on each side rose; but the curve matching the physical growth of the nuclear stockpiles with changes in their strategic implications stayed flat.

To the second strategic question, the question of how to deploy weapons to achieve their designated political purposes, the Kennedy administration had returned a two-part answer. Kennedy and McNamara had concluded, first, that a nuclear arsenal capable of weathering an attack and replying in crushing fashion was necessary to make certain that the Soviet Union would not launch such an attack. And the new missiles and submarines that each side acquired after 1963 added to the capacity of each side to retaliate against, and thus to deter, the other.

The administration had decided, second, that the threat of nuclear retaliation would deter only a narrow range of provocations, and that a more versatile, "flexible" military force than one composed simply of nuclear weapons would be needed, to deter if possible and to meet if necessary "subnuclear" challenges. The Cuban missile crisis had demonstrated that the canopy of nuclear deterrence was broader than Kennedy and McNamara had believed. It was a more "absolute" and less "proportional" matter than they had supposed because the uncertainty that a nuclear reply would not be triggered from a series of conventional "escalations" was powerful enough to discourage a wide spectrum of provocative behavior. The lesson of the missile crisis corresponded to the European view of deterrence. The Europeans counted on the American nuclear force to keep the Soviets at bay, and were unhappy at the prospect of any war, with or without nuclear weapons, being fought on their soil. Accordingly, they balked at contributing troops and equipment to make NATO's forces capable of conducting a nonnuclear war with the Soviet Union.

The European view ultimately prevailed, but in a curious, roundabout fashion. In 1967 the European members of NATO finally accepted the principle of "flexible response." They agreed on the need for nonnuclear strength to discourage Soviet adventures. But they declared that existing forces were adequate to the task. And no appreciable increase in the number of troops that the alliance fielded took place. The Europeans decided that they had been practicing a strategy of deterrence through the capacity for flexible response all along.[21]

A Soviet nonnuclear thrust in Europe did not exhaust the list of potential aggressions that McNamara and Kennedy believed the United States had to be prepared to repel. Other theaters and different tactics worried them as well. They worried especially about guerrilla conflicts in areas newly released from foreign rule. They gathered and trained men to fight guerrilla wars, who began to be dispatched to Southeast Asia between 1961 and 1963. Vietnam was first a laboratory for the techniques of unconventional warfare that Kennedy believed the United States should develop, then a full-fledged war, and finally a national disaster. And it was a disaster whose roots lay in the response to the second question of strategy in the nuclear age, that of "flexible response" that the Kennedy administration devised between 1961 and 1963.

The administration's response to the third strategic question, how to fight a nuclear war, also remained unshaken after 1963. No way was discovered to guarantee that a nuclear exchange would not bring more destruction on both parties than any political purpose could justify incurring. This conclusion was not universally popular,[22] but it seemed unavoidable. The hope of restoring the barriers to "absolute" war, which Clausewitz had identified and which nuclear weapons had the power to overcome, became increasingly faint.

One development in weapon technology did seem to hold out some promise of partly reconstituting those barriers, by making feasible one of the war-fighting programs that Kennedy and McNamara had considered. This development was the increasing accuracy of the ballistic missiles of both sides, which seemed to bring a "counterforce" targeting policy closer to the realm of possibility. When McNamara had announced in 1962 that in case of nuclear war with the Soviet

Union the United States would carry out strikes against military rather than civilian targets, the capacity of American bombers and missiles to avoid the latter while attacking the former was very much in doubt. Fifteen years later both sides could look forward to deploying missiles whose accuracies could be measured not in fractions of miles but in tens of feet.[23] Such weapons were capable of salvos with the kind of discrimination of which McNamara had prematurely spoken.

Some Americans feared that highly accurate Soviet missiles would tilt the relationship between the two nuclear giants against the United States. The fears, however, had to do not with the explicit contravention of the Kennedy administration's response to the third strategic question, but with the possibility that the Soviets might somehow draw political advantage from a more formidable missile force.[24] For even if one side obtained missiles of such power and pinpoint precision that they could wholly devastate the land-based missile fleet of the other in one sweeping attack, that side would still be prey to the warheads that could be launched from the other's submarines, and the bombs that could be dropped from its airplanes, both of which remained secure from a preemptive strike. But even missiles of pinpoint precision could not permit either side to mount a disarming attack, so large and diverse were both arsenals.

The strengthened "invulnerability" of the two nuclear forces and the diminished prospects for conducting a nuclear exchange within acceptable boundaries of destruction meant that the principal consequence of the growth in the two nuclear arsenals after 1963 was to reinforce the Kennedy response to the first strategic question. To this question, of the political purposes of force, the answer that Kennedy and McNamara affirmed was the answer that Eisenhower had given: The overriding purposes of the American stockpile of nuclear armaments was deterrence. Because the retaliatory power of each side was so vast, deterrence rested on more solid foundations in 1976 than it had in 1966, than Wohlstetter and others had feared might be the case in 1956, and than had been anticipated by almost all but Bernard Brodie in 1946.

And the American government acknowledged the durability and the mutuality in 1963 to abandon the claim to nuclear "superiority," and to concede that for practical purposes the Soviet Union was, or would shortly become, the nuclear equal of the United States. By the end of 1967 his public position had changed. He acknowledged that both sides possessed the secure capacity for "second strike," and that neither was likely to gain from acquiring more nuclear weapons.[25] Richard Nixon entered the presidency in 1969 with a pledge to restore "clearcut military superiority" over the Soviet Union.[26] In office, however, he proclaimed "sufficiency" the standard against which the American nuclear arsenal had to be measured, and signed the strategic arms limitation accords that conceded both the inevitability of each side's capacity for assured destruction and the equality of their respective striking forces.

In 1977 the first newly elected Democratic President since John Kennedy made clear, using Clausewitz's terms, that the strategic principles the Kennedy administration had established would remain the basis for American nuclear weapons policy. "In the nuclear era," Jimmy Carter told the United Nations General Assembly, "we can no longer think of war as merely a continuation of diplomacy by other means. Nuclear war cannot be measured by the standards of 'victory' or 'defeat.' This stark reality imposes on the United States and the Soviet Union an awesome and special responsibility."[27]

Nuclear war could not be like war in the past because nuclear weapons were radically different from previous armaments. Despite the revolutionary implications of the new weapons, nuclear strategy had been, at first, the continuation of the patterns of aerial bombardment in World War II. In 1946 atomic bombs were regarded as simply the most powerful variant yet developed of the explosives that had destroyed war plants, marshaling yards, and transit depots in Germany, and had demolished cities in Japan. The atomic bomb was just another weapon, to be worked into a nation's overall military calculations in time of war. By 1963 this had changed dramatically. Nuclear weapons had come to dominate strategic calculations. And strategy had undergone a kind of inversion. The chief, indeed, the only aim of nuclear weapons was to prevent, not to fight war.

Nuclear diplomacy underwent an equally decisive shift, but in a different direction. Through the first three decades it was driven by the "special responsibility" that the United States and the Soviet Union felt. But from a revolutionary beginning it reverted to a familiar, traditional pattern. The American nuclear diplomacy of 1946 had differed radically from previous approaches to negotiation. It had aimed at making the use of nuclear weapons impossible by removing them from the control of nation–states. By 1963 the aim and the method were far more modest – the adjustment of differences and the restraint of conflict. No longer did American officials aspire to do away with the bases of international conflict.

This inversion, in the one case, and reversion, in the other, bore out the prophecies of Bernard Brodie and Henry Stimson. The Kennedy administration ratified and adopted the nuclear strategy and diplomacy that they had foreseen at the dawn of the nuclear age. Their deductions had been accurate because they had grasped the features of international politics upon which strategy and diplomacy would depend.

Brodie had seen that the enormous physical force of the bomb was crucial for strategy: "Everything about it is overshadowed by the twin facts that it exists and that its power is fantastically great." Nuclear strategy was built around these twin facts, and the additional fact that two nations, not just one, had nuclear armaments. Stimson sensed that national sovereignty would persist in the nuclear age, that the international system would remain "anarchic." There was no point in trying to get the Soviets to relinquish the sovereign prerogative to maintain their "dreadful police state." It was wiser to seek some kind of accommodation, within the limits imposed by the resilience of sovereignty and the fundamental political differences between the Soviet Union and the United States, through direct, private negotiations.

Both Stimson and Brodie were proved right. The keystones of strategy and diplomacy that they had recognized – the enormous power of nuclear weapons and the stubborn persistence of the anarchic character of the international system – remained central to nuclear politics after 1963. So the strategic and diplomatic patterns to which they gave rise also endured.

Soviet nuclear strategy and diplomacy

The features of nuclear weaponry that Brodie and Stimson singled out were no less crucial for the Soviet Union than for the United States. The Soviets, too, had to learn to live with the bomb. They too, faced the task of adapting the venerable institutions of strategy and diplomacy to the singular challenges that nuclear weapons posed. How did they do so? And how closely did they follow the American example? If the documents, statements, and memoirs out of which the American side of the story has been fashioned were available to reconstruct the Soviet response to the problem of nuclear weapons, how closely matched would the two histories be?

The information necessary to piece together the history of Soviet nuclear weapons policy is not available. There is nothing for the Soviet Union remotely comparable to the public pronouncements of nuclear policy that Kennedy and especially McNamara made. There is no Soviet version of the annual "Posture Statement" by the Secretary of Defense, which McNamara made a practice of issuing and that his successors continued to produce. The leaders of the Soviet Union have not been wholly silent on the subject of nuclear weapons.[28] But what they have said does not add up to a clear picture of a coherent approach to nuclear weapons.

Soviet nuclear weapons policy between 1946 and 1976 was not entirely, to use Churchill's famous phrase, "a riddle wrapped in a mystery inside an enigma." American reconnaissance satellites provided detailed information about the weapons that the Soviets developed, built, and deployed. But that information came only from American, not Soviet sources. The Soviet government was no more forthcoming about its military programs in 1976 than it had been 30 years before.[29] And the available information did not include the reasons for deploying them, or the attitudes of the Soviet leaders toward the possibility of putting them to use.

The Soviet Union does profess allegiance to a set of principles that are supposed to guide its internal governance and shape its foreign policy. But the canons of Marxism – Leninism do not assist the understanding of official Soviet attitudes toward nuclear weapons. Naturally enough, neither Marx nor Lenin said anything about these weapons. Nor, however, did either go much beyond the injunction to beware of capitalist powers and to support "progressive" forces the world over on the subject of relations between communist and other states. And Soviet foreign policy has blurred even these guidelines.

Soon after taking power the Soviet government proclaimed the doctrine of "socialism in one country," according to which the ultimate goal of world revolution is best advanced by promoting the security and prosperity of the leading revolutionary state – the Soviet Union. This doctrine has served as a kind of elastic clause for Soviet foreign policy. It has been pressed into service to justify anything that the leaders of the Soviet Union have chosen to do, including cooperating with deadly enemies of local communists in China, in Germany, in France, and elsewhere at various times since 1917. Soviet foreign policy can, in fact, be explained quite adequately without reference to Marxism–Leninism, in terms of the ambitions and insecurities that have influenced all states (including the Bolsheviks' czarist predecessors) that have had to find their way in an "anarchic" international system.

The differences between the American and Soviet political systems have not, however, been entirely irrelevant to their approaches to nuclear weapons. In the American approach there have been traces of an attitude, basic to neoclassical economic thought, that international arrangements that advance the interests of all states are possible. This attitude is rooted in the liberal conviction that a natural harmony of interests among nations exists, a conviction that remained influential even after the abandonment of the liberal approach to nuclear diplomacy.

The Soviet Union seems to have taken a more "mercantile" view of international politics in general and nuclear issues in particular. One nation's gain, the Soviets appear to have believed, is necessarily another's loss. This view is summed up by a phrase that Lenin considered the key to understanding all politics, "kto kovo" — "Who is going to do what to whom?" — which denotes the assumption that in any political transaction one party is the perpetrator and the other party is the victim.[30]

So although the United States and the Soviet Union committed themselves to the same things in the accords that were signed between 1963 and 1976, they may well have had different motives for agreement. The Nonproliferation Treaty, for example, was attractive to the United States because the spread of nuclear weapons anywhere, under any circumstances, seemed undesirable. Nonproliferation was for Americans a kind of international public good. The Soviets, by contrast, may have been moved not by a commitment to the general principle of nonproliferation but by the fear that the states likeliest to acquire nuclear weapons would promptly train them on the Soviet Union.

Similarly, while the ABM treaty may have marked, for the United States, the ratification of the principle of mutual assured destruction as the basis for stability, and thus have seemed equally valuable to both sides, the Soviets may have regarded it as a means of stopping the contest to develop an ABM that, because of superior American resources for technical innovation, they were bound to lose.[31]

Motives, especially in politics, especially in international politics where they are the motives not of individuals but of states, are difficult to discern and disentangle. This is particularly so in the case of the Soviet Union, where so much is hidden. But however different their reasons for doing so, the United States and the Soviet Union did agree to a series of nuclear accords, beginning in 1963. They did sign the same treaties and communiques. For strategy, however, there was no such obvious common denominator.

Soviet nuclear strategy did come to resemble its American

counterpart in important respects. The Soviets clearly accepted Kennedy and McNamara's conclusion that a striking force capable of weathering a sudden assault and inflicting grave damage on the attacker in return was necessary for effective deterrence. Like the Americans the Soviets accumulated a large stockpile of nuclear armaments, placed their land-based missiles in concrete bunkers, and put a fleet of nuclear-armed submarines out to sea.

But there were differences also. The Soviets did not develop a comparable specialized vocabulary of nuclear terminology. There is no Russian equivalent, for example, of the American concept of "mutual assured destruction."[32] More importantly, official Soviet pronouncements, especially from the ranks of the military, have occasionally stressed that the Soviet Union would be the winner in a nuclear war with the "imperialist camp." The most authoritative Soviet treatise on the implications of nuclear weapons, Marshal V. D. Sokolovskiy's Soviet Military Strategy,[33] does not express the conviction, prominent in Western writing on strategy, that no victor would emerge from such a conflict; quite the contrary, the Soviet Union, Sokolovskiy insists, would prevail.

Rhetoric – and most Soviet pronouncements on nuclear weapons deserve no other title – proves nothing. And military men are unlikely to take positions that imply their own obsolescence. But doubts about the Soviet response to the third strategic question – how to fight a nuclear war – arose in the United States in the 1970s from the conjunction of Soviet rhetoric with two military programs that seemed to bespeak a belief that fighting and "winning" a nuclear war was indeed possible.

The first program was civil defense. The Soviet Union placed greater importance on, and invested more resources in, trying to protect its civilian population in case of nuclear attack than did the United States. Underground living spaces with special arrangements for party officials and caches of food that remained untapped even when poor harvests created shortages were scattered throughout the country.

The second program that reinforced the impression that the Soviet Union had adopted a different attitude than had the

United States toward the feasibility of fighting a nuclear war was the fleet of intercontinental ballistic missiles that the Soviets deployed in the late 1960s and 1970s. These were much larger than the American models. They could therefore hurl a heavier payload toward the United States, including greater numbers of warheads, than the Americans could launch at the Soviet Union. And this advantage, when combined with the highly accurate guidance systems that seemed likely to be available in the 1980s, promised to give the Soviets the capability to mount a crippling preemptive attack at the American fleet of land-based missiles, which would be as "vulnerable" in the 1980s as Albert Wohlstetter had warned they might be in the 1960s.

These programs were particularly worrisome because the United States had consciously abjured them. The Congress had declined to authorize a large-scale program of fallout shelters. And McNamara had purposely chosen the relatively small Minuteman missile as the heart of the American land-based striking force on the grounds that it was well suited for a retaliatory blow because more could be manufactured cheaply, ensuring "survivability," although it lacked the firepower for a first, preemptive, strike. The United States, by rejecting these two programs, had deliberately embraced deterrence and eschewed any hope of fighting a nuclear war. By adopting them the Soviet Union seemed, to some, to have made the opposite choice.

The curtain of secrecy behind which Soviet policy is made makes difficult the task deciding what nuclear choices the Soviet Union did make, or even estimating the extent to which the Soviets can justly be said consciously to have made any choices at all. But there are reasons for doubting that these two programs were inspired by an assessment of the possibilities for conducting nuclear war radically at odds with the one that the Kennedy administration made. Civil defense received greater attention from Soviet than American authorities, but their efforts held out little hope of averting loss of life and property on a colossal scale in the event of a nuclear exchange with the United States. For their civil defense preparations to have any appreciable effect, the Soviets would have to antici-

pate an attack in time to evacuate millions of people to protected areas; but early warning was anything but guaranteed,
and no large-scale rehearsal of evacuation procedures had, by
1976, been observed.[34]

There were, as well, possible reasons for fielding squadrons
of large missiles that did not imply the confidence that they
could be used in a disarming strike against the United States.
The Soviet version of the political "friction" that shaped the
American nuclear arsenal may have been responsible for these
weapons. The representatives of heavy industry, who have
charge of producing missiles, and the professional military,
who control them once they are built, are thought to have
disproportionate influence over decisions about the allocation
of resources in the Soviet Union. They can certainly be expected to have lobbied for extensive programs of nuclear construction, and may have had a particular preference for outsize
land-based intercontinental ballistic missiles. Or, the Soviet
military, which may hold sway over the procurement of armaments, may have a more sanguine view of nuclear combat
than the civilian leadership, which presumably has final responsibility for going to war.[35]

The Soviets may have deployed large missiles strictly for
the purpose of deterrence, not in an effort to achieve superiority of any sort. These missiles were designed in the mid-1960s,
when multiple warheads may have seemed necessary to pene-
trate an anticipated American ABM system. Lacking the
technology at that time to mount multiple warheads on small
land-based missiles and submarines, the Soviets may have
chosen to acquire missiles larger than their American counterparts. Even without ABMs, the Soviets may have expected
that the American Minuteman force would ultimately be able
to destroy much of the Soviet land-based arsenal in a preemptive strike, and, without a strategic bomber fleet and with
submarines far less efficient than those of the United States,
may have calculated that they needed large numbers of
warheads per missile to guarantee the capacity to strike back
effectively when the missiles themselves were vulnerable.[36]

Or, the Soviets may have felt the need to have large missiles
in order to draw even with the United States in nuclear might.

For although the Americans had smaller missiles, they held advantages in other areas: greater overall technical sophistication; wider-ranging and more sophisticated submarines; and a large fleet of intercontinental range bomber airplanes. Moreover, the three other states possessing nuclear weapons in 1976 — Britain, France, and the People's Republic of China — had all aimed their arsenals at the Soviet Union but not at the United States. The Soviets may have coveted more powerful missiles as compensation for these shortcomings. This, at any rate, is what they claimed during the negotiations to strike a balance between the two offensive forces.[37]

Or, it is conceivable, the Soviets may have acknowledged that their complement of missiles conferred an advantage upon them, but believed that such an advantage was necessary to deter the United States. Americans regarded their own intentions as self-evidently peaceful from the outset of the nuclear age, and consequently tended to the assumption that Soviet forces must have other than peaceful purposes. But the Soviets may not have shared this view.[38]

The Soviets may, finally, have believed that they could draw political benefits from a more muscular land-base striking force than the United States had built, but without including among those benefits the capacity to fight and win a nuclear war. Americans to whom that force seemed particularly menacing feared that it might make for more aggressive Soviet diplomacy, particularly during moments of crisis.[39] (But not even those most worried about the asymmetries between the two missile forces suggested that the Soviets could be certain of fighting a nuclear war with impunity by launching a successful preemptive attack on all of the American nuclear weapons. For however vulnerable the Minuteman force became, the submarines and bombers remained safe from preemptive destruction).[40]

The most tangible piece of evidence that the Soviet Union did not reach conclusions about nuclear war that differed significantly from those of the United States was the Soviet adherence to the 1972 ABM treaty. Whatever the motives for doing so, by agreeing to its terms the Soviets renounced the most promising (even if it was not at all promising in absolute terms) way of keeping the damage from a nuclear exchange within politically acceptable limits.

Evidence that is even more telling came from what Soviet leaders said about nuclear war. They said it would be disastrous. Marshal Andrei Grechko, the Defense Minister from 1967 to 1976, a time of rapid expansion of Soviet forces of all varieties, was reported to have said in 1971 that the decision to use nuclear weapons "could only be made by an idiot or a man who has lost his mind."[41] Although Soviet strategic writing from time to time claimed that a nuclear war could be won, no details of how this could be accomplished, or of precisely what would happen in such an exchange, were ever offered.[42] Nor did Soviet pronouncements betray an eagerness to engage in nuclear combat; only the undocumented assertion that if the enemy should choose to give battle, the Soviet forces would triumph.

The Soviet leaders, like their American counterparts, recognized that nuclear weapons differed dramatically from all the armaments of the past. And this recognition was made explicit at some cost in ideological purity. For one of the few axioms of Marxism—Leninism was the certainty of conflict between communist and capitalist states. Nuclear weapons forced the repudiation of that axiom. After first rebuking his rival, Georgi Malenkov, for daring to say it, Nikita Khrushchev declared that war could no longer be regarded as inevitable; since in the nuclear age war would not, as Lenin had imagined, bring about the triumph of communism.[43] As one of Khrushchev's colleagues put it, "A world thermonuclear conflict...would, of course, be a heavy loss for the cause of Communism.... For entire nations the question of the victory of Socialism would never arise at all, since they would simply disappear from the face of the earth."[44] The harnessing for military purposes of the power locked in the heart of matter had changed the laws of war and thus the laws of history. A statement by the Central Committee of the Communist Party put the proposition succinctly: "The atomic bomb does not adhere to the class principle; it destroys everybody within range of its destructive action."[45]

Fencers on a tightrope

They differed in the composition of their respective nuclear arsenals, the emphasis of their strategic doctrines, and the motives underlying their interests in nuclear diplomacy. But the United States and the Soviet Union agreed on one fundamental premise: the revolutionary character of nuclear weapons, stemming from explosive power that was, in Bernard Brodie's words, "fantastically great." And both accepted the consequence of this power. Each conducted its foreign policy so as to avoid collision with the other. Each behaved, where the interests of the other were engaged, in wary, cautious, moderate fashion. The word that best describes the foreign policy of each great power where the other was concerned is "prudence." The dictionary definition of "prudent" is "sagacious, discreet, worldy-wise."[46] It entails a quality of mind, a kind of behavior, and an experience from which these two arise. All three apply to the conduct of the United States and the Soviet Union in the nuclear age.

From 1946 to 1976 prudence, not the abolition of the possibility of war at which liberal diplomacy aimed, nor the reconciliation of all political differences between them, was the key to peace between the United States and the Soviet Union. Prudence was the answer to the basic question of the nuclear age: how to live with the bomb.

For prudential conduct in the postwar period the Cuban missile crisis was the exception that proved the rule. It was the most reckless act by either great power; but once its recklessness was made plain, the two hastened to resolve the issue that had provoked it. The lesson of the crisis was the need to avoid recklessness. But the effect of this lesson was difficult to detect. For prudence, like the successful deterrence that produces it, is invisible. Nuclear-induced prudence not only restrained the United States and the Soviet Union in crises, it encouraged policies designed to keep crises from occurring.

The two were more prudent after October 1962 than before. Relations between them were less fraught with the threat of war. The Berlin question faded in importance, although it was not formally settled until 1969. The use of force by each great power within its own sphere of direct concern, the United States in the Dominican Republic in 1965, the Soviet Union in Czechoslovakia in 1968, provoked nothing fiercer than angry denunciations from the other. Before 1962 as well, however, the use of force by one – the United States by proxy against Cuba in 1961, the Soviet Union against Hungary in 1956 – had triggered indignation, but not intervention, from the other. The lesson that prudence is of paramount importance in the nuclear age was reinforced by the Cuban missile crisis; it first emerged from the rubble of Hiroshima and Nagasaki.

Their common prudence was born of the odd relationship between the two nuclear giants. They could agree on nothing save the most important thing – the need for survival. Neither friendship nor isolation from the other was possible for either. They were at once mortal enemies and fraternal twins. One student of their relationship described it this way:

If you put a scorpion and a tarantula together in a bottle, the objective of their own self- preservation will impel them to fight each other to the death. For the moment, at least, no understanding between them is possible.... From the point of view of each, the basic situation is that the other is trying to kill him....[47]

The United States and the Soviet Union, like the scorpion and the tarantula, were at once deadly and fragile. And the two great powers were forced together by circumstances as unbreakable as the bottle holding the two lethal creatures. But the metaphor is faulty in one important way. The two great powers did not fight to the death. The recognition of their plight triumphed over their impulses for conflict.

In this respect they were more like fencers on a tightrope: each facing the other, weapon in hand, balancing precariously; neither willing to drop his weapon and give way to the other; each fearing to thrust decisively because such a thrust would topple them both, attacker and victim, to mutual disaster. Like fencers on a tightrope, the United States and the Soviet Union assumed the one posture that remained to them, given their convictions and their circumstances. They stood poised, ready, and waiting, in order to check the other, neither wanting to strike, but each making ready for a strike by the other. The United States and the Soviet Union learned to live with the bomb, and with each other, by wielding huge nuclear clubs menacingly, with the threat, implied if not fully stated, to bring them down with a terrible thump, and by not having to carry out the threat.

This state of affairs was foreseen by neither Stimson nor Brodie. But it was anticipated long before either wrote about the shape of the nuclear age, long before the nuclear age began, by Clausewitz. Clausewitz's concept of "armed wariness" prefigures the prudence that governed the relationship between the United States and the Soviet Union. This concept is the theoretical counterpoint, and the logical opposite, of "absolute war."[48] Clausewitz's characterization of the state of "armed wariness" is an apt description of politics in the shadow of nuclear weapons.

The effort to outdo the enemy, the violent and compulsive course of war, all stagnate for lack of real incentive. Neither side makes more than minimal moves, and neither feels itself seriously threatened...as the incentive fades away, the active element gradually becomes passive. Less and less happens, and guiding principles will not be needed. *The art of war will shrivel into prudence*, and its main concern will be to make sure the delicate balance is not suddenly upset in the enemy's favor and the half-hearted war does not become a real war after all.[49]

"Armed wariness" was, for Clausewitz, the product of modest war aims. It occurred when one side wanted only "a small concession" from the other. In the nuclear age, it was brought about by the enormity of the destruction risked, rather than by the modesty of the goal sought. The possibility of "absolute war" drove the United States and the Soviet Union to its opposite, the prudent passivity of "armed wariness."

The United States and the Soviet Union tried, in the 1970s, to define and ratify the prudence on which they both depended. In 1972, along with the limitations on offensive weapons and systems of ballistic missile defense, they agreed to a set of principles that read in part:

The USA and the USSR attach major importance to preventing the development of situations capable of causing a dangerous exacerbation of their relations and to preventing the outbreak of nuclear war... Both sides recognize that efforts to obtain unilateral advantage at the expense of the other, directly or indirectly, are inconsistent with these objectives... The USA and the USSR have a special responsibility, as do other countries which are permanent members of the United Nations Security Council, to do everything in their power so that conflicts or situations will not arise which would serve to increase international tensions.[50]

A year later they both signed an accord pledging to "act in such a manner as to prevent the development of situations capable of causing a dangerous exacerbation of their relations, as to avoid military confrontations, and as to exclude the outbreak of nuclear war between them and between either of the parties and other countries." They also promised that

If at any time relations between the parties or between either party and other countries appear to involve the risk of nuclear conflict, or if relations between countries not party to this agreement appear to involve the risk of nuclear war between the United States and the Union of Soviet Socialist Republics or between either party and other countries, the United States and the Soviet Union, acting in accordance with the provisions of this agreement, shall immediately enter into urgent consultations with each other and make every effort to avert this risk.[51]

The two agreements were drawn in general terms. Their specific referents were not clear. But if the letter of the accords was in each case uncertain, their common spirit was plain enough, and that spirit was violated by the Soviet Union only three months after the 1973 declaration was signed. Syria and Egypt struck Israel without warning at the beginning of October. The Soviet Union knew in advance of the attack, resupplied the two attackers while the war was in progress, and even exhorted other Arab states to join the fight. No warning was given to the United States. Soviet purposes in the 1973 Middle East War, as in other events since 1945 for which no documents or other direct evidence is available, remain hidden. Soviet policy can be interpreted as aggressive, goading the Arabs into action and underwriting their efforts. Or it may have been defensive; the Soviets may have felt forced to go along with plans laid independently in order to avoid appearing timid and losing influence in the region.

But whether they were leading the parade or running to catch up with it, what the Soviets did in October of 1973, and what they failed to do, ran counter to the implications of the 1972 and 1973 pledges of cooperation. They were not willing to sacrifice political interests in order to fulfill those pledges.

The 1973 war showed that efforts to translate prudence into formal terms were doomed to fail. It also showed that such efforts were redundant.

The war raised the danger of a collision between the United States and the Soviet Union. But that danger triggered the swift removal of its cause. After initial Arab successes the tide of battle turned. Israel pushed forward on both the northern and southern fronts and managed to cross the Suez Canal into Egypt itself. A ceasefire was arranged, but it broke down, and the Israelis surrounded the bulk of the Egyptian Army. Alarmed at the prospect of the annihilation of the Egyptian forces, the first Secretary of the Soviet Communist Party sent a note to the American President:

Let us together...urgently dispatch Soviet and American contingents to Egypt.... I will say it straight, if you find it impossible to act together with us on this matter, we should be faced with the necessity urgently to consider the question of taking appropriate steps unilaterally. Israel cannot be allowed to get away with the violations (of the ceasefire).[52]

The response came at two levels. First, American military forces were put on worldwide alert, as a signal that the United States would not permit unilateral Soviet intervention in the region. But second, the American government sent reassuring messages to Moscow, supported another ceasefire resolution in the United Nations Security Council, and, most important of all, forced the Israelis to stop short of the destruction of the Egyptian army.

The 1973 war qualified as a "crisis" in relations between the United States and the Soviet Union, because a threat to use force arose. It was a far paler, less serious crisis than the one provoked by the dispatch of missiles to Cuba in 1962. The two great powers confronted each other indirectly. It was not an initiative, like the emplacement of missiles, but the threat to take one, that prompted the crisis. And the two had similar aims; the United States, as it turned out, was no more anxious than the Soviet Union to permit a total Israeli victory. Neither side had reason to be as frightened as Khrushchev confessed he had been in October of 1962.

Nonetheless, the outline of events in 1973 corresponded to the missile crisis in several important respects; the threat of force brought an indignant response coupled with measures to solve the problem that had prompted the threat. The United States and the Soviet Union cooperated in 1973 not because of the pledges to cooperate that they had made but because of the imperatives of politics between the two great powers. These were apparent before 1972 — and before 1962 as well. The attempts to write rules of engagement for the great powers were not successful, but they did not have to be. Prudential conduct was the unwritten iron law of the nuclear age.

This raises a final question; What did the prudence that governed the foreign policies of both the United States and the Soviet Union from 1946 to 1976 owe to the nuclear strategy that they had forged and to the accords on nuclear weapons that they had reached? Khrushchev opined that "no sound-minded man would start a war." Was this soundness of mind rooted in, or independent of, the adaptations and refinements of the traditional instruments of statecraft that took place in those three decades, and especially between 1961 and 1963? There was, after all, nuclear peace before 1963, before the main lines of strategy and diplomacy had been fully worked out. Fencers on a tightrope do not need elaborate rules of conduct to behave cautiously; the logic of their predicament suffices. Would the examples of Hiroshima and Nagasaki have sufficed to keep the United States and the Soviet Union from each other's throat after 1945? If, in sum, neither side had carefully and explicitly worked out the answers, for nuclear weapons, to the three questions of strategy, and if no format for translating their common interests into formal treaties had been found — if, that is, the two giants had stood with their huge nuclear clubs poised to strike, and nothing more — would those three decades still have been free of nuclear shots fired in anger?[53]

The question cannot be answered. It is "counter-factual;" it asks what would have happened if things had been different. But things were not different. And history cannot be rerun without the strategic conclusions and the diplomatic approach of the Kennedy administration. What can be answered, however, is the question of why the revision of the principles of strategy and the renewal of the most familiar form of diplomacy, both inspired by the advent of nuclear weapons, took place.

The persistence of the "anarchic" structure of international politics, despite American attempts to reform it, prevented the erection of an insurmountable barrier to all wars. And the power of nuclear armaments pulled down the age-old barriers to absolute war that Clausewitz had identified; American efforts to replace these also failed. In their stead the United States, and the Soviet Union, put up the barriers to nuclear catastrophe that it was within their power to fashion. Nuclear strategy and nuclear diplomacy were designed to prevent nuclear war, even if questions of war and peace depended more on matters beyond the scope of these instruments of statecraft. In this they were like props for a tall tree, which may not be crucial to keeping it upright, but that are carefully set up because they might help to steady it, and because its fall would be so catastrophic as to justify any effort to prevent this.

Strategy and diplomacy were designed to enfeeble the "incentive for war" to which Clausewitz had referred in describing "armed wariness," by enhancing as far as possible the resistance to an attack that each could mount (in this case defined as the destruction that each could visit in retaliation), and by reducing as far as possible the political motives for war through gestures of conciliation and measures to advance jointly held interests. The first was the point of strategy; the second of diplomacy.

For thirty years the incentive for war was feeble. The history of the nuclear age has not been a tragedy; or rather, it has not been a tragedy of colossal, unprecedented destruction. It has been the continuation, with some modifications, of the history of politics among nations. The world has managed to live with the bomb. And this coexistence – of the age-old "anarchic" international system with the terrifying fruits of modern science – has arguably been the achievement, and unquestionably the purpose, of nuclear strategy and nuclear diplomacy.

Notes

Chapter 1. The nuclear question

1 Princeton, N.J., Princeton University Press, 1945, p. 226.

2 This theme pervades, for example, Joseph I. Lieberman, *The Scorpion and the Tarantula: The Struggle to Control Atomic Weapons, 1945 – 1949* (Boston: Houghton Mifflin, 1970); and Martin J. Sherwin, *A World Destroyed* (New York: Alfred A. Knopf, 1975).

3 Raymond Aron, *The Great Debate* (Garden City, N.Y.: Doubleday, 1965), p. 3.

4 Quoted in John Keegan, *The Face of Battle* (New York: Vintage, 1977), p. 264.

5 "Memorandum to Major General L. R. Groves from Brigadier General T. F. Farrell, Subject: Report on Overseas Operations – Atomic Bomb." Reprinted in Anthony Cave Brown and Charles B. MacDonald, editors, *The Secret History of the Atomic Bomb* (New York: The Dial Press/James Wade, 1977), p. 535.

6 Thomas Schelling, *Arms and Influence* (New Haven: Yale University Press, paperback, 1966), p. 191.

7 *Ibid.*

8 "Report of the Manhattan Project Atomic-Bomb Investigating Group," in Cave Brown and MacDonald, editors, *op. cit.*, p. 558.

9 Schelling, *op. cit.*, pp. 19 – 20.

10 Carl von Clausewitz, *On War*, edited and translated by Michael Howard and Peter Paret, Introductory Essays by Peter Paret, Michael Howard, and Bernard Brodie; with a Commentary by Bernard Brodie (Princeton, N.J.: Princeton University Press, 1976), p. 75.

11 "...Absolute war has never been achieved." *Ibid.*, p. 582.

12 Clausewitz, *op. cit.*, p. 69.

13 *Ibid.*, p. 607.

14 For an elaboration of "the inextricable connection between the war system and the states system," see Robert E. Osgood and Robert

225

W. Tucker, *Force, Order and Justice* (Baltimore: The Johns Hopkins University Press, paperback, 1967), p. 20.

15 Sherwin, *op. cit.*, p. 107.

16 See Chapter 2.

17 This is the spirit, if not the letter, of Martin Sherwin's argument in *A World Destroyed*. The thrust of the book is to suggest that if American officials had behaved differently before Hiroshima, imposing international control of some sort on atomic weapons afterward would have been easier. The author certainly demonstrates that these officials gave no systematic thought before the end of the war to what to do about atomic energy after it was over. If they had, would things have been different? It is, of course, impossible to say with certainty. Sherwin equivocates. Although the section of the book describing Niels Bohr's campaign for international control is called "The Road Not Taken," Sherwin does not make a strong case that the untraveled road led to a radically different destination, where nuclear weapons were concerned, than the one at which the world ultimately arrived. "The issue here, it must be emphasized," he writes of Roosevelt's refusal to approach Stalin on nuclear issues, "is not whether the initiative Bohr suggested might in fact have led to successful international control, but rather to what extent, if any, Roosevelt demonstrated serious interest in laying the groundwork for such a policy" (p. 107). But if such a policy had no chance of success, the issue of whether or not the groundwork for it was laid loses its importance. In his introduction, Hans Bethe is more forthright. "One is led to speculate...how differently Stalin might have acted had he been informed officially about the bomb" (p. xiii). One can indeed speculate, but nothing that is known about Stalin supports the speculation that he would have been willing to participate in a scheme for international control of atomic energy, no matter when it was put to him.

18 See Lieberman, *op. cit.*, chapter 21.

19 See Stanley Hoffmann, *The State of War* (New York: Frederick A. Praeger, 1965), chapter 3.

20 John H. Herz, *International Politics in the Atomic Age* (New York: Columbia University Press, paperback, 1962), p. 214n.

21 Sherwin, *op. cit.*, p. 9.

22 Definitions of the role of military force usually resolve around a distinction between "strategy" and "tactics." This one combines two such distinctions: Alfred Thayer Mahan's designation of strategy as the disposition of forces before they come in contact with the enemy, and tactics as their disposition afterward; and Clausewitz's rule that tactics involve the use of force in combat, while strategy entails the use of combat – battles – for political ends. The first "question" corresponds to what is generally regarded as the problem of foreign policy, the second to strategy, and the third to tactics.

23 See Raymond Aron, *Penser la guerre, Clausewitz, Vol. I; L'âge européen* (Paris: Editions Gallimard, 1976), pp. 84, 283, 335, 358.

24 Clausewitz, *op. cit.*, p. 89.

25 *Ibid.*, p. 79.

26 *Ibid.*, p. 357.

27 *Ibid.*, p. 120. "Uncertainty, ignorance, confusion, fatigue, error, countless other imponderables – all interfered with the effective application of force." Peter Paret, "The Genesis of *On War*," *ibid.*, p. 16. The analysis of military affairs has on occasion been compared to the study of economics, and some of Clausewitz's concepts are similar to the vocabulary of economists. Just as the heart of war is violence, so the essence of economic activity is production. And economic production, like violence, has three components: land, labor, and capital. The natural barriers to "absolute" war have a parallel in the principle of scarcity that all economists assume. And Clausewitz's injunction to keep military force under strict political control also has an economic analogue: the principle of efficiency.

28 Edward Luttwak has done something of this sort for imperial Rome in *The Grand Strategy of the Roman Empire* (Baltimore: The Johns Hopkins University Press, 1976).

29 Bernard Brodie, *Sea Power in the Machine Age* (Princeton, N.J.: Princeton University Press, 1941), chapters VI, VII.

30 Harold Nicolson, *The Evolution of Diplomatic Method* (New York: The Macmillan Company, 1954), p. 31; and Garrett Mattingly, *Renaissance Diplomacy* (Baltimore, Md.: Penguin Books, paperback, 1964), pp. 47 – 54.

31 Mattingly, *op. cit.*, chapters VIII and IX.

32 F. H. Hinsley, *Power and the Pursuit of Peace* (Cambridge: Cambridge University Press, paperback, 1967), p. 168.

33 Nicolson, *op. cit.*, pp. 69 – 70.

34 F. H. Hinsley, *op. cit.*, chapter 2. The idea of a world state differed from the strategy of empire in that it would come into existence peacefully, and no single party would dominate it.

35 *Ibid.*, p. 92. Socialists had the same view. See Kenneth Waltz, *Man, the State and War* (New York: Columbia University Press, paperback, 1965), chapter V.

36 Hinsley notes that during the nineteenth century the Great Powers came in the Congress system "as close to adopting the federalist ideas of the peace plans of the early eighteenth century as was consistent with their existence – and with their recent growth – as Great Powers;" *op. cit.*, p. 196. But the difference between the two ways of organizing international politics is precisely that one accepts national sovereignty, the other tries to reduce it.

37 Countries organized along nonliberal lines also participated, but the impetus generally came from the democracies.

38 For a brief survey of Soviet nuclear strategy and diplomacy, see chapter VIII.

39 Brodie, *Seapower in the Machine Age.*

40 New York, Harcourt, Brace and Company, 1946.

41 Bernard Brodie, "War in the Atomic Age," in Brodie, editor, *The Absolute Weapon*, p. 52.

42 *Ibid.*

43 This became the subject of intense debate twenty-three years later. But after the ABM controversy and the SALT I agreement, Brodie's assertion stands. See Chapter 5.

44 Brodie, "War in the Atomic Age," p. 63. The atomic scientists also assumed that other countries would soon make their own bombs. See David Lilienthal, *The Journals of David E. Lilienthal; Volume II: The Atomic Energy Years* (New York: Harper & Rowe, 1964); and Frederick Seitz and Hans Bethe, "How Close is the Danger?" in Dexter Masters and Katherine Way, *One World or None* (London: Latimer House, 1947), Chapter 9. But outside the scientific community the presumption that the United States could maintain its nuclear monopoly for a long time was widely held. Thus the first Soviet atomic explosion came as a shock.

45 Bernard Brodie, "Implications for Military Policy," in Brodie, editor, *The Absolute Weapon*, p. 73.

46 *Ibid.*, p. 76.

47 Henry Stimson and McGeorge Bundy, *On Active Service in Peace and War* (New York: Harper & Row, 1947), p. 645.

48 *Ibid.*, p. 641.

49 *Ibid.*, p. 645. Italics are added in the text, with the footnote, "This was the most important point of all."

Chapter 2. The failure of liberal diplomacy

1 Quoted in Emmett John Hughes, *The Ordeal of Power: A Political Memoir of the Eisenhower Years* (New York: Atheneum, 1965), p. 105.

2 Quoted in Adam Ulam, *Expansion and Coexistence: The History of Soviet Foreign Policy, 1917 – 67* (New York: Praeger, 1968), p. 416. A detailed outline of the proposal appears in Joseph Nogee, *Soviet Policy Towards International Control of Atomic Energy* (Notre Dame, Ind.: University of Notre Dame Press, 1961), p. 42.

3 Lloyd C. Gardner, *Architects of Illusion* (Chicago: Quadrangle Press, paperback, 1970), pp. 194 – 5.

4 See Alice Kimball Smith, *A Peril and a Hope: The Scientist's Movement in America, 1945 – 47* (Chicago: The University of Chicago Press, 1965).

5 *Ibid.*, pp. 13 – 14.

6 Bernhard G. Bechhoefer, *Postwar Negotiations for Arms Control* (Washington, D.C.: The Brookings Institution, 1961), p. 44.

7 Joseph I. Lieberman, *The Scorpion and the Tarantula* (Boston: Houghton Mifflin, 1970), p. 310; Nogee, *op. cit.*, pp. 36 – 9.

8 Leniece N. Wu, *The Baruch Plan: U.S. Diplomacy Enters the Nuclear Age.* Prepared for the Subcommittee on National Security Policy and Scientific Developments of the Committee on Foreign Affairs, U.S. House of Representatives, (Washington, D.C.: U.S. Government Printing Office, 1972). In his memoirs Vannevar Bush says of the Baruch Plan, "Of course, the approach to the United Nations got nowhere, but we all felt better for the try." Vannevar Bush, *Pieces of the Action* (New York: William Morrow, 1970), p. 298.

9 Smith, *op. cit.*, p. 129ff.

10 Wu, *op. cit.*, pp. 21 – 2.

11 *Ibid.*, p. 48.

12 "But before a country is ready to relinquish any winning weapons it must have more than words to reassure it. It must have a guarantee of safety, not only against the offenders in the atomic area but against the illegal uses of other weapons...why not? against war itself." Quoted in Lieberman, *op. cit.*, p. 300.

13 Walter Lippmann, "International Control of Atomic Energy," in Dexter Masters and Katherine Way, editors, *One World or None?* (London: Latimer House, 1947), p. 143.

14 Lieberman, *op. cit.*, pp. 282 – 3.

15 Quoted in Bechhoefer, *op. cit.*, p. 37.

16 Quoted in Wu, *op. cit.*, p. 33.

17 James Scott Brown, "Development of Diplomacy in Modern Times," in Edmund A. Walsh, editor, *The History and Nature of International Relations* (New York: Macmillan Co., 1922), p. 128. The author continues, "Any group of foreign states wishing to follow the example of the American states can. They do not need to confide so many powers upon the government of their creating unless they want to do so. But there are two things of fundamental importance which they should do, if they want their union to outlive its makers: they should eliminate the question of large and small States, as the wise men of the Federal Convention did, by providing that one of the chambers, which we call the Senate, should represent the States equally, and that a second chamber, which we call the House of Representatives, should represent the States according to population.... The Second requisite is that to the extent of its granted powers, the government of the Union should act upon each member of the State. States cannot act themselves, they must act by agents. An agent attempting to do an act contrary to the fundamental law can be restrained."

18 See Herbert Butterfield, "The New Diplomacy and Historical Diplomacy," in Herbert Butterfield and Martin Wight, editors, *Diplomatic Investigations* (Cambridge, Mass.: Harvard University Press, 1968), p. 181.

19 "Wilson sought to 'Lockeanize' or to Americanize, the global political system by creating a world society under law, to be preserved through the moral and material strength of the international social contract embodied in the League of Nations...a Wilsonian America was to be the historical agent of the world's transformation from chaos and imperialism to orderly liberal rationality." N. Gordon Levin, *Woodrow Wilson and World Politics* (New York: Oxford University Press, paperback, 1968), p. 4 – 5. Levin provides a good if sketchy general discussion of Wilson's international outlook, chiefly in the context of the issues that arose during the war and at Versailles. In *The Twenty Years' Crisis* (New York: Harper Torchbooks, 1964), first published in 1939, E. H. Carr offers an extensive critique of this liberal internationalism, which he regarded as "utopian."

20 This view was never officially proclaimed, but Stalin's policies were based upon it.

21 See Ulam, *op. cit.*, pp. 416 – 17. Nikita Khrushchev subsequently said as much. Through the Baruch Plan, he said, the United States "wanted to prevent the development of the atomic industry in other countries, leaving the monopoly of nuclear arms to the United States." He added, "We, of course, could not agree to this." Quoted in Chalmers Roberts, *The Nuclear Years* (New York: Praeger, 1971), p. 17.

22 Wu, *op. cit.*, p. 46.

23 John Lewis Gaddis, *The United States and the Origins of the Cold War* (New York: Columbia University Press, 1972), chapter 6.

24 Quoted in John W. Spanier and Joseph L. Nogee, *The Politics of Disarmament: A Study in Soviet –American Gamesmanship* (New York: Praeger, 1962), p. 56.
25 Quoted in Charles S. Maier, "Introduction: Science, Politics and Defense in the Eisenhower Era," in George Kistiakowsky, *A Scientist at the White House: The Private Diary of President Eisenhower's Special Assistant for Science and Technology* (Cambridge, Mass.: Harvard University Press, 1976), p. xxvii.
26 In retrospect this view seems at least partly correct; limited accords between the United States and the Soviet Union have made their coexistence easier by dissipating some of their mutual mistrust. But it also seems to many, in retrospect, that the Atoms for Peace plan was the wrong vehicle for reducing this antagonism. For the nuclear reactors whose world-wide distribution the program encouraged use fuel and produce byproducts that, with the proper treatment, can be converted to material from which nuclear weapons can be made.
27 Robert Gilpin, *American Scientists and Nuclear Weapons Policy* (Princeton, N.J.: Princeton University Press, 1962), pp. 142 – 3.
28 *Ibid.*, p. 150.
29 U.S. Arms Control and Disarmament Agency, *A Chronology of the Development of U.S. Disarmament Policy, 1953 – 60*, n.d., p. 23.
30 The effort to prevent others from matching these arsenals was also involved.
31 See Maier, *op. cit.*, p. xlviii.

Chapter 3. The origins of strategy

1 In *Proceedings of the American Philosophical Society* (Philadelphia, 1946), p. 48.
2 Robert Butow, *Japan's Decision to Surrender* (Stanford, Calif.: Stanford University Press, 1954), p. 3.
3 Henry Stimson and McGeorge Bundy, *On Active Service in Peace and War* (New York: Harper & Row, 1947), p. 630.
4 Gar Alperovitz has argued, in *Atomic Diplomacy* (New York: Simon & Schuster, 1965), that American motives for Hiroshima and Nagasaki had to do with resisting the spread of Soviet influence in Eastern Europe and Japan. His assertion rests on two propositions: the first is that American calculations about the bomb revolved *primarily* around the Soviet question. Alperovitz does show that the widening rift with Russia weighed on the minds of some American

policymakers in the spring and summer of 1945. One reason for trying to force Japan to surrender as quickly as possible was undoubtedly to prevent the Soviets from getting a foothold there. But the main reason was certainly to end the war with as little American bloodshed as possible. See Henry Stimson and McGeorge Bundy, *On Active Service in Peace and War* (New York: Harper & Row, 1947), pp. 620–30.

Alperovitz's second proposition is that Japan would have surrendered without the leveling of Hiroshima and Nagasaki, and that American officials realized this before the two bombs were dropped. It is difficult, even with close scrutiny in retrospect, to gauge precisely what role the bomb did play in Japan's decision to surrender. The authoritative account in English, by Robert Butow (*op. cit.*) gives some importance to Hiroshima and Nagasaki in pushing forward political forces already in motion within Japan, forces that ultimately brought about the capitulation. But Butow also stresses other events, in particular the concurrent Soviet decision to enter the war. (Butow, *op. cit.*, p. 151ff.) Still, even if it is conceded that the two nuclear attacks had little bearing on Japan's decision, it can scarcely be maintained that the Americans clearly and unanimously foresaw that this would be so. Alperovitz supports his assertion that they did so with postwar statements by military officers who had an interest in downplaying the importance of the new weapon, since their respective services didn't possess it (Alperovitz, *op. cit.*, p. 236ff.), or by officers who, like Eisenhower, had no direct command responsibility in the Pacific theater. Alperovitz also quotes Churchill's injunction that "It would be a mistake to suppose that the fate of Japan was settled by the atomic bomb. Her defeat was certain before the first bomb fell. . . ." (*op. cit.*, p. 238.) But the consideration governing those charged with deciding whether or not to use the bomb was not so much whether or not Japan would surrender as when, and at what cost. Perhaps Hiroshima and Nagasaki served to heighten Soviet suspicions and fears of the United States. And it is even possible that, as Martin Sherwin asserts, Henry Stimson "expected that once [the bomb's] power was demonstrated, the Soviets would be more accommodating to the American point of view on a wide range of issues. See Martin Sherwin, *A World Destroyed* (New York: Alfred A. Knopf, 1975), p. 190. Yet the evidence for even this tentative connection between the bomb and the Cold War is not overwhelming. And in neither case does it follow that in the official calculations of the United States, the decision to annihilate the two Japanese cities was made in order to impress the Russians.

Whether it was morally proper to use the two atomic bombs, even to end the war quickly and save American lives, is an endlessly debatable question. What can be said with some confidence is that it was scarcely debated at all by those in charge of American atomic policy in 1945. A related question is less easy to discuss: Why was the bomb not used in less destructive ways in pursuit of these unchallenged ends? One alternative, which the atomic scientists actively promoted, was to explode a bomb in an uninhabited part of Japan, perhaps offshore, to provide a vivid demonstration of its power and of the devastation that the Japanese risked if they did not surrender forthwith. The reasons why this suggestion, made in the "Franck Report" that came from the scientific group at the University of Chicago, was not accepted, are still not altogether clear. The logistics of a demonstration, however, would not have been easy to manage, and there was some worry that if a demonstration bomb did not explode the war effort would be set back. See David H. Frisch, "Scientists and the Decision to Bomb Japan," in Richard S. Lewis and Jane Wilson, editors, Alamogordo Plus Twenty-Five Years (New York: The Viking Press, 1971). Another alternative was waiting to see whether the destruction of Hiroshima would compel surrender, without mounting a second atomic attack on Nagasaki. The explanation (whether or not it is an adequate justification in another matter) for the second atomic raid is that the use of the two bombs was regarded as a single operation, which was designed, among other things, to "create the illusion that the United States had a stockpile of such weapons." See Walter Smith Schoenberger, "Decision of Destiny," in Paul R. Baker, editor, The Atomic Bomb (Hinsdale, Ill.: The Dryden Press, 1976), p. 182. On the morality of the use of the atomic bomb, see Michael Walzer, Just and Unjust Wars: A Moral Argument with Historical Illustrations (New York: Basic Books, 1977), pp. 263 – 8.

5   The Soviets certainly had some definite views. They wanted to make certain Germany could not strike eastward again. And they wanted reparations in some form for the damage they had suffered at German hands. But they seemed to have no blueprint for Germany's future. See Adam Ulam, Expansion and Coexistence: The History of Soviet Foreign Policy, 1917 – 67 (New York: Praeger, 1968), p. 440ff.

6   See Gaddis Smith, "Visions and Revisions of the Cold War," The New York Times Magazine (April 29, 1973), p. 48ff.

7 "NSC–68: A Report to the National Security Council by the Executive Secretary on United States Objectives and Programs for National Security," reprinted in the *U.S. Naval War College Review* (April 14, 1950), p. 54.

8 *Ibid.*, p. 66.

9 *Ibid.*, p. 108.

10 George Quester, *Nuclear Diplomacy* (New York: Dunellen, 1970), p. 7.

11 Warner R. Schilling, "The Politics of National Defense: Fiscal 1950," in Warner R. Schilling, Paul Y. Hammond, and Glenn H. Snyder, *Strategy, Politics and Defense Budgets* (New York: Columbia University Press, 1962), p. 35ff.

12 Samuel P. Huntington, *The Common Defense* (New York: Columbia University Press, 1961), p.44.

13 Quester, *op. cit.*, pp. 2–3.

14 For an estimate of its size, see *ibid.*, pp. 2–3.

15 For a discussion of the deterrent effects of increasingly destructive weaponry before 1945, see Robert Osgood, "The Expansion of Force," in Robert Osgood and Robert W. Tucker, *Force, Order and Justice* (Baltimore, Md.: The Johns Hopkins University Press, paperback, 1971), pp. 104–8; and for aerial bombardment in particular, see George Quester, *Deterrence Before Hiroshima* (New York: John Wiley, 1966).

16 "Mr. X" (George Kennan), "The Sources of Soviet Conduct," *Foreign Affairs* (July 1947).

17 Glenn H. Snyder, "The New Look of 1953," in Schilling, Hammond, and Snyder, *op. cit.*, pp. 406–10.

18 It may even have begun before that, since Soviet espionage probably provided some information about the Manhattan Project.

19 In March 1949 Churchill said, "It is certain that Europe would have been communized and London under bombardment long ago but for the deterrent of the atomic bomb in the hands of the United States." Huntington, *op. cit.*, p. 298. It was assumed in some quarters in the immediate postwar years that the American stockpile of atomic bombs, no matter how modest, served as a counter-weight to the large land armies that the Soviet Union deployed in Europe.

20 Huntington, *op. cit.*, pp. 304–5.

21 Bernard Brodie, "War in the Atomic Age," in Brodie, editor, *The Absolute Weapon* (New York: Harcourt Brace Jovanovich, 1946), p. 52.

22 Quoted in Norman Moss, *Men Who Play God* (New York: Harper & Row, 1968), p. 5.

23 The theme of the "liberation" of the Soviet satellites was especially favored by the right wing of the Republican Party in the early 1950s. Huntington, op. cit., p. 18.

24 Brodie, *The Absolute Weapon*, p. 76.

25 Dulles' speech is reprinted in Raymond O'Connor, editor, *American Defense Policy in Perspective: From Colonial Times to the Present Day* (New York: John Wiley, 1965), pp. 327 – 8.

26 See Snyder, op. cit., p. 465ff. ". . .The sum total of the administration's utterances gave the distinct impression that there had been a shift of policy in the direction of 'deterrence' by the threat of nuclear punishment." *Ibid.*, p. 467.

27 Edward Kolodziej, *The Uncommon Defense and Congress, 1945 – 1963* (Columbus: Ohio State University Press, 1966), p. 189ff.

28 *Ibid.*, p. 186.

29 "Transcript of Presidential Press Conference with Comment on Retaliation to Aggression," *The New York Times* (March 18, 1954), reprinted in W. Barton Leach, editor, *The New Look* (Air Command and Staff College, Maxwell Air Force Base, Ala., 1954), p. 320.

30 Dulles, "Remarks on Defense at News Conference," in *ibid.*, p. 311.

31 Snyder, op. cit., p. 388. See also George E. Lowe, *The Age of Deterrence* (Boston: Little, Brown, 1964), pp. 38 – 9.

32 The belief was still vivid a quarter century later, and the lesson still fresh for an American President. Gerald Ford cited it in the last of his three debates with Jimmy Carter. See *The New York Times* (October 23, 1976), p. 10.

33 See Jerome H. Kahan, *Security in the Nuclear Age* (Washington: The Brookings Institution, 1975), p. 19.

34 Edward S. Quade, "The Selection and Use of Strategic Bases: A Case History," in Quade, editor, *Analysis for Military Decisions* (Chicago: Rand McNally, 1966), p. 26.

35 Bruce L. R. Smith, *The RAND Corporation: Case Study of a Nonprofit Advisory Corporation* (Cambridge, Mass.: Harvard University Press, 1966), p. 229.

36 *Ibid.*

37 William Kaufmann, "The Requirements of Deterrence," in Kaufmann, editor, *Military Policy and National Security* (Princeton, N.J.: Princeton University Press, 1956), p. 21. This was originally published as Memorandum No. 7 of the Princeton Center of International Studies in 1954.

38 *Ibid.*, pp. 24 – 5.

39 *Ibid.*, p. 27.

40 *Ibid.*, p. 24.

41 William Kaufmann, "Limited War," in Kaufmann, editor, *op. cit.*, p. 104.

42 *Ibid.*, p. 107.

43 Other writers who stressed the need for a wider assortment of military capabilities were Robert Osgood, in *Limited War* (Chicago: University of Chicago Press, 1957), for example, pp. 60 – 1 and p. 126ff.; and Henry Kissinger, in *Nuclear Weapons and Foreign Policy* (New York: Harper & Row for the Council on Foreign Relations, 1957), for example, pp. 18 – 19.

44 Kolodziej, *op. cit.*, pp. 204 – 5. Ridgeway later published a memoir entitled *Soldier* that attacked the New Look.

45 Maxwell Taylor, *The Uncertain Trumpet* (New York: Harper & Row, 1959), p. 6.

46 See Kahan, *op. cit.*, pp. 30 – 1.

47 See Richard Cobden, *The Three Panics* (London: Wade, 1862).

48 Richard Aliano, *American Defense Policy From Eisenhower to Kennedy: The Politics of Changing Military Requirements* (Athens: Ohio University Press, 1975), p. 207; see also Marguerite Higgins, "How Many Pearl Harbors?" in Richard Witkin, editor, *The Challenge of the Sputniks* (Garden City, N.Y.: Doubleday, 1958).

49 Kolodziej, *op. cit.*, p. 270ff.

50 Aliano, *op. cit.*, pp. 1881 – 19.

51 Kahan, *op. cit.*, p. 14ff.

52 *Ibid.*, pp. 21 and 24; Kolodeziej, *op. cit.*, p. 294.

53 Quoted in Kahan, *op. cit.*, p. 33.

54 Secretary of Defense Neil McElroy was one. Aliano, *op. cit.*, p.114.

55 For an assessment of the reasons why the United States did not deploy missiles until the latter part of the decade, when the technology might have been perfected sooner if the government had turned its attention to the task earlier, see Edmund Beard, *Developing the ICBM: A Study in Bureaucratic Politics* (New York: Columbia University Press, 1976). For details of the various missile systems whose development began in the Eisenhower years, see Eugene M. Emme, editor, *The History of Rocket Technology* (Detroit: Wayne State University Press, 1964), especially chapters 7 and 8.

56 "Report to the President by the Security Resources Panel of the Office of Defense Mobilization Science Advisory Committee," the "Gaither Report," p. 1.

57 Albert Wohlstetter, "The Delicate Balance of Terror," reprinted in Henry Kissinger, editor, *Problems of National Strategy* (New York: Praeger, 1965), p. 54.

58 John F. Kennedy, *The Strategy of Peace* (New York: Harper & Row, 1960), p. 182.

59 *Ibid.*, pp. 61–3.

60 V. O. Key, Jr. (with the assistance of Milton C. Cummings, Jr.), *The Responsible Electorate* (Cambridge, Mass.: The Belknap Press of Harvard University Press, 1966).

61 Theodore H. White, *The Making of the President, 1960* (New York: Atheneum, 1961), p. 388.

Chapter 4. The foundations of stable deterrence

1 John F. Kennedy, *The Public Papers of the Presidents of the United States, 1961* (Washington, D.C.: United States Government Printing Office, 1964), p. 1.

2 *Ibid.*, p. 24.

3 The review consisted of reports by four task forces, on strategic forces and continental air defense, on the requirements for limited war, on research and development, and on military bases and installations. *Military Construction Authorization Bills, Number 9*, Committee on Armed Services, House of Representatives, Eighty-seventh Congress, 1961, p. 633.

4 And it was the third that year, since Eisenhower had delivered one before leaving office.

5 The remark is attributed to Robert McNamara. Henry Trewhitt, *McNamara: His Ordeal in the Pentagon* (New York: Harper & Row, 1971), p. 20.

6 Debates about what to do have taken place, but within party ranks. In 1952 a substantial fraction of the Republicans supported the presidential candidacy of Robert Taft, who favored an "isolationist" foreign policy. And in 1968 the Democratic Party was deeply split over the American war in Vietnam.

7 After the public pronouncements that made up the New Look, strategy did not receive as much public attention from Eisenhower and his associates as it got at the outset of the Kennedy presidency During the second Eisenhower term, there was a drift away from the principles of the New Look, especially the doctrine of "massive retaliation" as announced by Dulles in 1954, and toward meeting some of the strategic criticisms leveled against the administration. But there were few, if any, explicit, authoritative statements setting forth these changes.

8 Kennedy, *The Public Papers, 1961*, p. 230.

9 This ranking excludes the Attorney General, who, as the President's brother, had a special status.

10 Carl W. Borklund, *Men of the Pentagon: From Forrestal to McNamara* (New York: Praeger, 1966), p. 220.

11 *Military Procurement Authorization, Fiscal Year 1964.* Hearings before the Committee on Armed Services, United States Senate, 88th Congress, First Session, on HR 2440(S843), p. 89.

12 Kennedy, *The Public Papers, 1961*, p. 196, 231.

13 John F. Kennedy, *The Public Papers, 1962* (Washington, D.C.: United States Government Printing Office, 1963), p. 276.

14 Kennedy, *The Public Papers, 1961*, p. 211.

15 *Ibid.*, p. 231.

16 *Military Construction Authorization Bills*, Number 9, p. 634.

17 *Department of Defense Appropriations for 1962:* Subcommittee of the House Committee on Appropriations, 87th Congress, First Session, volume 7, part 3, p. 102.

18 Jerome H. Kahan, *Security in the Nuclear Age* (Washington, D.C.: The Brookings Institution, 1975), p. 95.

19 *Department of Defense Appropriations for 1962*, p. 4.

20 *Ibid.*

21 Finally forty-one submarines were built.

22 *Military Procurement Authorization, Fiscal Year 1964*, p. 74.

23 *Department of Defense Appropriations for 1962*, p. 128.

24 *Hearings on Military Posture and HR 2440*, Committee on Armed Services, House of Representatives, 88th Congress, First Session, January 30, 1963, p. 384.

25 Alain Enthoven and K. Wayne Smith, *How Much Is Enough?* (New York: Harper & Row, paperback, 1972), p. 9ff.

26 Quoted in William W. Kaufmann, *The McNamara Strategy* (New York: Harper & Row, 1964), p. 48.

27 Quoted in Henry Trewhitt, *op. cit.*, pp. 22 – 3.

28 The term is used by William T. R. Fox in his foreword to Michael Armacost, *The Politics of Weapons Innovation: The Thor-Jupiter Controversy* (New York: Columbia University Press, 1969), p. vii.

29 The history of procurement has a considerable literature. It begins with Samuel P. Huntington, *The Common Defense: Strategic Programs in National Politics* (New York: Columbia University Press, 1961), and includes a number of case studies of particular weapon systems, notably: Robert Art, *The TFX Controversy* (Boston: Little, Brown, 1968); Robert Coulam, *The Illusion of Choice* (Princeton, N.J.: Princeton University Press, 1977); and Ted Greenwood, *Making the MIRV* (Cambridge, Mass.: Ballinger, 1975); in addition to others mentioned elsewhere in this book. All these cases emphasize the internal political determinants of weapons programs, as distinct from external "strategic" considerations. More general discussions of "bureaucratic politics" can be found in Graham Allison, *Essence of Decision* (Boston: Little, Brown, 1971) and Morton Halperin, *Bureaucratic Politics and Foreign Policy* (Washington, D.C.: Brookings Institution, 1973).

30 *Department of Defense Appropriations for 1962*, House Appropriations Committee, p. 7.

31 See *Military Procurement Authorization, Fiscal Year 1964*, Senate Committee on Armed Services, p. 7.

32 See Enthoven and Smith, *op. cit.*, pp. 243 – 51.

33 *Military Procurement Authorization, 1964*, pp. 96 – 97. On Skybolt, see Richard Neustadt, *Alliance Politics* (New York: Columbia University Press, 1971), Chapter II, and Harold Macmillan, *At the End of the Day* (New York: Harper & Row, 1973), p. 357ff. Macmillan reports that at his meeting with Kennedy in Nassau the President "said at once that the decision to abandon Skybolt was not made for political reasons." The administration also offended the corporations that had contracted to build Skybolt. "Review of the World Scene: Television Interview with the President," December 17, 1962, in Richard P. Stebbins, editor, *Documents on American Foreign Relations, 1962* (New York: Harper & Row, 1963), p. 49.

34 Enforcing doctrinal integrity that the Kennedy administration officially adopted meant political combat. McNamara was brave and determined, but he was not a glutton for punishment, as a story told by one of his aides indicates: "One extremely frustrating experience I had was over my effort to eliminate the Nike-Hercules missiles around bomber bases in the South. We should never have had any air defense in the South in the first place, but Southern Congressmen had wanted them. This was bad enough, but to have Nike-Hercules missiles around them was absurd for these were completely ineffective. So I did a fancy analysis of their effectiveness in transferring them to protecting ICBMs. McNamara ignored the analysis in a preemptory and arbitrary way. He said that we just are not going to move them and that the same political problems were involved if we transferred them instead of eliminating them altogether. Besides, he continued, if we transferred them, that would have implied that I supported some effectiveness for Nike-Hercules, which was not the

case." Clark A. Murdock, "Impact of McNamara's Analytic Innovations on Civil – Military Relations," paper prepared for presentation
at The International Studies Association Convention, March 18,
1971, San Juan, Pueíto Rico.
35 "Projects to be Assigned Within the Department of Defense,"
Defense, 1-6/61, President's Office File, John F. Kennedy Library, p.
2.
36 Statement by Secretary of Defense Robert S. McNamara before
the House Committee on Armed Services on the Fiscal Year 1963 –
67 Defense Program and 1963 Defense Budget, January 24, 1962
(1962 Posture Statement). Mimeographed, p. 15.
37 *Hearings on Military Posture and HR 9751. To Authorize Appropriations during Fiscal Year 1963 for Aircraft, Missiles, and
Naval Vessels for the Armed Forces and for other Purposes.* The
Committee on Armed Services, House of Representatives, Eighty-
seventh Congress, Second Session, p. 3291. See also 1962 Posture
Statement, p. 15.
38 Enthoven and Smith, *op. cit.*, p. 175.
39 Theodore C. Sorensen, Recorded interview by Carl Kaysen,
March 26, 1964, John F. Kennedy Library, p. 4.
40 See Roger Hilsman, Recorded Interview by Joseph O'Connor,
August 14, 1970, John F. Kennedy Library, p. 14; Sorensen, Interview, p. 13; Desmond J. Ball, *The Strategic Missile Programme of the
Kennedy Administration, 1961 –63,* unpublished manuscript,
Strategic and Defence Studies Centre, Australian National University, Canberra, Australia, especially part three, chapter one.
41 McNamara later gave 800 as the optimal size for the Minuteman
fleet. See Desmond J. Ball, *op. cit.*, p. 269, 468. Ball's long and
exhaustively detailed manuscript addressed the question, "Why did
the Kennedy administration authorize 1,000 Minutemen, especially
since the missile gap turned out not to exist?" The answer he gives
has to do with the institutional preferences and political power of
the "quasi-sovereignties" within the executive branch of the federal
government.
42 McNamara, Defense Posture Statement, 1962, pp. 16 –17.
43 *Military Procurement Authorization, Fiscal Year 1964,* p. 39.
44 Statement by Secretary of Defense Robert S. McNamara before
the House Committee on Armed Services on the Fiscal Year 1964 –
68 Defense Program and 1964 Defense Budget (1963 Posture Statement). Mimeographed, January 30, 1963, p. 4.
45 *Military Procurement Authorization, Fiscal Year 1964,* Senate
Armed Services Committee, p. 126.

46 *Hearings on Military Posture*, House Armed Services Committee, January 30, 1963, p. 416.
47 *Military Procurement Authorization, 1964*, Senate Armed Services Committee, p. 335.
48 *Ibid.*, p. 330.
49 Quoted in Trewhitt, *op. cit.*, p. 116.
50 Accused of permitting a "nuclear stalemate," he replied, "It is our objective to maintain nuclear superiority measured in terms of numbers of warheads versus the Communist bloc." *Military Procurement Authorization 1964*, Senate Armed Services Committee, p. 88. According to one of his biographers, "There is no question that for a time McNamara deliberately obscured the outlook for an eventual nuclear standoff, long after he understood the prospect himself." Trewhitt, *op. cit.*, p. 115.
51 The figures are from Ball, *op. cit.*, pp. 140, 547.
52 Quoted in Bernard Brodie, *War and Politics* (New York: Macmillan, 1973), p. 377.
53 Quoted in George E. Lowe, *The Age of Deterrence* (Boston: Little, Brown, 1964), p. 106.
54 See Stewart Alsop, "Kennedy's Grand Strategy," *The Saturday Evening Post*, 235:13 (March 31, 1962).
55 See these messages in Kennedy, *The Public Papers of the President, 1961*, and Enthoven and Smith, *op. cit.*, p. 75.
56 Robert Amory, Recorded interview by Joseph E. O'Connor, February 9, 1964, John F. Kennedy Library, p. 80; Roswell Gilpatric, recorded interview by Dennis J. O'Brien, May 5, 1970, John F. Kennedy Library, p. 80.
57 John Newhouse, *U.S. Troops in Europe* (Washington, D.C.: The Brookings Institution, 1971), p. 12.
58 The proper division of responsibility for this tension remains a matter of debate. At the time, of course, the Americans blamed it on the Russians, and vice versa. Subsequently, it has been argued that Kennedy's rhetoric of international challenge and national sacrifice, and the steep increase in military expenditures that he ordered, had the effect of alarming the Soviets, and fueling their belligerence. The Russian bear started to growl, runs this line of argument, out of fear of being attacked. And if Kennedy's policies are laid to misperceptions by the Americans — overestimations of Soviet military might and a misreading of Khrushchev's "wars of national liberation" speech in early January of 1961 — then the events of 1961 – 2 come to appear as the consequence of a spiral of mutual misunderstanding. There is no way to test this interpretation without the records of the

deliberations of the Soviet government during the period, which are not likely soon to be available. It is plausible. But there is evidence to contradict it. The spell of aggressive Soviet conduct began before Kennedy took office, with the cancellation of the 1960 summit meeting. On the other hand, it may be that this cancellation represented not the opening round of a deliberate Soviet campaign of belligerence, but a reaction to the public disclosure of regular U-2 flights, to which Khrushchev felt he had to respond, and that the Soviets were prepared for smoother relations with the new administration.

59 Abram Chayes, recorded interview by Eugene Gordon, May 18, 1964, John F. Kennedy Library, p. 224.

60 "We are in a very dangerous period in our world history." Kennedy, *The Public Papers, 1961*, p. 30. "Our way of life is under attack. Those who make themselves our enemy are advancing around the globe. The survival of our friends is in danger." *Ibid.*, p. 336. See also *Ibid.*, pp. 261–2, 478, 431, for other references to the urgency of the Cold War.

61 *Ibid.*, p. 3.

62 "I don't believe the President had very much more in mind than opening, or strengthening, the channels of communications between himself and Khrushchev. He had no ambitious plans on what the meeting would accomplish, or any objectives to be secured, or any concessions he would wring out of Khrushchev. It was simply a fact that they were toe to toe in a great many specific areas and likely to be on a good many others, yet they had never met. They controlled, in a very real sense, the future of the world between them, and it was logical that they should meet instead of the President relying on what others told him about Khrushchev." Sorensen, interview, p. 29.

63 See Charles E. Bohlen, Recorded interview by Arthur Schlesinger, Jr., May 21, 1964, John F. Kennedy Library, p. 4. Sorensen claims that the encounter did not shake Kennedy as much as has been popularly supposed. Theodore C. Sorensen, *Kennedy* (New York: Harper & Row, 1965), p. 550. But Khrushchev recollected that during his last meeting with the President in Vienna, Kennedy "looked not only anxious but deeply upset." *Khrushchev Remembers: The Last Testament*. Translated and edited by Strobe Talbott (Boston: Little, Brown, 1974), p. 499. Of course neither Sorensen nor Khrushchev qualifies as a disinterested party on this subject.

64 Kennedy, *The Public Papers, 1961*, p. 442.

65 Sorensen, *Kennedy*, p. 584.

66 Sorensen, interview, pp. 32–4.

67 Kennedy, *The Public Papers, 1961,* p. 535.
68 *Ibid.,* p. 534.
69 *Ibid.,* p. 539.
70 *Ibid.,* p. 534.
71 See Seyom Brown, *The Faces of Power* (New York: Columbia University Press, 1968), p. 249, and *Khrushchev Remembers, The Last Testament,* p. 506ff.
72 Kennedy, *The Public Papers, 1961,* p. 558.
73 Draft Special Defense Message, Defense Message 1/6-62-2/1/62: Sorensen, 6f. President's Office File. John F. Kennedy Library, p. 7.
74 There was a third inducement to exploring the character of nuclear war. It was believed to make deterrence more credible. This belief carried the reasons for flexible response beyond the nuclear threshold. By being prepared to conduct a nuclear war the United States could keep the Soviet Union from starting one. "Unless one has a force that has capabilities for actual operations [in nuclear warfare]," McNamara testified in 1963, "and a force for which one has an operational plan, one, in my opinion, does not have a creditable deterrent." *Military Procurement Authorization, 1964,* Senate Armed Services Committee, p. 106.

Chapter 5. The rise and fall of nuclear war

1 Quoted in Bernard Brodie, "Technical Change, Strategic Doctrine, and Political Overtones," in Klaus Knorr, editor, *Historical Dimensions of National Security Policy* (Lawrence, Kansas: University of Kansas Press, 1976), p. 267.
2 Alain Enthoven and K. Wayne Smith, *How Much is Enough? Shaping the Defense Program, 1961 – 1962* (New York: Harper & Row, paperback, 1971), p. 124.
3 *Ibid.*
4 New York: Harper and Brothers for the Council on Foreign Relations, 1958.
5 See, for example, William W. Kaufmann, "The Crisis in Military Affairs," *World Politics,* X:4 (July 1958). "Apparently in his [Kissinger's] version of warfare, airmen do not get panicky and jettison their bombs or hit the wrong targets, missiles do not go astray, and heavily populated areas – whether rural or urban – do not suffer thereby. Surely this is wistful thinking." See also, James E. King, Jr., "Nuclear Weapons and Foreign Policy," *The New Republic,* CXXXVII, "I. Limited Defense," (July 1, 1957), pp. 18 – 21; "II. Lim-

ited Annihilation?" (July 15, 1957), pp. 16 – 18; and Bernard Brodie, "More About Limited War," *World Politics*, X:I (October 1957).

6   P. M. S. Blackett, *Studies of War; Nuclear and Conventional* (New York: Hill and Wang, 1962), p. 63.

7   See Henry Kissinger, "Limited War: Nuclear or Conventional?" in Donald Brennan, editor, *Arms Control, Disarmament, and National Security* (New York: Braziller, 1961).

8   John F. Kennedy, *A Compilation of Speeches, Statements and Remarks Delivered During His Service in the Congress of the United States.* Prepared by the Legislative Reference Service, Library of Congress, (Washington, D.C.: United States Government Printing Office, 1964), p. 915.

9   George H. Quester, *Nuclear Diplomacy: The First Twenty-five Years* (New York: Dunellen, 1970), p. 225. There was some doubt about precisely what this would mean in practice, how long the United States would be willing to wait, and how much ground it was willing to lose before loosing its atomic bolts. But it certainly underscored the Kennedy administration's extreme reluctance to loose them.

10   Enthoven and Smith, *op. cit.*, p. 128. A former CIA official recalled "a maneuver that was held in '60, '61, or '62 in the Tennessee – Mississippi area in which they sort of 'war gamed' on the ground the use of tactical nuclear weapons. And that did show a hell of a lot of destruction. If played on a highly populated area such as West Germany, there isn't much difference between whether you use tactical nukes than big nukes. Christ, if you'd fight a modern war as it would be fought with these things, remembering that these so-called nominal bombs are all about the size of the Hiroshima bomb, you'd have damn little left." Robert Amory, recorded interview by Joseph E. O'Connor, February 9, 1964, John F. Kennedy Library, p. 97.

11   Enthoven and Smith, *op. cit.*, p. 125.

12   *Ibid.*, pp. 126, 127.

13   "Statement of Secretary of Defense Robert S. McNamara before the House Armed Services Committee, The Fiscal Year 1964 – 68 Defense Program and 1964 Defense Budget" (1963 Posture Statement). Mimeographed, January 30, 1963, p. 18.

14   *Military Authorization, Fiscal Year 1964*, Hearings before the Committee on Armed Services, United States Senate, p. 85.

15   *Ibid.*, p. 159.

16   Richard Fryklund, *One Hundred Million Lives; Maximum Sur-*

vival in a Nuclear War (New York: Macmillan, 1962), chapter 2: and Desmond J. Ball, "The Strategic Missile Programme of the Kennedy Administration," unpublished manuscript, Australian National University, 1976, chapter II, pp. 62 – 8.

17 Fryklund, *op. cit.*, p. 32.

18 Jerome H. Kahan, *Security in The Nuclear Age: Developing U.S. Strategic Arms Policy* (Washington: The Brookings Institution, 1975), p. 227.

19 Ball, *op. cit.*, p. 379ff.

20 *Department of Defense Appropriations for 1963*, Part 2, House Appropriations Committee, p. 250. "We may have to retaliate with a single massive attack. Or, we may be able to use our retaliatory forces to limit damage done to ourselves, and our allies, by knocking out the enemy's bases before he has had time to launch his second salvo." Speech in Chicago, February 17, 1962, quoted in *The New York Times*, February 18, 1962.

21 "Memorandum to the President from McGeorge Bundy, Defense 1-6/62," President's Office File, John F. Kennedy Library.

22 McNamara's speech is reprinted in Richard Stebbins, editor, *Documents on American Foreign Relations, 1962* (New York: Harper & Row, 1963), p. 233.

23 *Ibid.*, p. 232.

24 *Ibid.*

25 "...Relatively weak national nuclear forces with enemy cities as their targets are not likely to be sufficient to perform even the function of deterrence. If they are small, and perhaps vulnerable on the ground or in the air, or inaccurate, a major antagonist can take a variety of measures to counter them. Indeed, if a major antagonist came to believe there was a substantial likelihood of its being used independently, this force would be inviting a preemptive strike against it." *Ibid.*

26 Harold Macmillan, the British Prime Minister, later observed that McNamara "could hardly have done anything more calculated to upset both his French and his British allies." Harold Macmillan, *At the End of the Day; 1961 – 63* (New York: Harper & Row, 1973), p. 334.

27 The city-avoidance strategy, like the decision to cancel the Skybolt program, represented the triumph of strategic over political considerations. In both cases the administration adopted policies that it regarded as advantageous in its military duel with the Soviet Union, but that, because they were not popular with European members, damaged the cohesion of the Atlantic Alliance. The Multilateral Force (MLF) reflected the opposite preference. It made (or at least was designed to make) political relations with the allies easier, but complicated the military confrontation with the Soviet Union. In keeping with one of the axioms of the "bureaucratic politics" school of analysis – that "where you stand depends on where you sit" – the city-avoidance doctrine emanated from a corner of the government, the Office of the Secretary of Defense, that interested itself exclusively in strategic matters. The MLF was hatched by men in the Policy Planning Staff of the State Department, for whom, by contrast, international political considerations were paramount. The final verdict on both, as on most foreign policy matters of significance, however, rested with the President.

28 "McNamara's Strategy," *The New Republic,* (July 2, 1962), p. 5.

29 William V. O'Brien, "The Fate of Counterforce," *The Commonweal* (May 17, 1963), p. 218.

30 See Henry Kissinger, *The Troubled Partnership: A Reappraisal of the Atlantic Alliance* (Garden City, N.Y.: Doubleday Anchor Books, paperback, 1966), p. 101.

31 See James Wadsworth, "Counterforce," *The Saturday Review* (July 28, 1962), p. 22.

32 *Ibid.,* p. 29.

33 Michael Brower, "Controlled Thermonuclear War," *The New Republic* (July 30, 1962), p. 12.

34 McNamara interviewed by Stewart Alsop, *Saturday Evening Post* (December 1, 1962), p. 18.

35 *Military Procurement Authorization, Fiscal Year 1964,* Hearings before the Committee on Armed Services, United States Senate, 88th Congress, First Session, on HR 2440 (S843), p. 125. "I believe that the current Soviet strategy would most probably lead to a strike against our urban areas in the event of nuclear war and I am inclined to think that the [deleted] force which appears to us that they are planning for near future, say the next 2 to 3 years, would imply a continuation of that strategy." *Ibid.,* p. 143.

36 "In the Ann Arbor speech I believe I stated essentially the policy that I believe today and that we are following today; that our total force requirement is determined on an assumption that we must have sufficient strategic forces to absorb a full Soviet strike, and survive with sufficient strength to absolutely destroy the Soviet Union. Secondly, that in determining the force required to destroy the Soviet Union, we consider the possibility, but it is only a possibility, that we may wish to launch that force in waves, if you will.

"Now the fact that it is launched in waves means that certain portions of it are exposed to potential further destruction during the period it is withheld prior to launch. This, in turn, increases our requirements for secure communications, secure command and control centers, and invulnerable forces." *Military Procurement Authorization, Fiscal Year 1964*, Senate Armed Services Committee, p. 317.

37 Jerome Kahan, *Security in the Missile Age* (Washington, D.C.: The Brookings Institution, 1975), p. 91ff.
38 Benson D. Adams, *Ballistic Missile Defense* (New York: American Elsevier, 1971), p. 10.
39 *Ibid.*, p. 11.
40 There are three parts to the task. A ballistic missile defense system must detect incoming missiles. It must discriminate between the warheads and the decoys that have been sent with them. And it must then destroy the missiles. (*Ibid.*, p. 78.) For these three operations a missile defense system needs radars to sight and track its quarry, computers to plot their trajectories and sort out the true missiles from the bogus ones that have been sent to confound the system, missile interceptors that carry their own weapons to destroy the incoming ones, and an interconnected command, control, and communications system. (*Ibid.*, p. 3.) All this requires an exceedingly complicated piece of machinery.

Defense systems have come in two models, which differ in the territory they can protect. A "point defense" system intercepts the intruding missile in the final stage of its trajectory, and thus cannot defend much territory by itself. An "area defense," on the other hand, is designed to cut off tho flight of incoming weapons in midcourse, and can patrol a wider patch of its own country. Each has advantages and shortcomings. Although area defense spreads a broad net over a populated area, that net is relatively flimsy. In the phases of the missile's flight at which it is aimed "blank bullets" — decoys — are extraordinarily difficult to distinguish from live ones, and the chances are good that some of each will get through the protective net to their targets. (See *Military Procurement Authorization, Fiscal Year 1963*, Senate Armed Services Committee, p. 36.) And of course the intercepting "bullet" in an area defense system has much further to travel. Point defense systems have more reliable "kill" ratios, but more units are needed to erect a shield over most of a nation's population. And point defense presents a special problem. Defense systems ordinarily use nuclear weapons to destroy the incoming (and also, presumably, nuclear) missiles. Since they would detonate inside the earth's atmosphere, perhaps only a few miles above its surface, a city defended by a point system might, while escaping the full force of an approaching missile, would still find itself pelted with the radioactive fallout that resulted from the explosion.

41 Adams, *op. cit.*, p. 22.

42 Quoted in *ibid.*, p. 19.

43 "In our lifetime, I assume that the development of the bomb and the missile has been the great change in the balance of power up to now, and that the next great change will come as a result of the development of a successful anti-missile missile." McNamara testimony in *Hearings on Military Posture, Fiscal Year 1963*, House Armed Services Committee, p. 3217.

44 Quoted in Adams, *op. cit.*, p. 28, who comments: "This was the first of the eight successive and almost identical pronouncements by Secretaries of Defense which, while development activities would continue, would consider production and deployment of an ABM as being premature." *Ibid.*, p. 29.

45 *Department of Defense Appropriations for 1962*, Subcommittee of the House Committee on Appropriations, 87th Congress, First Session, p. 16.

46 *Ibid.*, p. 76.

47 *Ibid.*

48 *Ibid.*

49 "Statement by Secretary of Defense Robert S. McNamara before the House Committee on Armed Services on the Fiscal Year 1963 – 67 Defense Program and 1963 Defense Budget" (1962 Posture Statement). Mimeographed, January 24, 1962, p. 25.

50 The President took the same position: "One of the problems that we have now, he said at the end of the year, "is the question of whether we should begin to put out the Nike-Zeus system, which is an anti-missile system around this country. We hope sometime to develop a systen which will permit us to fire a missile at a missile coming towards us and destroy it, and thereby prevent an atomic attack on the United States. But it will cost billions. There is no sense going ahead until that system is perfected. Some think now is the time, but we are going to wait for a further period of investigation." "Review of the World Scene: Television Interview with the President, December 17, 1962," in Stebbins, editor, *op. cit.*, p. 50.

51 "Statement by Secretary of Defense Robert S. McNamara before the House Committee on Armed Services on the Fiscal Year 1964 – 68 Defense Program and the 1964 Defense Budget" (1963 Posture Statement). Mimeographed, January 30, 1963, pp. 46 – 8. See also Adams, *op. cit., p. 50.*
52 1963 Posture Statement, p. 49.
53 *Military Procurement Authorization, Fiscal Year 1964,* Senate Armed Services Committee, p. 70.
54 *Military Procurement Authorization, Fiscal Year 1964,* House Armed Services Committee, p. 548.
55 Stebbins, editor, *op. cit.,* pp. 50 – 1. Proponents of missile defense have often conceded that the striking force on each side must be limited for defense to be effective.
56 See Morton H. Halperin, "The Decision to Deploy the ABM: Bureaucratic and Domestic Politics in the Johnson Administration," *World Politics,* XXV:1 (October 1972).
57 The original ABM treaty permitted deployment of two ABM systems. The number was later reduced to one. But the United States has built none. For further discussion, see Chapter VIII.
58 *Civil defense, 1961,* Hearings before a Subcommittee on Government Operations, House of Representatives, Eighty-seventh Congress. First Session,·Military Operations Subcommittee, p. 6.
59 1963 Posture Statement, p. 49.
60 A notable one was Chet Holifield of California. See Thomas J. Kerr, "The Civil Defense Shelter Program: A Case Study of the Politics of National Security Policy Making," unpublished doctoral dissertation. Syracuse University, 1970, p. 45.
61 *Ibid.,* p. 229.
62 John F. Kennedy, *The Public Papers of the Presidents of the United States, 1961* (Washington, D.C.: United States Government Printing Office, 1962)-, p. 339.
63 Harland Moulton, *From Superiority to Parity: The United States and the Strategic Arms Race, 1961 – 1971* (Westport, Conn.: Greenwood Press, 1972) p. 58.
64 Carl Kaysen, "Memorandum on Civil Defense: Appendix: Draft Program," Staff Memorandum, Sorensen, 1961 – 63, President's Office File, John F. Kennedy Library.
65 Kennedy, *The Public Papers, 1961,* p. 402. Theodore Sorensen says that Kennedy felt "as a matter of conscience that, in the event of a nuclear exchange of any kind, major or minor, rational or irrational, it would be a terrible thing to have any number of civilians killed who might have been saved had the President made an effort

to save them through his civil defense shelter program." Theodore Sorensen, recorded interview by Carl Kaysen, March 26, 1964, John F. Kennedy Library, p. 8. See also Arthur Schlesinger, Jr., *A Thousand Days: John F. Kennedy in the White House* (Boston: Houghton Mifflin, 1965), p. 47. Sorensen also says that Kennedy believed that a national civil defense program would strengthen his bargaining power with the Soviets and reinforce the strength of the American deterrent. "He thought he could act more freely and flexibly if the civilian population of the country could be protected from the attack another country might launch as a part of our involvement in international affairs." Sorensen, *op cit.*, p. 8. See also George H. Quester, *Nuclear Diplomacy: The First Twenty-Five Years* (New York: Dunellen, 1970), p. 231. This logic would have applied, of course, to any war-fighting program.

66 "Everyone thought. . .that Governor [Nelson A.] Rockefeller was likely to be his opponent in 1964. Rockefeller was a constant advocate of a large shelter program, and the President felt it was inconsistent with his own posture to be advocating less than the Republicans in an area which appeared to represent an example of American lag." Sorensen interview, p. 8. There was also political pressure within Kennedy's own party. Senator Stuart Symington, whose presidential hopes had bloomed briefly in 1960 and then wilted, and who, as a former Secretary of the Air Force, had weighty credentials in defense matters, told McNamara in April of 1961: "It would seem vitally important, based on past history and the current nuclear age, that if we are attacked, there must be people with training and authority to tell people where to go and what to do. It seems to me that more and more we are faced with the fact that civil defense is just as much a part of defense as all other forms of defense. Therefore, Mr. Chairman, I would ask that the Chairman of the Joint Chiefs, or anybody Secretary McNamara decided on, make a statement of the position of the Department of Defense on civil defense at this time." *Department of Defense Appropriations, Fiscal Year 1962*, House Appropriations Committee, p. 101.

67 *Department of Defense Appropriations for 1962*, Senate Appropriations Committee, p. 1637.

68 *Ibid.*

69 Kennedy, *The Public Papers, 1961*, p. 402.

70 *Department of Defense Appropriations, Fiscal Year 1964*, House Appropriations Committee, p. 577. Congressman Long made the estimate, and McNamara concurred with it.

71   *Ibid.* p. 578.
72   Sorensen, interview p. 8.
73   *Ibid.* See also Schlesinger, *op. cit.*, p. 747.
74   Sorensen, interview, p. 8.
75   Kennedy, *The Public Papers, 1961,* p. 536.
76   Schlesinger, *op. cit.*, p. 748.
77   *Civil Defense, 1961,* House Military Operations Subcommittee, p. 143. Downtown Detroit was not considered a safe place at night even under conditions of nuclear peace.
78   *Military Applications of Nuclear Technology,* Hearing before the Subcommittee on Military Applications of the Joint Committee on Atomic Energy of the Congress of the United States, Ninety-third Congress, First Session, May 22 and June 29, 1973, p. 107.
79   *Ibid.*, p. 35.
80   See Desmond J. Ball, "Déjà Vu," California Arms Control Seminar, 1976.
81   For details see Steuart Pittman, in Eugene Wigner, editor, *Who Speaks for Civil Defense?* (New York: Scribner, 1968).
82   "My personal characterization of our strategy as it relates to our strategic forces is one of nuclear deterrence. I think the important question is not do we or don't we have a deterrent strategy. The important question is what will our nuclear forces deter. . . .I feel quite certain that if the Soviets are rational, our strategic forces program will deter the Soviets from launching a first strike against this country." *Hearings on Military Posture for Fiscal Year 1964,* House Armed Services Committee, p. 415.
83   *Ibid.*, p. 392.
84   *Ibid.*, p. 391.
85   Carl von Clausewitz, *On War*, edited and translated by Michael Howard and Peter Paret (Princeton, N.J.: Princeton University Press, 1976), p. 605.
86   And if it were possible to fight a nuclear war it would become difficult to deter one, since there would no longer be mutual assured destruction. Hence deterrence through the threat of assured destruction and damage-limitation are, in a sense, alternatives.

Chapter 6. The great fright: the Cuban missile crisis

1   Quoted in Norman Cousins, *The Improbable Triumvirate* (New York: Norton, 1972), p. 46.

2 *Military Procurement Authorization*, Fiscal Year 1964, Hearings before the Committee on Armed Services, United States Senate, Eighty-eighth Congress, First Session, p. 85.

3 Robert F. Kennedy, *Thirteen Days* (New York: Norton, 1969), p. 17.

4 Theodore C. Sorensen, *Kennedy* (New York: Harper & Row, 1965), p. 679.

5 Two principals have set down their recollections directly; Robert Kennedy, in *Thirteen Days*, and Theodore C. Sorensen, in *Kennedy*, Chapter XXIV. Sorensen covers the same ground, but with some additional information, in his Oral History Interview for the John F. Kennedy Library. Three other accounts of the crises are tantamount to primary sources: Arthur M. Schlesinger, *A Thousand Days* (Boston: Houghton Mifflin, 1965), Chapter XXX; Roger Hilsman, *To Move a Nation* (Garden City, N.Y.: Doubleday, 1965), Part V; and Elie Abel, *The Missile Crisis* (Philadelphia: Lippincott, 1966). Schlesinger and Hilsman, although neither took direct part in shaping American policy during the missile crisis, had access to those who did as high officials in the Kennedy administration. And Abel conducted extensive interviews with the participants. Finally, a number of official documents from the missile crisis have been declassified, notably the crucial personal correspondence between President Kennedy and Chairman Khrushchev. The record for the Soviet side is far less complete. It includes public statements, Khrushchev's letters to Kennedy, and the two volumes of memoirs published in the west under the title *Khrushchev Remembers*, translated and edited by Strobe Talbott (Boston: Little, Brown, 1971 and 1974; the second volume has the subtitle *The Last Testament*.) Both these volumes touch on the events of October 1962. They are the fruit of the ramblings and ruminations into a tape recorder of an old man without access to official records, whose memory could scarcely have been flawless and who had not cultivated the habit of telling all he knew. But the words are his, as tests of the tapes from which they are taken verify. And they make a valuable addition to the literature of the crisis.

6 Sorensen, *Kennedy*, p. 671

7 *Ibid.*, p. 668.

8 Robert Kennedy, *op. cit.*, p. 25.

9 Sorensen, *Kennedy*, p. 668.

10 On the failure of intelligence to detect the missiles sooner, see Abel, *op. cit.*, p. 18.

11   David L. Larson, editor, *The "Cuban Crisis" of 1962: Selected Documents and Chronology* (Boston: Houghton Mifflin, 1963), p. 17.

12   Robert Kennedy, *op. cit.*, p. 52.

13   Sorensen, *Kennedy*, p. 674.

14   The group included: Secretary of State Dean Rusk, Under-Secretary George Ball, Latin-American Assistant Secretary Edwin Martin, Deputy Under Secretary Alexis Johnson, and Soviet expert Llewellyn Thompson; Secretary of Defense Robert McNamara, Deputy Secretary Roswell Gilpatric, Assistant Secretary Paul Nitze, and Chairman of the Joint Chiefs of Staff General Maxwell Taylor; Director of the Central Intelligence Agency John McCone; Attorney General Robert Kennedy, Treasury Secretary Douglas Dillon, and White House aides McGeorge Bundy and Theodore Sorensen. Others sitting in on one or more meetings were Ambassador to France Charles ("Chip") Bohlen, Deputy CIA Director Marshall Carter, Vice-President Johnson, White House aide Kenneth O'Donnell, deputy USIA Director Donald Wilson, and Adlai Stevenson, Dean Acheson, and Robert Lovett. *Ibid.*

15   See Robert Kennedy, *op. cit.*, p. 167.

16   The Soviets never explicitly promised not to put *nuclear* weapons in Cuba. They repeatedly foreswore offensive ones, and steadfastly insisted throughout the crisis that the MRBMs and the IRBMs were in place for strictly *defensive* purposes. It is not likely, however, that the crisis was touched off by a misunderstanding. See Graham T. Allison, *Essence of Decision: Explaining the Cuban Missile Crisis* (Boston: Little, Brown, 1971), p. 6.

17   Robert Kennedy, *op. cit.*, p. 169.

18   *Ibid.*, p. 168.

19   Allison, *op. cit.*, p. 64.

20   Robert Kennedy, *op. cit.*, p. 109.

21   *Ibid.*, p. 205.

22   *Ibid.*, p. 211.

23   Alexander George in Alexander George, David K. Hall, and William E. Simons, *The Limits of Coercive Diplomacy* (Boston: Little, Brown, 1971), and Ole Holsti, in *Crisis, Escalation, War* (Montreal: McGill-Queens, 1972), for example, take the missile crisis to be an example of a general feature of international politics; "coercive diplomacy" in the first instance; a crisis, defined as a rapid sequence of events leading toward war, in the second.

24   Fidel Castro may not have been wholly enthusiastic about receiving the missiles. See *Khrushchev Remembers: The Last Testa-*

ment, p. 511, and Arthur M. Schlesinger, Jr., *Robert Kennedy and His Times* (Boston: Houghton Mifflin, 1978), p. 502 – 3. For a discussion of the role of international law and organization in the crisis, see Abram Chayes, *The Cuban Missile Crisis: International Crises and The Role of Law* (New York: Oxford University Press, 1974).

25 Robert Kennedy, *op. cit.,* pp. 166 – 7.

26 David L. Larson, editor, *op. cit.,* p. 3.

27 Khrushchev insisted to the end that the missiles were defensive in character. See his letters of October and his conversation with American businessman William Knox, described in Abel, *op. cit.,* p. 151ff. This is not to say that the crisis came about through a misunderstanding, and that if Kennedy had only made his warning clearer the missiles would never have been sent. It is rather to argue that the political provocation that the missiles represented was less severe than it would have been if their deployment had more directly and explicitly violated a warning by the American President.

28 In theory the President's September warnings were not directed against strictly *nuclear* weapons, but in fact they were. The letter of his statements would have prohibited nonnuclear ground-to-ground missiles, and allowed nuclear defensive ones. But there is no evidence that the Soviets wanted to install the first, or had built the second. See also George Quester, *Nuclear Diplomacy* (New York: Dunellen, 1970), p. 237.

29 "Press Conferences, 9/13/62: Background III." President's Office File, John F. Kennedy Library. For some reasons why it may have been decided not to issue the statement in this form, see Quester, *op. cit.,* p. 237.

30 Quester, *ibid.,* p. 239; Roberta Wohlstetter and Albert Wohlstetter, *Controlling the Risks in Cuba,* Adelphi Papers, Number 17 (London: The Institute for Strategic Studies, 1965). Of course the Americans could not be certain that, once installed, the weapons would remain forever under Soviet control.

31 Robert Kennedy, *op. cit.,* p. 166.

32 Abel, *op. cit.,* p. 51.

33 Roswell Gilpatric, Recorded interview by Dennis J. O'Brien, February 9, 1964, John F. Kennedy Library, p. 53.

34 Abel, *op. cit.,* p. 52. Interpretations after the fact also differ on this point. Arthur Schlesinger downgrades the effect of the missiles on the military (as distinct from the political) balance between the United States and the Soviet Union. Schlesinger, *op. cit.,* p. 796. But Arnold L. Horelick and Myron Rush, *Strategic Power and Soviet*

Foreign Policy (Chicago: University of Chicago Press, 1966), p. 137ff, as well as Allison, *op. cit.*, pp. 53 – 4, and Wohlstetter and Wohlstetter, p. 11, count them as important contributions to the Soviet strategic force, while admitting their political value as well. Of course, the Soviets might have sent more missiles to Cuba. But this would have taxed their capacity to control them. See Quester, *op. cit.*, p. 239. In any case it seems clear that the political import of the missiles weighed most heavily with the President.

35 Quoted in Bernard Brodie, *Escalation and the Nuclear Option* (Princeton, N.J.: Princeton University Press, 1966), p. 52.

36 *Khrushchev Remembers*, p. 493.

37 "Messages Exchanged by President Kennedy and Chairman Khrushchev During the Cuban Missile Crisis of October 1962," *The State Department Bulletin*, November 19, 1973, p. 636.

38 *Ibid.*, p. 638.

39 *Ibid.* It is arguable that these, too, were calculated for effect, to impress the Americans with the risks they were running. But the correspondence, especially the long, rambling first letter of October 26, does not seem wholly calculated in tone.

40 The United States had 156 ICBMs fully operational in October 1962, and between 188 and 190 were placed on Emergency War Order. The Soviet Union had deployed only about 30; and few were in a state of war readiness. Desmond J. Ball, *The Strategic Missile Program of the Kennedy Administration, 1961 – 1963*, unpublished manuscript, Australian National University, 1977, pp. 131, 542.

41 Robert Kennedy, *op. cit.*, p. 98.

42 "Messages," p. 65.

43 *Ibid.*, p. 637.

44 *Ibid.*, p. 654.

45 Among the other objections to a blockade were "the obvious invitation to the Soviets to respond by blockading Berlin. . .[and] that it was difficult to see the logical connection between the Soviet action and our responses." Theodore Sorensen, Recorded Interview by Carl Kaysen, March 26, 1964, John F. Kennedy Library, p. 52. Robert Kennedy's preference for a blockade rather than an air strike stemmed in part from moral qualms about surprise attacks and the killing of civilians. Schlesinger, *Robert Kennedy*, p. 509 – 10.

46 Sorensen, Interview, p. 152. Much the same account, but without naming Acheson as the individual involved, referring to him only as a "consultant," appears in Sorensen, *Kennedy*, p. 685.

47 Robert Kennedy, *op. cit.*, p. 76 – 77.

48 Ibid., p. 82. See also Abel, op. cit., p. 172.

49 Robert Kennedy, op. cit., p. 58.

50 See Alexander George in George, Hall, and Simons, op. cit., p. 126ff.

51 Sorensen, Interview, p. 61; George, op. cit., p. 97.

52 Sorensen, Kennedy, p. 716.

53 The quote is from Barbara Tuchman, The Guns of August (New York: Macmillan, 1962), p. 49. For McNamara's expression of this fear, see Schlesinger, Robert Kennedy, p. 510.

54 Robert Kennedy, op. cit., p. 99. See also Sorensen, Interview, p. 52.

55 Robert Kennedy, op. cit., p. 127.

56 The term was coined, and the distinction from deterrence drawn first, by Thomas C. Schelling, in Arms and Influence (New Haven, Conn.: Yale University Press, 1966), p. 69ff.

57 Jack M. Schick, The Berlin Crisis (Philadelphia: University of Pennsylvania Press, 1971), p. 209.

58 I am indebted for this analogy to Samuel Weiss.

59 Writing several years later, Bernard Brodie commented unfavorably upon the tendency of American participants in the missile crisis to "think or at least talk in absolute terms." Escalation and the Nuclear Option, p. 118. And perhaps war in the Caribbean in 1962 would not have become nuclear war. (See Wohlstetter and Wohlstetter, op. cit., p. 25.) What is important is that the Americans, and the Russians, feared that it would, and that this common fear shaped their policies. And Brodie admitted that such thinking might recur: "One has to be ready, it appears, for a kind of crisis induced regression to older patterns of thinking about war and peace." Brodie, Ibid. By the final days of the crisis, American intelligence had established that the Soviet troops guarding the missile sites were equipped with tactical nuclear weapons and this, it might be argued, made the chance that war would turn into nuclear war greater than it would have been under other circumstances. See George, op. cit., p. 728. But military options were open to the American side that would not have engaged these weapons directly, like bombing the missile sites. (The invasion of Cuba would have been another matter.) And the President was extremely diffident about attacking even before the tactical nuclear weapons were discovered.

60 See Michael Mandelbaum, "International Stability and Nuclear Order: The First Nuclear Regime," in David C. Gompert, et al., Nuclear Weapons and World Politics (New York: McGraw-Hill, 1977), p. 17.

61 CIA Memorandum, October 24, 1962. Executive Committee Meetings 1–5, 10/23/62–10/25/62, National Security File, John F. Kennedy Library.

62 "Messages," p. 636.

63 *Ibid.*

64 Larson, editor, *op. cit.*, pp. 11, 131.

65 The phrase is Dean Rusk's.

66 George, *op. cit.*, pp. 102–3.

67 Draft Telegram to American Embassy in Brazil, Cuba, General, 10/26–10/27, 1962, National Security File, John F. Kennedy Library. Also Sorensen, interview, p. 50; and Schlesinger, *Robert Kennedy*, p. 513.

68 See *The New York Times* (September 23, 1973), p. 16.

69 "Messages," p. 642.

70 Robert Kennedy, *op. cit.*, pp. 202–3.

71 *Ibid.*, p. 207.

72 *Ibid.*, p. 216.

73 "Letter from Stevenson to the President, November 22, 1962," Cuba, 1962, President's Office File, John F. Kennedy Library. The reluctance to make a public pledge not to invade the island is indicated in "Briefing Paper for the President's Press Conference. Subject: Limits of Your No-Invasion of Cuba Pledge," Press Conference, 11/20/62, Background II. President's Office File, John F. Kennedy Library.

74 "There is some disagreement about whether Stevenson thought this trade a good one, or merely suggested that it be considered, or warned that the Russians might request it." Abel, *op. cit.*, pp. 94–6. See also Sorensen, *Kennedy*, pp. 695–6.

75 Gilpatric, Interview, p. 52.

76 Robert Kennedy, *op. cit.*, p. 95.

77 *Ibid.*, p. 119. But on Friday evening, several members of the Executive Committee did "develop a contingency plan for withdrawing the Turkish Jupiters, should such a step become necessary." Gilpatric, Interview, p. 52.

78 Robert Kennedy, *op. cit.*, p. 199. The Soviets may have incorrectly detected an official signal in Walter Lippmann's New York Herald Tribune column suggesting a Cuban-for-Turkish missile exchange. Abel, *op. cit.*, p. 57.

79 Robert Kennedy, *op. cit.*, pp. 108–9.

80 John F. Kennedy, *The Public Papers of the Presidents of the United States, 1963* (Washington, D.C.: United States Government Printing Office, 1964), p. 98. In his memoirs Khrushchev says of

Kennedy's concession on Turkish missiles: "We knew perfectly well that this pledge was of a symbolic nature: the American rockets in Turkey and Italy were already obsolete, and the Americans would promptly replace them with more modern ones. Besides, the U.S. was already equipping its navy with Polaris missiles. Nevertheless, by agreeing even to symbolic measures, Kennedy was creating the impression of mutual concessions." Khrushchev, *Khrushchev Remembers, The Last Testament*, p. 512. He may have underrated their importance. They certainly had some political value to the Turks, in the same way that the Western Europeans believed that the tactical nuclear weapons stationed within their borders bound the United States to their defense. See Quester, *op. cit.*, p. 238; George, *op. cit.*, p. 132; and Schlesinger, *Robert Kennedy*, p. 518 – 22.

81 See Chapter 1, The Two Schools of Diplomacy.

82 Without firm evidence, any assessment of the Soviet reasons for putting the missiles in Cuba in the first place must fall into the realm of speculation. Extensive interpretations appear in Arnold Horelick and Myron Rush, *op. cit.*, and Herbert Dinerstein, *The Making of a Missile Crisis, October 1962* (Baltimore: Johns Hopkins University Press, 1976). See also Adam Ulam, *Expansion and Coexistence: The History of Soviet Foreign Policy, 1917 – 67* (New York: Praeger, 1968), chapter XI. Allison, *op. cit.*, has a useful summary of the various hypotheses about Soviet motives.

83 Sorensen, *Kennedy*, p. 700; Sorensen, Interview, p. 50.

84 Larson, editor, *op. cit.*, p. 48.

85 *Ibid.*, p. 50.

86 Abel, *op. cit.*, p. 169. Another international body, the Organization of American States, also became involved in the missile crisis. But here, again, the United States used the OAS not to work out a solution to the affair, but to muster support for the American position. See *ibid.*, p. 127ff.

87 Henry Pachter, *Collision Course: The Cuban Missile Crisis and Coexistence* (New York: Praeger, 1962), p. 97. In his October 28 letter transmitted the day before to Khrushchev accepting the offer to settle the crisis, Kennedy noted that "the distinguished efforts of Acting Secretary General U Thant have greatly facilitated both our tasks." *Robert Kennedy*, *op. cit.*, p. 213.

88 The details of the Soviet withdrawal were supposed to be worked out under UN auspices. But the talks in New York turned into private discussions between John McCloy, Adlai Stevenson, and Roswell Gilpatric for the United States, and Deputy Foreign Minister

Vasily Kuznetsov for the Soviet Union. Since Fidel Castro forbade inspection teams from visiting Cuba, the United Nations took no real part in liquidating the crisis.

89 Schlesinger, *A Thousand Days*, p. 821.

90 "Memorandum for the President from Pierre Salinger," October 30, 1962: Pierre Salinger, President's Office File, John F. Kennedy Library. Salinger reported Norman Cousins, editor of the *Saturday Review*, telling Zhukov that while "he could only speak for himself," he "felt confident that the President would not crow about such a victory nor would he do anything to humiliate the Soviet Union; that the President was always a firm but reasonable man."

91 Abel, *op. cit.*, p. 175.

92 *Ibid.*, p. 76. Schlesinger, *A Thousand Days*, p. 825 – 6.

93 Abel, *op. cit.*, p. 177.

94 Robert Kennedy, *op. cit.*, p. 24.

95 *Ibid.*, pp. 65 – 6; Schlesinger, *A Thousand Days*, p. 817.

96 Robert Kennedy, *op. cit.*, p. 107 – 9.

97 Nikita Khrushchev, *Khrushchev Remembers*, p. 499.

98 *Ibid.*, p. 497 – 8.

99 He continues, "he came to our embassy and expressed on behalf of the President, a desire to reach agreement. He also consented to transmit our demands to the President." Nikita Khrushchev, *Khrushchev Remembers: The Last Testament*, pp. 511 – 12.

100 Abel, *op. cit.*, p. 112. De Gaulle apparently replied, "I am in favor of independent decisions." Kennedy did speak frequently to Harold Macmillan during the week of the blockade. Afterward, Macmillan allowed that the British had "played our part perfectly. We were 'in on' and took full part in (and almost responsibility for) every American move." "Introduction" to Robert Kennedy, *op. cit.*, p. 25. But Macmillan learned of the missiles only hours before de Gaulle did. The President informed the British Ambassador to Washington, David Ormsy-Gore, of the blockade before word of it reached allied heads of state, but after the decision to impose one had been taken. His trans-Atlantic conversations may have fortified or comforted the American President, but they do not appear to have influenced his conduct during that week.

101 And in his letter to Kennedy of October 28, in which he agreed to withdraw the missiles, Khrushchev complained that an American reconnaissance plane had violated Soviet air space. Kennedy replied that it had strayed off course. "Messages," p. 654.

102 Sorensen, *Kennedy*, p. 711.

103 Robert Kennedy, *op. cit.*, p. 203.

104 *Ibid.*, p. 207.

105 Abel, *op. cit.*, p. 210. See also "Briefing Paper for the President. Subject: Castro's 'Five Points.'" Press Conference, 11/20/62, Background II, President's Office File, John F. Kennedy Library.

106 He did lift the blockade on November 20, when the last IL-28 airplane had left the island.

107 At his November 20 news conference he said that "serious problems remain as to verification and reassurance, and therefore, this matter of our negotiations are not – have not been completed, and until they're completed, of course, I suppose we're not going to be fully satisfied that there will be peace in the Caribbean." John F. Kennedy, *The Public Papers, 1962*. See also Robert McNamara's testimony in *Hearings on Military Posture for Fiscal Year 1964*, Committee on Armed Services, House of Representatives, p. 274.

108 Robert Kennedy, *op. cit.*, p. 215.

109 "Briefing Paper for the President's Press Conference, November 20, 1962. Subject: Ascertaining that all offensive weapons are out of Cuba." Press Conference, 11/20/62, Background II. President's Office File, John F. Kennedy Library.

110 It added, however, that "Castro reportedly was very strongly opposed. . .[and that] they would resist any further violations of their airspace." But the surveillance continued, suggesting that the Cubans changed their minds – perhaps at the behest of the Russians. "The Crisis USSR/Cuba: CIA Review, 1 November 1962." Executive Committee Meetings, 10/29 – 11/1/62. National Security File, John F. Kennedy Library.

111 Khrushchev, *Khrushchev Remembers*, p. 499.

112 *Hearings on Military Posture, Fiscal Year 1964*, House Armed Services Committee, pp. 254 – 5. McNamara said that the United States had had an "almost uninhibited opportunity to scrutinize the island very closely." *Ibid.*, p. 266.

113 It is sometimes suggested that the "lesson" of the Cuban missile crisis is that nuclear superiority, of the sort that the United States enjoyed over the Soviet Union in October 1962, yields "victory" in local confrontations. This is a dubious lesson to draw. At the time President Kennedy was far more impressed with the potential horrors of any nuclear exchange than with the chances of emerging from such an exchange less damaged than the Soviets. The result of the crisis was not, as noted, unambiguously an American "victory"; the United States made concessions as well. Insofar as it was a victory, this may have been due to things other than the nuclear balance; the preponderance of American nonnuclear force in the Caribbean, for example. Finally, insofar as the missile crisis was an American victory based on nuclear superiority, it is of limited relevance to the future of Soviet-American relations because the high levels of nuclear force that both sides have acquired make a nuclear balance as lopsided as the one that existed in the fall of 1962 exceedingly unlikely.

114   Robert Kennedy, *op. cit.*, p. 169.

115   *Ibid.*, p. 20.

116   "Messages," p. 651.

117   *Ibid.*, p. 214. During the crisis the President said to Ormsby-Gore, ". . .It really is an intolerable state of affairs when nations can threaten each other with nuclear weapons. . . . We really must try to get on with disarmament if we get through this crisis. . .because this is just too much." Schlesinger, *Robert Kennedy*, p. 530.

118   Kennedy, *The Public Papers, 1962*, p. 825. He included the words in a lengthy toast to the visiting German Chancellor, Konrad Adenauer, who, with his deep suspicion of the communist bloc, may not have been happy to hear them.

Chapter 7. The first step: The Limited Test Ban Treaty of 1963

1   Quoted in Theodore C. Sorensen, *Kennedy* (New York: Harper & Row, 1965), p. 737.

2   John F. Kennedy, *The Public Papers of the Presidents of the United States, 1961* (Washington, D.C.: United States Government Printing Office, 1962), p. 387. Also, Richard P. Stebbins, editor, *Documents on American Foreign Relations, 1961* (New York: Harper & Row, 1962), p. 108.

3   Stebbins, *op. cit.*, p. 201.

4   *Ibid.*

5   *Ibid.*, p. 203.

6   *Ibid.*, p. 204.

7   The administration did not have unanimous and unqualified confidence that the plan was practicable. Arthur Schlesinger, certainly no opponent of arms control, confessed that he found himself "in the unaccustomed position of sharing the doubts of the Joint Chiefs of Staff" about part of the plan. Arthur M. Schlesinger, Jr., *A Thousand Days: John F. Kennedy in the White House* (Boston:

Houghton Mifflin, 1965), p. 476. When the idea of presenting it at the United Nations was discussed in August, according to Schlesinger, the President "saw little present chance of significant progress and therefore looked to disarmament primarily as a measure of political warfare, feeling at the same time that, if the political warfare were to be effective, our plan, unlike its predecessors in the fifties, must offer an honest basis for negotiation." *Ibid.*, p. 479. See, on the other hand, Theodore Sorensen, Recorded interview, by Carl Kaysen, March 26, 1964, John F. Kennedy Library, p. 93, for the assertion that Kennedy never put forward a proposal he wasn't prepared to stand behind.

8 Schlesinger, *op. cit.*, p. 476.

9 See William F. Bader, *The United States and the Spread of Nuclear Weapons* (New York: Pegasus, 1968), p. 26.

10 *Ibid.*, pp. 40 – 1. Bader notes that the resolution drew a distinction between "control" and "ownership," and that whatever its origins, "the language of the 1959 resolution was tailored to the developing American position on the proliferation question, that is, willingness to pledge adherence to any doctrine creating barriers to any additional independent nuclear forces but maintaining the right to provide information, weapons, and technology to any established nuclear power as long as the United States maintained 'control' of the firing system."

11 *Ibid.*, p. 44, quoting Raymond Aron.

12 Kennedy, *The Public Papers, 1961*, p. 2. The spread was not particularly steady, nor was it as clear then as it proved to be later that the Soviet Union shared Kennedy's alarm. He reiterated the theme in his State of the Union Message: "We must prevent. . .[the] arms race from spreading to new nations, to new nuclear powers, and to the reaches of outer space." *Ibid.*, p. 26.

13 It was fundamental to his successor's foreign policy as well; under Lyndon Johnson's stewardship the United States managed to enact the Non-Proliferation Treaty of 1968, and coax or coerce most allied governments to sign it. See Chapter 8.

14 Still, the Kennedy administration hoped to avoid a serious rupture in the alliance and in 1962 entertained seriously the possibility of assisting the French nuclear program. But in the end the decision came down from the President against this, and the French went their own way. "Draft Memorandum for the President from McGeorge Bundy, January 30, 1963. Subject: The U.S. and de Gaulle – The Past and the Future." "France, 1963," President's Office File, John F. Kennedy Library, p. 7. See also Sorensen, interview, p. 1.

15 To try to resolve this dilemma, the State Department cobbled together a plan for a Multilateral Force (MLF), with men of different nationalities manning nuclear submarines, whose ultimate control was never spelled out with full clarity. The plan surfaced and sank several times before it finally perished in 1964. See John Steinbruner, *The Cybernetic Theory of Decision* (Princeton, N.J.: Princeton University Press, 1973).

16 Harold Karan Jacobson and Eric Stein, *Diplomats, Scientists, and Politicians: The United States and the Nuclear Test Ban Negotiations* (Ann Arbor: The University of Michigan Press, 1966), p. 410.

17 *Ibid.*, p. 411.

18 Philip J. Klass, *Secret Sentries in Space* (New York: Random House, 1971), p. 112.

19 "I think the President felt that the country was narrowly divided, that it was terribly important to have as much national unity as possible in foreign policy questions, and that Republicans in and out of Congress would be much less likely to attack a McCloy or a McCone, McNamara or Dillon, than they would a Stevenson, Bowles, or Kaysen." Sorensen, Interview, p. 68. Schlesinger concurs: "Knowing he had to protect disarmament against suspicions of softness, idealism, one-worldism and so on, he followed his customary practice of seeking a conservative to execute a liberal policy. The appointment of John J. McCloy as his special disarmament advisor was thus a deliberate effort to prepare the political ground. . . ." Schlesinger, *op. cit.*, p. 72.

20 Schlesinger, *op. cit.*, p. 459.

21 *Ibid.*

22 Sorensen, Interview, p. 77.

23 Kennedy, *The Public Papers, 1961*, p. 589.

24 This was certainly true for the American President. No one disputed his responsibility for deciding what to do about the shipment of the missiles to Cuba. He informed congressional leaders of the blockade only minutes before he went on television to announce it to the world, and he felt no need to get approval of the terms of settlement from anybody else. Khrushchev's paramountcy during the crisis is less clear, since the Soviet side is far less well documented. There is some evidence that the Soviet leadership was divided over some of the issues they faced then. See Herbert S. Dinerstein, *The Making of a Missile Crisis: October 1962* (Baltimore:

Johns Hopkins University Press, 1976), chapter 6. But Khrushchev, at least – and he alone – signed the private communications from the Soviet side during the crucial week.

25   Kennedy, *The Public Papers, 1962*, p. 839.

26   A seismic area is one where earthquakes occur frequently.

27   Edward Skloot, "Organizing for Peace: Disarmament Politics and the State Department, 1958 – 60," unpublished manuscript, p. IX-3.

28   *Ibid.*, chapters IX and X.

29   Jacobson and Stein, *op. cit.*, pp. 434 – 5.

30   John F. Kennedy, *The Public Papers, 1962*, p. 205.

31   *Ibid.*, p. 280.

32   Harold Macmillan, *At the End of the Day: 1961 – 63* (New York: Harper & Row, 1973), p. 468. See also Kennedy, *The Public Papers of the Presidents of the United States, 1963* (Washington: United States Government Printing Office, 1964), p. 343.

33   Kennedy, *The Public Papers*, ibid.

34   *Ibid.*, p. 377.

35   See Michel Tatu, *Power in the Kremlin*, translated by Helen Kabel (New York: Viking, 1969), p. 352ff.

36   "It became clear subsequently that the Cuban affair marked the end of the great Soviet design on Berlin, of the rocket-rattling that had served Khrushchev so well since his 1957 space achievements – in short, of a long period of Soviet initiatives." *Ibid.*, p. 273.

37   Walter C. Clemens, Jr., *The Arms Race and Sino-Soviet Relations* (Stanford, Calif.: The Hoover Institute on War, Revolution, and Peace, 1968), p. 24.

38   "As one observes the course of Soviet foreign policy throughout 1962, one cannot but conclude that the priorities in the minds of the Soviet leaders were as follows: (1) to prevent China from acquiring nuclear weapons, or somehow to limit and control Chinese nuclear armament. . . ." Adam Ulam, *Expansion and Coexistence, The History of Soviet Foreign Policy, 1917–67* (New York: Praeger, 1968), p. 661.

39   *Ibid.*, p. 665.

40   Quoted in Walter C. Clemens, Jr., "The Nuclear Test Ban and Sino-Soviet Relations," in Morton Halperin, editor, *Sino-Soviet Relations and Arms Control* (Cambridge, Mass.: The MIT Press, 1966), p. 149.

41   Ulam, *op. cit.*, p. 675.

42   *Ibid.*, p. 676.

43 He alluded to Albania's attacks on him and other Soviet leaders, and then said; "I remember that in in the miners' towns foulmouths used to do this: they would find a little boy who had barely learned to repeat words and did not understand their meaning; they would teach him the dirtiest oaths and would tell him: 'go under the windows of people's homes and say these words to the people.' Or, worse, they would say to such a child: 'Go to your mother and repeat these words to her. Here is three kopeks for this, and afterwards we shall give you five more.'

"The child would run under the windows of houses or run around to his mother, repeating the oaths; this would provide a form of entertainment for the foulmouths.

"Now the Albanian leaders are acting like those silly boys. Someone taught them to pronounce foul words, and they walk under windows and shout hooligan curses at the Communist Party of the Soviet Union. But this is their mother." Quoted in Alexander Dallin, editor, *Diversity in International Communism: A Documentary Record, 1961 – 63* (New York: Columbia University Press, 1963), p. 676. Khrushchev's nominee for the role of the foulmouthed miners, who put Albania up to its childish pranks, is not difficult to guess.

44 *Ibid.*

45 *Ibid.*, p. 675.

46 Schlesinger, *op. cit.*, p. 891.

47 See Tatu, *op. cit.*, p. 891.

48 Department of State Telegram from Moscow to the Secretary of State, No. 2141. February 28, 1963. USSR, 1963, President's Office File, John F. Kennedy Library, p. 1.

49 Kennedy, *The Public Papers, 1963*, p. 19.

50 He had changed, by his own account, because the Soviets themselves had changed. They no longer posed as immediate a menace to Western Europe as they had a few short years before. "Our present difficulties in Europe," he said in the spring of 1963, "while annoying in a sense, or burdensome, are not nearly as dangerous as they were" at a comparable time two years previously. *Ibid.* In recognition of this reformed behavior, Kennedy trod softly around the disputes that had earlier threatened to flare into open warfare. When he visited Germany in June of 1963, and made his famous declaration, "Ich bin ein Berliner," he took an extremely guarded, circumspect line on what was then the tensest issue in East – West relations. He pledged allegiance to the idea of a united Germany, but

warned that the "peaceful reunification of Berlin and Germany will
. . .not be either quick or easy." *Ibid.*, p. 527. There was, he told
the Germans, "no immediate solution" (*Ibid.*, p. 506) to the German
problem.

51 Schlesinger, *op. cit.*, p. 898.

52 Sorensen, interview, p. 72.

53 Kennedy, *The Public Papers, 1963*, p. 462.

54 *Ibid.*, p. 461.

55 *Ibid.*

56 Department of State Telegram from Moscow to the Secretary of
State, No. 3124, June 11, 1963. Disarmament –Nuclear Test Ban,
4/62 – 8/63, President's Office File, John F. Kennedy Library. The
jamming of all American broadcasts ceased shortly afterward. See
Sorensen, *Kennedy*, p. 733.

57 Department of State Telegram from Moscow to the Secretary of
State, No. 3130, June 11, 1963. Disarmament – Nuclear Test Ban,
4/62 – 8/63, President's Office File, John F. Kennedy Library.

58 Sir Humphrey Trevelyan, recorded interview by Joseph E.
O'Connor, John F.Kennedy Library, p. 7.

59 He told Averell Harriman that it was "the greatest speech by
any American President since Roosevelt," Schlesinger, *op. cit.*, p.
904.

60 Nikita S. Khrushchev, Letter to Robert Kennedy, June 29, 1964,
John F. Kennedy Library, p. 2.

61 Tatu, *op. cit.*, p. 352.

62 Clemens, "The Nuclear Test Ban," in Halperin, editor, *op. cit.*,
p. 151.

63 The sequence continued on July 24, when agreement was
reached on a limited test ban, on July 26, when the Chinese denounced it vehemently, and on August 2, when the Soviets responded with equal vehemence.

64 Tatu, *op. cit.*, p. 352.

65 See *Military Procurement Authorization, Fiscal Year, 1964*,
Hearings before the Committee on Armed Services, United States
Senate, Eighty-eighth Congress, First Session (McNamara tes-
timony), p. 136; also *Nuclear Test Ban Hearings*, Senate Committee
on Foreign Relations, Eighty-eighth Congress, First Session (Rusk
Testimony), p. 89.

66 Helmut Sonnenfeldt, "The Chinese Factor in Soviet Disarmament Policy," in Halperin, editor, *op. cit.*, p. 111; Ulam, *op. cit.*, p.
661.

67 Trevelyan, interview, p. 9.

68 Tatu, op. cit., part three, chapter 4.

69 Schlesinger, op. cit., p. 904.

70 Trevelyan, interview, p. 9.

71 Sorensen, interview, p. 74.

72 Seyom Brown, The Faces of Power (New York: Columbia University Press, 1968), p. 279.

73 Roswell Gilpatric, Recorded interview by Dennis J. O'Brien, February 9, 1964, John F. Kennedy Library, p. 10.

74 Schlesinger, op. cit., p. 903. Schlesinger also quotes Chairman Khrushchev as saying, "Harriman is a responsible man." Ibid.

75 Richard P. Stebbins, editor, Documents on American Foreign Relations, 1963 (New York: Harper & Row, 1964), p. 130.

76 Kennedy, Ibid., p. 133; Rusk in Test Ban Hearings, Senate Foreign Relations Committee, 1963, p. 20.

77 Stebbins, editor, Documents, 1963, p. 130.

78 Ibid., pp. 129 – 30.

79 Jacobson and Stein, op. cit., p. 456.

80 Schlesinger, op. cit., p. 907.

81 They were Secretary of State Rusk, Under-Secretary Ball, Defense Secretary McNamara, CIA Director McCone, former Ambassador to the Soviet Union Llewellyn Thompson, and Arms Control and Disarmament Agency chief William Foster. As in the Cuban missile crisis, Kennedy chose, at a crucial juncture, to move outside normal channels.

82 Sorensen, Kennedy, p. 735.

83 Schlesinger, op. cit., p. 905.

84 Quoted in Stephen Ambrose, Rise to Globalism: American Foreign Policy, 1938 – 1970 (Baltimore: Penguin, paperback, 1971), p. 294.

85 Sorensen, Interview, p. 82.

86 Ibid., p. 75.

87 Several Republicans, including the Minority Leader, Everett Dirksen, declined to go. Sorensen, Kennedy, p. 737. But Dirksen subsequently voted for the treaty.

88 "His activities paralleled few other efforts which took place during the three years of the Kennedy presidency and no other strictly foreign policy effort. . . .He personally talked with a great many senators, he worked through the Senate leadership, the Vice President, the legislative liaison officers in the White House and in the State Department. He kept in daily touch with the tactics being used both by the proponents and opponents of the treaty. . . ." Sorensen, Interview, p. 84.

89 *Ibid.*, p. 74.

90 *Test Ban Hearings*, p. 372.

91 Quoted in Herbert York, "The Great Test Ban Debate," *Scientific American*, 227:5 (November 1972), p. 22.

92 *Test Ban Hearings*, p. 541.

93 Maxwell Taylor, the Chairman of the Joint Chiefs of Staff, when asked whether the Russians might be able to achieve a technical breakthrough that would confer a decisive strategic advantage, replied, "Frankly I cannot visualize that situation." He added, however, that "obviously one never visualizes all the possibilities of the future." *Ibid.*, p. 310.

94 Moreover, it was argued, the United States could still build huge bombs if it were decided that they were desirable. The treaty would also restrict tests of the strength of the concrete silos in which missiles were housed to protect them against preemptive attack. But the two sides would be restricted equally. And the resulting uncertainty would reinforce deterrence, not undercut it, for neither the United States nor the Soviet Union could be confident that the other's missiles would *not* survive an attack.

95 *Test Ban Hearings*, p. 568.

96 *Ibid.*, p. 109.

97 He said at one point that he was "not certain that we will be able to develop the other components of the system [besides the warhead] to the point where they will justify deployment." *Ibid.*, p. 174.

98 Herbert York, a former Defense Department Director of Research and Engineering, testified: "In any development race between antiballistic missiles and ballistic missiles, I believe the offense will always, and by a wide margin, have the advantage over the defense." *Ibid.*, p. 758. Norris Bradbury, Director of the Los Alamos Scientific Laboratory in New Mexico, expressed very much the same view. *Ibid.*, p. 603.

99 *Ibid.*, p. 114.

100 *Ibid.*, pp. 132 – 5.

101 Kennedy, *The Public Papers, 1963*, p. 609.

102 *Ibid.*, pp. 720ff, 724ff, 727ff, 735ff.

103 *Test Ban Hearings*, p. 3.

104 *Ibid.*, p. 114.
105 The Chinese did, of course, ultimately acquire nuclear armaments.
106 Kennedy, *The Public Papers, 1962,* p. 871.

Chapter 8. Fencers on a tightrope

1 Nikita S. Khrushchev, Letter to Robert Kennedy, June 29, 1964, John F. Kennedy Library, p. 3.
2 In 1974 India also set off a nuclear explosion, although by 1979 the Indians had not chosen to fabricate a nuclear weapon, or at least not to announce publicly that they had done so.
3 Not the least important part of the 1972 accord on offensive weapons was the definition of which weapons would be limited. The definition included those nuclear weapons in the arsenal of each side capable of striking the homeland of the other; intercontinental-range ballistic missiles based on land and carried by submarines, and bomber aircraft based in one country with the capacity for a round-trip to the territory of the other.
4 But because of a lead in the technology of multiple warheads, the United States had 5,700 warheads – that is, bombs that could be delivered to a target – to the Soviets' 2,500.
5 This agreement was never submitted to the Senate for ratification. See below, p. 291.
6 In 1976 ninety-nine nations had signed the Nonproliferation Treaty and 88 had ratified it. The corresponding figures for the Limited Test Ban Treaty were 109 and 91. *Arms Control and Disarmament Agreements: Text and History of Negotiations.* (Washington, D.C.: U.S. Arms Control and Disarmament Agency, 1977), pp. 44 and 91.
7 The People's Republic of China and France declined to sign.
8 States that did not wish to waive the right to acquire nuclear weapons simply refused to sign the treaty. By the end of 1976 Israel, Egypt, India, and Pakistan, among others, had not signed. And any signatory could legally withdraw, on six months' notice, "if it decides that extraordinary events, related to the subject matter of this Treaty, have jeopardized the supreme interests of its country." *Arms Control and Disarmament Agreements,* pp. 87 – 8.
9 *Ibid.,* p. 134.
10 The cruise missile, a small pilotless jet aircraft capable of carry-

ing nuclear explosives to distant targets at subsonic speeds but at very low altitude, thus eluding most radar defenses, seemed to fit into this second category. Small, and easy both to manufacture in quantity and to conceal, it seemed to be a weapon whose inclusion in an overall limitation on offensive forces would be exceptionally difficult.

11 The United States did offer to permit the inspection of American facilities devoted to "non-military" purposes. But the Soviets declined to follow suit.

12 The provision for inspection of "peaceful" explosions is reported in *The New York Times*, May 29, 1976.

13 John Newhouse's account of the making of the 1972 agreements, *Cold Dawn* (New York: Holt, Rinehart, Winston, 1973) provides a detailed picture of the negotiations *within* the American government.

14 See Chapter 7.

15 The Vladivostock agreement was flawed, as well, because it did not provide for two strategic nuclear weapons whose importance loomed larger and larger after December 1974; the American cruise missile and the Soviet "Backfire" bomber, which under some circumstances could have intercontinental range.

16 John F. Kennedy, *The Public Papers of the Presidents of the United States, 1963* (Washington, D.C.: United States Government Printing Office, 1964), p. 777.

17 Department of State Telegram from Moscow to the Secretary of State, No. 1601, November 8, 1963, USSR, 1963, President's Office File, John F. Kennedy Library.

18 The UN forums were also permanent. But since they were public, participating in them denoted the the two great powers' common recognition that nuclear weapons were a potent international political issue, not a common resolve to find accommodation.

19 The figures are from Desmond J. Ball, *The Strategic Missile Programme of the Kennedy Administration*, unpublished manuscript, Australian National University, 1976, pp. 140, 537, 548.

20 See Chapter 5, under "Ballistic Missile Defense."

21 See Henry Trewhitt, *McNamara: His Ordeal at the Pentagon* (New York: Harper & Row, 1971), p. 290ff.

22 See, for example, Fred C. Iklé, "Can Nuclear Deterrence Last Out the Century?" *Foreign Affairs* (January 1972), for an appeal for an alternative to an equilibrium between the United States and the

Soviet Union based on a mutual capacity for assured destruction.

23 Accuracy is measured by "circular error probable" (CEP), which is the radius of a circle about a target within which 50 percent of the missiles aimed at that target will fall.

24 For a statement of the importance of matching the Soviets in important categories of nuclear hardware, see *Annual Defense Department Report* (Defense Posture Statement), FY 1976, p. I – 13. For an assertion of the possible political perils of conspicuous asymmetries in the two principal nuclear arsenals, see Paul Nitze, "Assuring Strategic Stability in an Era of Detente," *Foreign Affairs*, vol. 54, no. 2 (January 1976). For a skeptical appraisal of such dangers, see Michael Mandelbaum, "International Stability and Nuclear Order: The First Nuclear Regime," in David C. Gompert, *et. al.*, *Nuclear Weapons and World Politics* (New York, McGraw-Hill, 1977), pp. 40 – 7; and Robert Jervis, "Why Minuteman Vulnerability Doesn't Matter," unpublished paper.

25 Jerome H. Kahan, *Security in the Nuclear Age: Developing U.S. Strategic Arms Policy* (Washington, D.C.: Brookings Institution, 1975), p. 117.

26 Newhouse, *op. cit.*, p. 134.

27 "Text of President Carter's Address to the United Nations General Assembly," *The New York Times*, October 6, 1977, p. A12.

28 They have been conspicuously less voluble since the fall of Khrushchev in 1964. Under Khrushchev's leadership disputes about military policy frequently made their way, in thinly disguised form, into official publications. See Thomas Wolfe, *Soviet Strategy at the Crossroads* (Cambridge: Harvard University Press, 1964), chapter II; and Thomas Wolfe, *Soviet Power in Europe, 1945 – 1970* (Baltimore: Johns Hopkins University Press, 1970), chapters VII and XVI.

29 John Newhouse has noted the reluctance to share information even within the Soviet Government. In the discussions leading up to the 1972 agreements, the American negotiators "discoursed fluently about the military hardware of both sides, much to the annoyance of the military members of the Soviet delegation: At one point, Colonel-General Nikolai Ogarkov, who was listed as the second-ranking Soviet delegate but who is also the First Deputy Chief of the General Staff, took aside an American delegate and urged that he and others discontinue talking so specifically about Soviet military hardware; such matters, he said, need not concern his civilian colleagues." Newhouse, *op. cit.*, p. 192.

30 See Walter C. Clemens, Jr., "A Balance Sheet on Sixty Years of Soviet Foreign Policy — Part II," *Worldview* (January – February 1978), p. 51.

31 American nuclear diplomacy has hardly been an exercise in unadulterated altruism. The spread of nuclear weapons, if not as gravely menacing as to the Soviet Union, did not promise to advance American interests. Rather, it threatened lessened control over states that acquired them, and unpredictable political consequences wherever they were introduced for the first time. And in the negotiations to limit offensive weaponry, the Americans were as intent on constraining Soviet armaments as vice versa.

32 See Thomas Wolfe, *The SALT Experience: Its Impact on U.S. and Soviet Strategic Policy and Decisionmaking*, Rand R-1686-PR, September 1975, p. 118; and Marshall Shulman, "SALT and the Soviet Union," in Mason Willrich and John B. Rhinelander, editors, *SALT: The Moscow Agreements and Beyond* (New York: Free Press, 1974), p. 118.

33 New York, N.Y., Crane Russak and Company, 1975. A translation, edited with analysis and commentary, by Harriet Fast Scott, of *Voyenna Strategiya*, 3rd edition (Moscow: Voyenizdat, 1968). On Soviet nuclear weapons doctrine, see Richard Pipes, "Why the Soviet Union Thinks It Could Fight and Win a Nuclear War," *Commentary* 64:1 (July 1977); "Letters to the Editor," *Commentary* 64:3 (September 1977); Bernard Brodie, "The Development of Nuclear Strategy," *International Security* 2:4 (Spring 1978); and Raymond Garthoff, "Mutual Deterrence and Strategic Arms Limitation in Soviet Policy," *International Security* 3:1 (Summer 1978).

34 See Fred Kaplan, "The Soviet Civil Defense Myth," *The Bulletin of the Atomic Scientists*, vol. 34, nos. 3 and 4 (March and April 1978).

35 For informed speculation about the influence of those with a vested interest in producing more and more weaponry, see Arnold Horelick, "The Strategic Mind-Set of the Soviet Military," *Problems of Communism* (March – April 1977), p. 81; and Newhouse, *op. cit.*, p. 245. For speculation about splits within the Soviet hierarchy over the feasibility of fighting a nuclear war, see Thomas Wolfe, *The SALT Experience*, p. 154ff. Henry Kissinger suggested that "the pressures from military men, who by profession are obliged to weigh security dangers but not to take political initiatives, are just as great in Moscow as in Washington." See "Kissinger Looks to Public Debate on Moscow Ties," *The New York Times*, July 7, 1974.

36 See Jan. M. Lodal, "Assuring Strategic Stability: An Alternate

View," *Foreign Affairs*, 54:3 (April, 1976), pp. 467–9.

37 See Wolfe, *The SALT Experience*, p. 73.

38 See Raymond Garthoff, "On Estimating and Imputing Intentions," *International Security* 2:3 (Winter 1978), p. 27ff. There has been, historically, a tendency on the part of the Russians to accumulate military force beyond the real requirements of the Russian state. See, for example, George F. Kennan, "A Last Warning: Reply to My Critics," *Encounter* (July 1978), p. 16.

39 See Nitze, *op. cit.*

40 See Wolfe, *The SALT Experience*, p. 143.

41 Quoted in Hedrick Smith, "Soviet Politburo Shuffled: Gromyko Among 4 Raised," *The New York Times* (April 28, 1973).

42 See Thomas Wolfe, *Soviet Strategy at the Crossroads*, p. 226ff.

43 For a discussion of the debate over Lenin's dictum, see Wolfe, *Soviet Strategy at the Crossroads*, chapter VI.

44 Quoted in Joseph Coffey, *Strategic Power and National Security* (Pittsburgh, Penn.: University of Pittsburgh Press, 1971), p. 78.

45 Quoted in *Ibid.*

46 *The Concise Oxford Dictionary of Current English*, Fifth Edition (Oxford: The Clarendon Press, 1964), p. 987.

47 Louis J. Halle, *The Cold War as History* (New York: Harper & Row, 1967), p. xiii. It is from this passage that Joseph I. Lieberman takes the title of his book about the Baruch Plan.

48 See Raymond Aron, *Penser la guerre, Clausewitz. Volume II, L'âge planétaire* (Paris: Editions Gallimard, p. 183). Although Clausewitz did not develop this idea fully, Aron believes that he would have done so had he been able to revise his manuscript, which represents only a first draft, before his death.

49 Carl von Clausewitz, *On War*. Edited and translated by Michael Howard and Peter Paret. (Princeton, N.J.: Princeton University Press, 1976), p. 604. Emphasis added.

50 "Basic Principles of Relations Between the United States of America and the Union of Soviet Socialist Republics." May 29, 1972. In Willrich and Rhinelander, editors, *op. cit.*, pp. 310–11.

51 Text reprinted in *The New York Times* (June 23, 1973), p. 8.

52 Quoted in Marvin and Bernard Kalb, *Kissinger* (Boston: Little, Brown, 1979), p. 490.

53 It is arguable that there would have been no war between the United States and the Soviet Union after 1945, even if neither had had nuclear weapons, on the grounds that the nonnuclear armaments available at the end of World War II were formidable enough for effective deterrence. See Mandelbaum, *op. cit.*, p. 19.

Index

ABM, see ballistic missile defense
"absolute war," 3–4, 9–10, 97–8, 127, 205
Acheson, Dean, 25–6, 28, 139, 152
Air Force, 54, 61, 63, 84, 86, 115
Arms Control and Disarmament Agency, 159
Army, 60, 81, 115
Arnold, H. H., 115
Aron, Raymond, 154
atomic scientists, see scientists

B-52 bomber, 84, 100
B-70 bomber, 84
ballistic missile, the, 64, 66, 73
ballistic missile defense, 113–19, 124–5, 183–4; debate over, 203; details of, 247–8; prohibition of, 192, 194, 211, 215
Baruch Plan, 23–6, 42; and inspection, 37–8; as liberal diplomacy, 27–8, 149; criticisms of, 54; failure of, 32–3; in comparison with the Limited Test Ban Treaty, 177–9; motives for, 34–5; origins of, 156; similarity to "massive retaliation," 53
Benz, Carl, 45
Berlin, 43, 61, 93–6, 122
"Bhagavad Ghita," 8
Bohr, Niels, 6–7, 24, 28, 30–1
Brezhnev, Leonid, 198, 200
Brodie, Bernard: as strategic prophet, 55, 76, 85, 206, 208; on nuclear strategy, 19–20; quoted, 49–50, 73, 217
Brown, Harold, 182–3
Bush, Vannevar, 24–5

Canada, 19
Carter, Jimmy, 207
Castro, Fidel, 136, 146; 149, 151, 153
Churchill, Winston, 31; and British strategy, 52; and Niels Bohr, 6–7; on diplomacy, 12; on nuclear stability, 89; on the hydrogen bomb, 49; on the Soviet Union, 209

civil defense, 98, 125, 212–13
Clausewitz, Carl von: on "absolute war," 127; on "armed wariness," 219, 223; on diplomacy, 12, 40; on morale, 119; on the "genius for war," 106; on the nature of war, 3–4, 9–10, 96–8; on the superiority of the defense, 113
Cold War, the, 33–4, 39, 40, 42, 93
"compellence," 141–2
Conant, James, 24–5
counterforce doctrine, 110–12, 125–6, 205–6
Cousins, Norman, 172
Cuban missile crisis: accounts of, 252; aftermath of, 156–7; and deterrence, 133–4, 134–44; as diplomacy, 134, 144–54; compared with 1973 Middle East War, 221, events of, 128–34; significance of, 133, 142–3, 154–6, 170, 198, 204, 217, 260–1

Dean, Arthur, 166, 168
de Gaulle, Charles, 152, 163
deterrence: "absolute," 60, 62, 204; as American policy, 49, 51, 75, 206; British conception of, 52; by nuclear weapons, 50–1; definition of, 47; effect of technical progress on, 182–3; "graduated," 59, 90, 127, 204; in the Cuban missile crisis, 141–4; requirements of, 56–60, 63, 75–8, 85–6, 92, 111, 128, 204; see also "massive retaliation"
diplomacy: definition of, 8, 12; incentives for, 34; "liberal," 16–17, 22, 29, 149; requirements for success of, 12, 33, 39, 148–9, 165, 175, 198; "traditional," 13–14, 17, 149, 179, 194, 197, 208
Dobrynin, Anatoly, 130, 148, 151
Dulles, John Foster, 50–1

Einstein, Albert, 7
Eisenhower administration, the, 52; and civil defense, 120; and fiscal frugality,

274